Metropolitan Opera House

ebruary 25, 1902 — Gala performance in honor of Prince Henry of Prussia.

pril 27, 1903 — Farewell gala performance for Grau.

ovember 23, 1903 — Opening night. Heinrich Conried regime begins with *Rigoletto* (debut of nrico Caruso; Sembrich, Louise Homer, Antonio Scotti).

ecember 24, 1903 — First staged performance of *Parsifal* outside Bayreuth (Milka Ternina, lois Burgstaller, Anton Van Rooy, Marcel Journet).

ecember 5, 1904 — Only Metropolitan performance of Donizetti's *Lucrezia Borgia* (Maria di acchi, Edyth Walker, Caruso, Scotti).

anuary 7, 1905 — In first act of *Carmen,* heavy bridge collapses from height of eighteen feet. urtain lowered while eight members of the chorus are rushed to hospitals.

anuary 22, 1907 — First American performance of *Salome* (Olive Fremstad, Marion Weed, ippel, Van Rooy).

ebruary 11, 1907 — First Italian-language production in America of *Madama Butterfly* (Ger-dine Farrar, Homer, Caruso, Scotti). Production supervised by Puccini, who receives an ovation.

anuary 23, 1908 — Debut of Gustav Mahler, conducting *Don Giovanni* (Eames, Johanna Gad-ci, Sembrich, Alessandro Bonci, Scotti, Feodor Chaliapin).

pril 18, 1908 — Conried regime ends with *Götterdämmerung* (Martha Leffler-Burckhard, Homer, urgstaller, Robert Blass).

ovember 16, 1908 — First opening night of the Gatti-Casazza regime. Debut of Arturo Tos-nini, conducting *Aida* (Emmy Destinn, Homer, Caruso, Scotti).

arch 18, 1910 — Frederick Converse's *The Pipe of Desire* (Riccardo Martin, Homer, Clarence hitehill, Herbert Witherspoon) is the first opera by an American composer to be performed at e Metropolitan.

ecember 10, 1910 — World premiere of *La Fanciulla del West* (Destinn, Caruso, Pasquale mato). Staged by David Belasco; production supervised by Puccini.

arch 14, 1912 — World premiere of Horatio Parker's *Mona* (Homer, Martin, Witherspoon), ·st opera by an American composer to be commissioned by the Metropolitan.

ebruary 27, 1913 — World premiere of Walter Damrosch's *Cyrano de Bergerac* (Frances Alda, artin, Amato).

arch 19, 1913 — First American performance of *Boris Godounov* (Adamo Didur, Homer, Paul lthouse).

ecember 9, 1913 — First American performance of *Der Rosenkavalier* (Frieda Hempel, Otto oritz, Margaret Ober, Anna Case).

pril 3, 1916 — Opening of a series of performances by the Diaghilev Ballet Russe, as part of gular Metropolitan subscription season. Principal dancers include Vaslav Nijinsky and Leonid assine.

pril 13, 1917 — *Tristan und Isolde* (Gadski, Jacques Urlus, Margaret Matzenauer, Whitehill); adski's farewell performance. Last German-language production at the Metropolitan for nearly ree years.

arch 23, 1918 — World premiere of Charles Wakefield Cadman's *Shanewis* (Sophie Braslau, athleen Howard, Althouse).

ovember 11, 1918 — *Samson et Dalila* (Homer, Caruso, Robert Couzinou). Opening night incides with armistice ending World War I.

ecember 14, 1918 — World premiere of Puccini's three one-act operas *Il Tabarro* (Claudia uzio, Giulio Crimi, Luigi Montesanto), *Suor Angelica* (Farrar, Flora Perini), *Gianni Schicchi* lorence Easton, Crimi, Giuseppe de Luca).

BOOKS by JOHN BRIGGS

THE COLLECTOR'S TCHAIKOVSKY AND THE FIVE

LEONARD BERNSTEIN
The Man, His Work and His World

THE COLLECTOR'S BEETHOVEN

REQUIEM FOR A YELLOW BRICK BREWERY
A History of the Metropolitan Opera

REQUIEM
for a
Yellow Brick Brewery

by JOHN BRIGGS

REQUIEM

for a

Yellow Brick Brewery

A History of the Metropolitan Opera

LITTLE, BROWN AND COMPANY

Boston • *Toronto*

*Published simultaneously in Canada
by Little, Brown & Company (Canada) Limited*

PRINTED IN THE UNITED STATES OF AMERICA

To E. B.

". . . the new yellow-brick brewery on Broadway . . ."

—Early characterization
of the Metropolitan Opera House,
ascribed to COLONEL JAMES HENRY MAPLESON

As down the stage again,
With Spanish hat and plumes, and gait inimitable,
Back from the fading lessons of the past, I'd call, I'd
  tell and own
How much from thee! the revelation of the singing voice
  from thee!
(So firm — so liquid-soft — again that tremulous, manly
  timbre!)
How through those strains distill'd — how the rapt ears,
  the soul of me absorbing
Fernando's heart, Manrico's passionate call, Ernani's,
  sweet Gennaro's . . .
From these, for these, with these, a hurried line, dead tenor,
A wafted autumn leaf, dropt in the closing grave, the shovel'd
  earth
To memory of thee.

      —WHITMAN, *Leaves of Grass*

For all the dead-and-gone opera singers (those in particular
whose obituaries one wrote, and lived to see published in the paper):
Requiem aeternam dona eis, Domine,
  Et lux perpetua luceat eis.

Contents

Contents

Illustrations

Prologue

Un nido di memorie
In fondo all'anima
Cantava un giorno . . .

— I PAGLIACCI,
Prologue

IT WAS A HOUSE of memories. People used to go there just as their parents, and sometimes their parents' parents, had gone, and through their own recollections they called back those of the years gone by.

Sitting in the darkened auditorium, with the six-story gold proscenium aglow from the footlights, one could imagine Caruso singing his last *Vesti la giubba*, cracking on the high A as the excruciating pain struck his side.

In 1897, baritone Armand Castelmary had died on the stage, in full view of the audience during a performance, as baritone Leonard Warren was to do sixty-three years later. Castelmary's death was the most disastrous event to take place within view of a Metropolitan audience until January 7, 1905. On that date, in the first act of Carmen, a heavy bridge collapsed from a height of eighteen feet. Fortunately, there were no fatalities, and after the curtain had been lowered while eight members of the chorus were rushed to hospitals, the performance resumed.

Enrique Granados had taken his bows here after the premiere of his *Goyescas*, for which he insisted on being paid in gold. He was carrying it when the torpedoed *Sussex* went down — a convincing refutation of the notion that you can't take it with you.

Tchaikovsky had sat here, exquisitely bored, to hear a program of his own works and an oratorio by Max Vogrich. (When Tchaikovsky made a speech of thanks, in French, a lady threw a bouquet that struck him full in the face.)

Puccini had hurried here from his just-docked ship in time for a performance of *Manon Lescaut*, creating a furor when he appeared in the director's box. Four of his operas — *Suor Angelica, Gianni Schicchi, Il Tabarro* and *La Fanciulla del West* — had been given their first performances here.

American audiences had seen their first sight of Gustav Mahler in this house, as he labored to rouse performers to an incandescence that matched his own. Arturo Toscanini, a Vesuvius in eruption when rehearsals went badly, had made these walls reverberate with English and Italian profanity.

From the first, it had been a magnet that drew singers from everywhere, often at lower fees than other houses paid them. All the great ones had been here, beginning with those reviewed by the youthful George Bernard Shaw as a London music critic — Adelina "the divine" Patti; Etelka Gerster, whose high notes, said Shaw, chimed like bells in the florid passages of the Queen of the Night aria; the de Reszkes, Jean and Edouard ("Brer Edouard's endowment is mainly vocal; if the De Reszkes had been an English country family, he would almost certainly have gone into the Church"); baritone Jean Lassalle; soprano Amalie Materna ("the comfortable way in which she arranged herself for a stage faint on the arm of her partner presented a spectacle of matronly decorum before which the house recoiled"); Francesco Tamagno ("shrill and tremulous") and Victor Maurel ("wooly and nasal"), chosen by Verdi himself to create the roles of Otello and Iago.

The house had seen the mezzo-soprano Sofia Scalchi, whose face was plain but whose legs in tights were the shapeliest that critic H. E. Krehbiel remembered in thirty years of operagoing. There had been Americans who had made good both here and abroad — baritone David Bispham, sopranos Marie Van Zandt, Sybil Sanderson and Emma Eames.

A portrait of Eames, done by her painter husband Julian Story soon after their marriage, hung in Sherry's Restaurant on the Grand Tier. It showed a beautiful woman who looked radiantly in love. But some listeners thought her singing cold. After her first Aida, the irrepressible critic James G. Huneker had written: "Last night there was skating on the Nile."*

American-born Lillian Nordica sang dramatic roles; Lilli Lehmann sang everything. Basso Pol Plançon had a trill that would have done credit to a coloratura soprano. So would have the high notes of mezzo-soprano Emma Calvé.

Some old-timers called it "the Golden Age of Song," but the Metropolitan had barely started. The age of Caruso and Farrar was still to come.

Only two great names were missing from the roster — those of baritone Mattia Battistini, who was afraid to travel by water, and of tenor Fernand Ansseau, who didn't want to bother. Once, when the Paris Opéra begged him to interrupt his summer holiday to replace an indisposed colleague, Ansseau wired back: DANS L'ÉTÉ, JE PECHE.

At the Sunday night concerts that continued until the regime of Rudolf Bing, the house had heard great instrumentalists — Bernhard Stavenhagen, Eugène Ysaÿe, Franz Ondricek, Bronislaw Huberman, Moritz Rosenthal, Lady Hallé, Arthur Friedheim, Vladimir de Pachmann, Fritz Kreisler, Jan Kubelik, Jacques Thibaud, Josef Hofmann, Ossip Gabrilowitsch, Albert Spalding, Sergei Rachmaninoff, Mischa Elman, Ferruccio Busoni, Sigismund Stojowski, Harold Bauer, Efrem Zimbalist, Josef Lhévinne and Leopold Godowsky were some.

Sarah Bernhardt had played a "Positively Farewell" performance here in 1892, another farewell twenty-five years later. Eleonora Duse had played Ibsen's *Lady from the Sea*, in Italian, a few months before her death. Edwin Booth's Hamlet, Maude Adams's Joan of Arc and Sir Herbert Beerbohm Tree's Svengali had been other nonmusical events. George Bernard Shaw had spoken here, confessing that the surroundings gave him an almost uncontrollable desire to sing. Comedians Weber and Fields had shared a bill, in 1912, with Al Jolson, Lillian Nordica and the Dolly Sisters.

---

* After hearing Eames in a London performance of *Werther* in 1894, Shaw wrote: "Whoever has not seen Miss Eames as Charlotte has not realized the full force of Thackeray's picture of the young lady who, when she saw the remains of her lover

> *Borne before her on a shutter,*
> *Like a well-conducted person*
> *Went on cutting bread and butter.*

For everyone there was some point at which Metropolitan history began to blend with his own memories. Typically, memories began with student-day performances heard from the topmost balcony, or from standing room behind the brass rail; then progressed to the more comfortable vantage point of a box or a seat on the aisle.

For a few whose duties took them behind the scenes, there was the added dimension of going backstage at intermission to pick up the latest opera-house gossip; or of seeing a performance from the special viewpoint of the prompter's box; or of standing in the wings while, at one's elbow, Zinka Milanov nervously hummed arpeggios as she awaited the cue for her first entrance in *Ernani.*

There were recollections of glamor and of grubbiness; of the splendor of stage sets as seen from the audience and their shabbiness when viewed at close range; of coffee in a cardboard container in the press department and champagne at Sherry's Restaurant; of stagehands in overalls and Mrs. George Washington Kavanaugh's blazing diamond tiara.

Everyone's memories were different — but all of them were memorable.

Chronology

April 7, 1880 — "Three Vanderbilts, two Roosevelts, Iselins, Goelets, Astors, Morgans and others" subscribe $800,000 to build a new opera house in New York.

May 24, 1883 — In the new Metropolitan Opera House, completed at a cost of $1,732,978.71, shareholders of the Metropolitan Opera House Company, Ltd, draw lots for boxes.

October 22, 1883 — Opening night. *Faust* (Christine Nilsson, Italo Campanini, Franco Novara) in Italian.

April 21, 1884 — Manager Henry E. Abbey, $600,000 in debt from his first season, is dropped as manager but given the use of the house for a benefit. Marcella Sembrich performs as coloratura soprano, violinist and pianist.

November 17, 1884 — *Tannhäuser* (Auguste Kraus, Anton Schott, Adolf Robinson) opens the first of Leopold Damrosch's seasons of opera in German.

February 15, 1885 — Damrosch dies of pneumonia after a brief illness. He is succeeded by Anton Seidl.

January 4, 1886 — First American performance of *Die Meistersinger* (Auguste Seidl-Kraus, Marianne Brandt, Albert Stritt, Emil Fischer).

December 1, 1886 — First American performance of *Tristan und Isolde* (Lilli Lehmann, Brandt, Albert Niemann, Robinson).

November 9, 1887 — First American performance of *Siegfried* (Lehmann, Seidl-Kraus, Max Alvary, Fischer).

January 25, 1888 — First American performance of *Götterdämmerung* (Lehmann, Seidl-Kraus, Niemann, Fischer).

January 4, 1889 — First American performance of *Das Rheingold* (Fanny Moran-Olden, Hedwig Reil, Alvary, Fischer).

January 9, 1891 — First American performance of *Diana von Solange*, by Ernst II, Duke of Saxe-Coburg-Gotha. Upon receipt of a petition signed by 300 opera-lovers, a later performance is canceled.

March 21, 1891 — *Die Meistersinger* (Marie Jahn, Charlotte Huhn, Andreas Dippel, Fischer) ends era of German opera. Abbey returns as manager.

December 14, 1891 — Opening night. First American performance of Gounod's *Roméo et Juliette*. Debuts of Emma Eames, Jean de Reszke, Edouard de Reszke.

August 27, 1892 — Interior of the Metropolitan wrecked by fire. Collapse of the Metropolitan Opera House Company, Ltd, and reorganization as the Metropolitan Opera and Real Estate Company.

November 27, 1893 — Opening night for the reconstructed opera house (*Faust*, with Eames, Jean Lassalle, the de Reszkes).

February 4, 1895 — First North American performance of *Falstaff* (Eames, Sofia Scalchi, Giuseppe Campanari, Victor Maurel).

November 27, 1895 — First appearance of Lillian Nordica, singing *Tristan und Isolde* in German, with the de Reszkes.

October 17, 1896 — Death of Abbey. Maurice Grau, new manager, takes a year off to reorganize. No resident company occupies the house in 1897–1898.

February 10, 1897 — Armand Castelmary collapses and dies onstage during a performance of *Martha*.

March 30, 1900 — First Metropolitan production of *The Magic Flute* (Sembrich, Eames, Dippel, Pol Plançon).

February 25, 1902 — Gala performance in honor of Prince Henry of Prussia.

April 27, 1903 — Farewell gala performance for Grau.

November 23, 1903 — Opening night. Heinrich Conried regime begins with *Rigoletto* (debut of Enrico Caruso; Sembrich, Louise Homer, Antonio Scotti).

December 24, 1903 — First staged performance of *Parsifal* outside Bayreuth (Milka Ternina, Alois Burgstaller, Anton Van Rooy, Marcel Journet).

December 5, 1904 — Only Metropolitan performance of Donizetti's *Lucrezia Borgia* (Maria di Macchi, Edyth Walker, Caruso, Scotti).

January 7, 1905 — In first act of *Carmen*, heavy bridge collapses from height of eighteen feet. Curtain lowered while eight members of the chorus are rushed to hospitals.

January 22, 1907 — First American performance of *Salome* (Olive Fremstad, Marion Weed, Dippel, Van Rooy).

February 11, 1907 — First Italian-language production in America of *Madame Butterfly* (Geraldine Farrar, Homer, Caruso, Scotti). Production supervised by Puccini, who receives an ovation.

January 23, 1908 — Debut of Gustav Mahler, conducting *Don Giovanni* (Eames, Johanna Gadski, Sembrich, Alessandro Bonci, Scotti, Feodor Chaliapin).

April 18, 1908 — Conried regime ends with *Götterdämmerung* (Martha Leffler-Burckhard, Homer, Burgstaller, Robert Blass).

November 16, 1908 — First opening night of the Gatti-Casazza regime. Debut of Arturo Toscanini, conducting *Aida* (Emmy Destinn, Homer, Caruso, Scotti).

March 18, 1910 — Frederick Converse's *The Pipe of Desire* (Riccardo Martin, Homer, Clarence Whitehill, Herbert Witherspoon) is the first opera by an American composer to be performed at the Metropolitan.

December 10, 1910 — World premiere of *La Fanciulla del West* (Destinn, Caruso, Pasquale Amato). Staged by David Belasco; production supervised by Puccini.

March 14, 1912 — World premier of Horatio Parker's *Mona* (Homer, Martin, Witherspoon), first opera by an American composer to be commissioned by the Metropolitan.

February 27, 1913 — World premiere of Walter Damrosch's *Cyrano de Bergerac* (Frances Alda, Martin, Amato).

March 19, 1913 — First American performance of *Boris Godounov* (Adamo Didur, Homer, Paul Althouse).

December 9, 1913 — First American performance of *Der Rosenkavalier* (Frieda Hempel, Otto Goritz, Margaret Ober, Anna Case).

April 3, 1916 — Opening of a series of performances by the Diaghilev Ballet Russe, as part of regular Metropolitan subscription season. Principal dancers include Vaslav Nijinsky and Leonid Massine.

April 13, 1917 — *Tristan und Isolde* (Gadski, Jacques Urlus, Margaret Matzenauer, Whitehill); Gadski's farewell performance. Last German-language production at the Metropolitan for nearly three years.

March 23, 1918 — World premiere of Charles Wakefield Cadman's *Shanewis* (Sophie Braslau, Kathleen Howard, Althouse).

November 11, 1918 — *Samson et Dalila* (Homer, Caruso, Robert Couzinou). Opening night coincides with armistice ending World War I.

December 14, 1918 — World premiere of Puccini's three one-act operas *Il Tabarro* (Claudia Muzio, Giulio Crimi, Luigi Montesanto), *Suor Angelica* (Farrar, Flora Perini), *Gianni Schicchi* (Florence Easton, Crimi, Giuseppe de Luca).

January 31, 1920 — World premiere of Henry Hadley's *Cleopatra's Night* (Alda, Orville Harrold, Jeanne Gordon).

December 24, 1920 — *La Juive* (Easton, Caruso, Leon Rothier, Harrold). Caruso's 607th and last appearance at the Metropolitan.

March 24, 1922 — First American performance of *Così fan tutte* (Easton, Lucrezia Bori, de Luca, Didur).

March 21, 1925 — First Metropolitan performance of *Pelléas et Mélisande* (Bori, Edward Johnson, Whitehill, Rothier).

November 16, 1926 — First American performance of *Turandot* (Maria Jeritza, Giacomo Lauri-Volpi, de Luca).

February 17, 1927 — World premiere of Deems Taylor's *The King's Henchman* (Easton, Johnson, Lawrence Tibbett).

January 25, 1930 — First American performance of Rimsky-Korsakoff's *Sadko* (Ina Bourskaya, Gladys Swarthout, Johnson).

February 7, 1931 — World premiere of Taylor's *Peter Ibbetson* (Bori, Johnson, Tibbett).

December 25, 1931 — *Hänsel und Gretel* (Editha Fleischer, Queena Mario, Dorothee Manski) is first opera to be broadcast complete from the Metropolitan. Its coast-to-coast and international shortwave network is largest ever assembled up to that time.

December 3, 1932 — First Metropolitan performance of *Elektra* (Karin Branzell, Gertrude Kappel, Rudolf Laubenthal, Friedrich Schorr).

January 7, 1933 — World premiere of Gruenberg's *The Emperor Jones* (Tibbett, Marek Windheim).

February 25, 1933 — Public fund-raising campaign begins during matinee broadcast of *Manon* (Bori, de Luca, Richard Crooks). Deficit from previous season is $497,213, the largest in many decades.

February 10, 1934 — World premiere of Howard Hanson's *Merry Mount* (Göta Ljungberg, Swarthout, Arnold Gabor, Tibbett).

March 19, 1935 — Farewell gala for retiring Gatti-Casazza. Acts and scenes from six operas performed by twenty-seven artists.

May 10, 1935 — Herbert Witherspoon, named as Gatti's successor, dies of a heart attack. Edward Johnson takes over as general manager.

July–August, 1935 — Metropolitan Opera Guild founded under leadership of Mrs. August Belmont.

December 16, 1935 — First Johnson season opens with *La Traviata* (Bori, Crooks, Tibbett).

May 12, 1937 — World premiere of Walter Damrosch's *The Man Without a Country* (debut of Helen Traubel; Arthur Carron, George Rasely).

February 26, 1938 — Giovanni Martinelli collapses during matinee broadcast of *Aida* (Zinka Milanov, Bruna Castagna, Carlo Tagliabue). Performance resumes in less than half an hour as Frederick Jagel hurries to the Metropolitan to fill in.

1939–1940 season — Million-dollar fund campaign raises $1,042,000. Largest sum from a single source — $327,000 — comes from radio audience.

June 28, 1940 — Metropolitan Opera Association takes title to Metropolitan Opera House from Metropolitan Opera and Real Estate Company.

February 20, 1942 — World premiere of Gian-Carlo Menotti's *The Island God* (Astrid Varnay, Raoul Jobin, Leonard Warren).

December 18, 1943 — Marjorie Lawrence, after being stricken with polio, returns to sing Venus in *Tannhäuser* (Traubel, Lauritz Melchior, Herbert Janssen), a role in which it is not necessary to stand. She later appears as Isolde.

1944–45 season — For the first time in its history, not one foreign-born singer is added to the Metropolitan's roster.

January 11, 1947 — World premiere of Bernard Rogers's *The Warrior* (Regina Resnick, Mack Harrell).

October 25, 1947 — Edward Ziegler dies, ending thirty-year association with the Metropolitan.

June–August, 1948 — Season threatened by labor disputes. Billy Rose offers to operate the Metropolitan for one year "without loss," if "given a free hand and allowed to clean house."

November 29, 1948 — Opening night. *Otello* (Licia Albanese, Ramon Vinay, Warren) is first opera to be telecast from the Metropolitan.

March–May, 1949 — Rudolf Bing of the Glyndebourne Opera, after paying a courtesy call on Edward Johnson, is invited to become Johnson's successor as general manager. Is signed to a three-year contract beginning June 1, 1950.

February 28, 1950 — Formal farewell to Johnson follows *Tosca* (Ljuba Welitch, Ferruccio Tagliavini, Tibbett). Performance, at a $20 top, raises $46,000 for the Edward Johnson Opera Fund.

November 6, 1950 — Bing's first opening night. *Don Carlo* (Delia Rigal, Fedora Barbieri, Jussi Bjoerling, Robert Merrill, Cesare Siepi), a work not heard at the Metropolitan since 1923, staged by Shakespearean director Margaret Webster.

January 22, 1951 — Kirsten Flagstad returns as Isolde. Receives nineteen curtain calls.

January 7, 1955 — Marian Anderson makes her debut as Ulrica in *Un Ballo in maschera*, becoming first Negro to sing a solo role at the Metropolitan.

July–August, 1955 — John D. Rockefeller III announces plans for Lincoln Center for the Performing Arts. Sends architect Wallace K. Harrison, stage director Herbert Graf and assistant manager Herman Krawitz to Europe to study design of European opera houses.

January 15, 1958 — World premiere of Samuel Barber's *Vanessa* (Eleanor Steber, Rosalind Elias, Nicolai Gedda, Giorgio Tozzi).

October 27, 1958 — Metropolitan opens seventy-fifth anniversary season with *Tosca* (Renata Tebaldi, Mario del Monaco, George London).

March 4, 1960 — Warren dies onstage during a performance of *La Forza del destino*.

November 8, 1960 — Clothilde Operti Gobbi, onetime Metropolitan chorister and last surviving member of 1883 opening-night company, dies in Bellevue Hospital at age of 104.

August 9, 1961 — Season temporarily canceled because of dispute with musicians' union. Dispute settled by intervention of President Kennedy, who sends Secretary of Labor Arthur J. Goldberg as mediator.

May 21, 1964 — Metropolitan travels by air during spring tour for first time. Three planes airlift 266 members of the company from Dallas to Minneapolis.

April 16, 1966 — The Metropolitan presents it last operatic performances: a matinee *La Bohème* (Gabriella Tucci, Heidi Krall, Richard Tucker, Jerome Hines), and a final gala, featuring eleven conductors and sixty vocalists.

REQUIEM

for a
Yellow Brick Brewery

1

The People

THE TIDE HAD BEGUN to turn. The postwar slump that had culminated in the Panic of 1873 was over; European crop failures were making American wheat farmers rich. To haul the tremendous crops to market, railroads were lacing the prairies with networks of steel. At Promontory Point, Utah, Ex-governor Leland Stanford had driven a golden spike to link the rails of the Central Pacific with the Union Pacific, and the continent was spanned. Railroad building in the coming decade would eclipse everything that had gone before.

Congress had shored up the sagging wartime greenbacks with bars of gold. For the first time since 1862 paper money was worth its face value in hard coin. Once again it was possible to take paper money to the bank and receive gold or silver in exchange.

And there was more where that came from. Gold had been found at Deadwood Gulch, South Dakota; silver strikes had been made at Leadville, Colorado, and the Great Bonanza Mine in Nevada.

From all over the country, money generated by railroads, mining, manufacturing and commerce was flowing into New York. New fortunes were being made — fortunes like those of Collis P. Huntington, who grubstaked California goldminers in return for a share of their claims; Commodore Cornelius Vanderbilt, who foresaw the railroads' future at a time when prudent money was in canal bonds; or J. P. Morgan, who moved dexterously through the then-unregulated jungles of Wall Street, in which market manipulation was not only openly practiced but also satirized in the cartoons of Thomas Nast.

The stock market reflected the prevailing optimism. The Cowles index, precursor of the Dow-Jones average, opened the year 1879 at 24.85 and closed it at 30.27.

New ideas were in the air. Within the past decade, tennis and polo had been introduced from England. San Francisco had solved the transportation problem of its roller-coaster hills by installing cable cars. New Haven had opened the first telephone switchboard, with twenty-one subscribers. The Remington Fire Arms Company had begun to manufacture typewriters. William Deering had invented his grain binder; George Eastman had begun to manufacture his dry photographic plate; Thomas A. Edison had invented the mimeograph, the phonograph and the electric light; and the town of Wabash, Indiana, was soon to be completely illuminated in a spectacular display of the Brush electrical system.

In New York, the goldbrick swindle, a fraud exceeded in popularity among confidence men only by the selling of the Brooklyn Bridge, had just been introduced by Reed Waddell of Springfield, Illinois.

At the Academy of Music, Colonel James Henry Mapleson was in his second season as New York's leading opera impresario.

The Academy was on East Fourteenth Street, where the Consolidated Edison building now stands. It had a striking resemblance to the famous Academy of Music in Philadelphia. Although chartered by the State of New York as a quasi-educational institution, the Academy over the years had evolved into New York's fashionable opera house. Ironically, it had displaced the Astor Place Opera House for the same reason that would later bring its own downfall — the Astor didn't have enough boxes to go around.

A colorful and knowledgeable description of a typical evening at the Academy is given in a newspaper article by Walt Whitman. Whitman, who loved both Italian opera and spectacles of all kinds, was on the "free list" at the Academy during his newspaper days, and obviously made good use of the privilege. The names of thirteen operas and dozens of allusions to music are found in *Leaves of Grass*. The poem quoted at the beginning of this book was written late in Whitman's career, in 1884, when he was no longer able to hear the operas which had charmed and fascinated him as a young man. A note in Whitman's handwriting identifies it as a memorial

4

tribute to Pasquale Brignoli, the operatic idol of New York in the decade
before the Civil War.*

Contemporary accounts suggest that Brignoli was more than a little of
what would today be called a ham; but he obviously had a voice that communicated. Even so hardened a professional as Krehbiel would write in
1908: "Shall we, because a critic did not like him, be ashamed for having
thrilled a little when we heard his 'Coot boy, sweetheart, c-o-o-o-t boy!'
thirty years ago? I trust not. . . . I had been four years in the turmoil of
New York's musical life when Brignoli died; I cannot recall an unkind
word that was ever spoken of him."

The Academy had seen opera presented by a variety of impresarios.
One disastrous season, under the Norwegian violinist Ole Bull, lasted only
two weeks, and during one three-year period there had been five
impresarios.

Colonel James Henry Mapleson was one of the most colorful of the lot.
He had been an opera singer under the name of Enrico Mariani, a profes-
sional viola player and finally for twenty-seven years an impresario in
London and New York. How he came by his military title is not known.

Those who knew him testified to the Colonel's extraordinary powers of
persuasion. Once a theatrical costumer with a long-overdue bill for $1,500
swore out a warrant for Mapleson's arrest. After talking with the Colonel
for half an hour, he called off the sheriff and lent Mapleson an additional
seventy-five.

Mapleson was said to be the only man alive who could persuade Adelina
"the divine" Patti to sing before she had received her fee. (Patti once
sent word to an impresario who had not paid in advance that she was
ready to perform, except for her shoes. Taking the hint, the impresario
quickly scrounged half the agreed-upon fee. Word came back that Patti
had put on one slipper and would don the other when the rest of the money
arrived.) Colonel Mapleson kissed her hand, buttered her up with flattery and ended by owing money to Patti as well as to everyone else.

Patti was the unrivaled bright star of Mapleson's New York company.

---

* The "Fernando" of Whitman's poem is the hero of Donizetti's *La Favorita*, the unhappy lover who discovers that his adored sweetheart is the King's mistress: "*Favorita
del Re!*" Manrico in *Il Trovatore* and Ernani are still familiar to modern listeners.
"Sweet Gennaro" is the hero of *Lucrezia Borgia* by Donizetti, the supposed lover who
in reality is Lucrezia's son by an earlier marriage.

Another member, considerably less bright, was a tenor named Nicolini, who was Patti's husband. He sang only when Patti did but not always then. The story was widely circulated that Patti charged two separate fees: six thousand francs for herself alone and four thousand francs for herself and Nicolini.*

At some point during Colonel Mapleson's 1879–1880 season occurred the incident described by Lilli Lehmann in her memoirs: "As, on a particular evening, one of the millionairesses did not receive the box in which she intended to shine because another woman had anticipated her, the husband of the former took prompt action and caused the Metropolitan Opera House to rise."

Nowadays it seems odd to think of Vanderbilts as being among the "new people." But the $94,000,000 left by Commodore Vanderbilt in 1877 was a much more recent fortune than those, for example, of the Lorillards or Goelets. The Lorillards had been profitably concerned with tobacco since the eighteenth century. The Goelets were descended from Peter Goelet, a pre-Revolutionary ironmonger who, at a time when it was held unthinkable that civilization could ever advance so far uptown, had bought what eventually became mid-Manhattan, from Union Square to Forty-seventh Street.

Lorillards, Goelets, Bayards, Beekmans, Schuylers and other old Manhattan families, some going back to the days of New Amsterdam, made up the "Knickerbocker aristocracy." It was a select inner circle to which virtually all the boxholders at the Academy of Music belonged. By 1880, however, the wealth and power of the Knickerbockers was being eclipsed by the immense fortunes the "new people" were piling up.

"This social decay," one historian wrote, "began about 1840, and culminated in the Vanderbilt ball of 1882, to which nearly all the leaders of the old Knickerbocker aristocracy accepted invitations. . . . Sagacious and far-sighted Knickerbockers began to realize that as a caste they no longer possessed sufficient money to sustain social ascendancy, and that it behooved them to form an intimate alliance with the *nouveaux riches*."

Accommodation with the *nouveaux riches*, however, did not go so far as

---

* The dollar had been so recently stabilized that European artists, some with searing memories of inflation and currency devaluation, did not wholly trust it. As late as 1903, Caruso's first contract was paid in gold Swiss francs.

to include the boxes at the Academy of Music. Accordingly, the Vanderbilt money began making its power felt.

On April 3, 1880, George Henry Warren, a Vanderbilt-connected lawyer and stockbroker, called on the German-born banker who had changed his name from Augustus Schönberg to its French form, August Belmont, and risen to eminence in the firm of Kuhn, Loeb & Company. It says something for Belmont's *savoir faire* that while other newcomers waited outside the magic circle, he was president of the Academy of Music's board of directors.

It seems clear that there had been earlier discussions in which Warren had intimated that since there were not enough boxes at the Academy to go around, he and his associates intended to build an opera house of their own. Academy officials could not have failed to be alarmed at the prospect of such formidable competition. At the April 3rd meeting, Belmont and his fellow directors Lorillard, Van Hoffman and Dinsmore submitted a compromise plan. It was a design for remodeling the interior of the Academy that would add twenty-six new boxes.

It wasn't enough. On April 7, Warren told the New York *Times* that he and a group of associates had subscribed $800,000 to purchase a site and build a new opera house.

The *Times* story listed some of the associates. Cyrus Field, who, after long delays and frustrations, had succeeded in laying the first transatlantic cable. Jay Gould, Commodore Vanderbilt's archenemy in the railroad wars, who, when not in New Jersey as a fugitive from New York justice, conducted his affairs from the theatre on West Twenty-third Street that had been built for the dual purpose of housing the Erie Railroad's offices and displaying the charms of Josie Mansfield.

William C. Whitney, Secretary of the Navy in Cleveland's cabinet, who had begun his ascent to riches as an inspector of New York City schools. Darius Ogden Mills, who had made his fortune from mining; James Harriman, from railroads; James Gordon Bennett, from the New York *Herald*, and William Rockefeller, from oil. George F. Baker, who had attained the presidency of the First National Bank of New York by a process he once described when asked whether it was a good time to sell stocks: "I don't sell stocks, I only buy them."

Although many of the founding group were "new people," there were also Roosevelts — in those days impeccable Knickerbocker aristocrats — Iselins, Astors, Goelets and others who either wished to move with the times or were merely bored with the Academy.

An important group of founders was made up of Vanderbilts and their associates — William H., William K. and Cornelius Vanderbilt, Warren and cotton broker R. T. Wilson, whose daughter Grace married Cornelius Vanderbilt III. Another group centered around the elder J. P. Morgan, whose favorite opera was *Il Trovatore* and who had emphatic ideas about how the music should be performed. The Morgan group included George P. Wetmore, Levi P. Morton, J. Hood Wright and G. G. Haven, all Morgan business associates. It also included Henry C. Clews, whose *Fifty Years in Wall Street* is one of the great classics of the market in its buccaneering days and whose firm still does business at Number 2 Broadway.

The group formed a corporation, the Metropolitan Opera House Company, Ltd. (Any American corporation may use the British designation "Limited" rather than "Incorporated" if it cares to.) Sixty-five founding members each subscribed to 150 shares of stock in the new company at a hundred dollars a share, which entitled them to a box when the opera house was built. In addition, Warren, George Peabody Wetmore, William K. Vanderbilt and Robert and Ogden Goelet each subscribed for a second box. On the other hand, J. N. A. Griswold, first president of the Metropolitan Opera House Company, Ltd, does not appear to have reserved a box at all.

The site originally chosen for its new opera house by the Metropolitan Opera House Company was the block bounded by Vanderbilt and Madison avenues, East Forty-third and East Forty-fourth streets, where the Hotel Biltmore now stands. While its lawyers went about acquiring title to the property, the company invited four architectural firms to submit designs for the new opera house. The firms were those of G. E. Harvey, George B. Post, Potter & Harrison, and Josiah Cleaveland Cady. Each firm was given a $3,000 retainer and three months' working time. On October 15, 1880, it was announced that Cady's design had won.

Cady, designer of the American Museum of Natural History, Saint Andrew's Church, the Hudson Street Hospital and numerous college buildings, was a zealous Sunday School teacher and amateur organist. He had never been to Europe, never seen the world's great opera houses, nor, for that matter, attended an opera performance. But when his design won the competition, Cady sailed for Europe to fill the operatic gap in his knowledge. The egg-shaped acoustical chamber he installed under the Metropolitan stage may have been copied from the similar one at La Scala. Cady also studied the plans of Covent Garden. They were made available by impresario Ernest Gye, who hoped to obtain the producing rights at the new opera house.

For European experience and a knowledge of operatic tradition, Cady relied heavily on a twenty-four-year-old Swiss draftsman, Louis de Coppet Bergh. But when the Metropolitan contract was awarded, Bergh was so elated that he married his fiancée and went to Lake Mohonk for a honeymoon. Cady was forced to send three urgent telegrams summoning him back to his drawing board.

Meanwhile the lawyers had run into an obstacle. The deeds to several plots on the Vanderbilt Avenue site specifically forbade their use as "places of amusement," a term elastic enough to embrace an opera house. On March 8, 1881, the Vanderbilt Avenue site was abandoned. Instead the Metropolitan Opera House Company purchased the block bounded by West Thirty-ninth Street, Broadway, West Fortieth Street and Seventh Avenue.

Cady must have been thunderstruck. His building had been designed for a rectangular plot; whereas the new site, because of Broadway's list to port as it veers uptown, was an irregular block no two sides of which were equal in length. It might have been wiser to start afresh with a new design. But since it was his original design that had won the competition, Cady used it again, and by cutting and fitting, he managed to wedge it into the Broadway site.

The $1,100,000 raised by the initial subscription soon proved insufficient. Boom times had brought rising costs for labor and materials. By the time the $125,000 foundation was completed, building costs had risen so sharply that it was suggested the group abandon its opera-house project and put up an apartment building instead. A narrow majority of stockholders voted to go ahead; the rest voted against it or abstained. The capitalization was increased to $1,700,000; when finally completed, the house would cost $1,732,978.71.

Since the memory of recent disastrous theatre fires, notably the destruction of the Burgtheater in Vienna, was vivid, no aspect of the building received more careful attention than its fireproofing. The building was solid masonry throughout; there was not a stud partition in it. Floors were iron beams and brick arches. The roof was of iron, masonry and slate, supported by iron roof beams more than a hundred feet long, which were mounted on rollers to allow for expansion and contraction. The ceiling of the auditorium was of iron, as were the proscenium, the tier balustrades and the partitions between the boxes. To meet the specifications for the boxes, the ironwork contractor had had to erect his own mill for bending and rolling the beams. Fire exits were numerous and well designed; the house could be completely emptied in less than three minutes.

The stage was supported not by wooden beams but by more than four thousand sectional irons, which could be removed to open the stage floor. In addition, since theatre fires almost invariably originate on the stage, Cady devised a backstage sprinkler system. A large skylight was counterweighted so as to fall open in case of fire. Above the skylight was a great water tank, feeding a network of pipes that were stoppered with quick-melting solder. The heat from even a small fire would melt the solder to release a drenching cascade of water. In addition, a heavy asbestos curtain could be quickly lowered to keep the flames backstage.

On May 24, 1883, the newly completed Metropolitan Opera House was put to its first official use. President Griswold called a meeting of Metropolitan Opera House Company shareholders to draw lots for the boxes. The lots were drawn by the daughters of shareholders Warren and John Peter Townsend. While young Miss Warren drew names from one hat, Miss Townsend drew numbers from another.

At the same meeting, each shareholder was assessed five thousand dollars to finance completion of the storefronts to be rented on the Broadway side of the building. The thrifty shareholders felt the Metropolitan Opera House Company, Ltd, ought to return *something* on their investment.

2

The House

EVEN IN A CITY with its fair share of grotesque nineteenth-century architecture, the Metropolitan stood out. Very early it was derisively called "the new yellow-brick brewery on Broadway," and, in all candor, that is just what it looked like. Its façade was the target of so much criticism that Cady felt obliged to defend himself in a letter to the *Tribune*, in which he maintained that "probably no other building in the country has received so much care and thought."

Its foyer was small and not very impressive; it looked rather like a prosperous suburban bank. There was no dramatic central staircase for opera patrons to ascend and descend in glittering evening dress. The house was deficient in the studios, rehearsal rooms and practice stages found in most well-equipped opera houses, where extra rehearsal space is needed because at any given moment during the season a number of rehearsals are simultaneously going on. Leading artists may be coaching their roles in *Carmen*, for example, while the chorus rehearses *Lucia di Lammermoor* and brass players of the orchestra play a *"Tuben-rehearsal"* for *Lohengrin*.

Until the time of Gatti-Casazza, who came to the Metropolitan as general manager in 1908, the only rehearsal stage was that of the auditorium itself. The ballet rehearsed in what later became Sherry's Restaurant. Chorus rehearsals were held in the ladies' parlor or the smoking room of the Grand Tier.

Many a prima donna accustomed to European theatres received a shock at the sight of her cramped dressing room, with its unenclosed toilet and washbasin. It was one of the duties of a prima donna's maid to come down on the afternoon of a performance with a screen to hide the "conveniences." These were found only on the women's side of the house; in the men's dressing rooms there was no plumbing at all.

The Metropolitan's most serious and costly defect was its lack of provision for storing scenery. Backstage storage space was not merely inadequate; it was nonexistent. With his left hand on the rearmost flat of a stage set, one could touch the Seventh Avenue wall of the building with his right.

The burden imposed on the company by its cramped backstage facilities can hardly be overstated. From the beginning, the Metropolitan functioned as a repertory company rather than a stock company — that is, it presented a different opera every night, and two on Saturday. In most well-equipped repertory theatres there is space for storing the scenery for at least one or two productions besides the current one. At the Metropolitan, however, the only way to get a new set in was to move the old one out.

Walking down Seventh Avenue in foul winter weather, one flinched to see Joseph Urban sets stacked against the rear wall of the building, protected only by a tarpaulin. A caterer would have taken better care of his marquees. It is disheartening to think of the dollars washed away in the slush and grime.

The financial burden became heavier and heavier as the cost of doing business with the stagehands' union increased year by year. Today a Broadway producer with a hit will think long and earnestly before transferring it to a larger theatre, because of the cost of trucking scenery across town. The Metropolitan, however, was in the position of moving a production six to eight times weekly, to five different warehouses located all over the city.

It is easy to blame Cady's inexperience and ignorance of operatic requirements for the lack of storage space. Yet, in fairness to the architect, it is hard to see where he could have put it. Only with difficulty had he shoehorned his original design into the irregular Broadway plot. To provide the desired number of boxes, the auditorium needed to be a certain minimum size. The stage had to be in proportion to the auditorium, and the depth of the stage in proportion to its height. By that time, the rear of

12

"The new yellow-brick brewery on Broadway"

the stage was touching Seventh Avenue and the box office was on Broadway. Expansion upward was impossible; a New York City ordinance forbade building anything on top of a theatre.

Cady believed a space beneath the stage would be adequate for storing scenery and it was, until a fire in 1892 showed what a hazard painted canvas could be. Thereafter, sets went back to the warehouse after a performance.

So many things about the opera house were crude, inadequate makeshifts that almost as soon as the building was completed, there was talk of erecting a new one. When Gatti-Casazza took over as general manager in 1908, board chairman Otto Kahn advised him not to waste money on new scenery. In a few years completion of the new opera house would make the sets obsolete. Both men would have been incredulous at the idea that the old house would be functioning more than fifty years later.

The Metropolitan, however, had one virtue that made up for many shortcomings: superb acoustics. It is astonishing that Cady, a rank tyro at theatrical design, should have hit the target so squarely on his first attempt. Acoustical excellence, even today, is an elusive thing. London's Royal Festival Hall, built in 1951, New York's 1962 Philharmonic Hall and Berlin's 1963 Philharmonie all turned out to be badly planned from an acoustical point of view.

A peculiarity of Metropolitan acoustics was that the singer could not hear himself. In most halls there is a slight reverberation, an echo that is audible even though lasting only a fraction of a second. But at the Metropolitan the sound appeared to be dissipated into the void. Singers appearing there for the first time consequently had a tendency to panic and to force their voices. The first ovation, however, assured them they *were* being heard.

Its size and its acoustics made the Metropolitan unique among the great opera houses of the world. Not La Scala, not Covent Garden, not the opera houses of Paris, Berlin or Vienna approached its capacity of nearly four thousand seats. And it was possible to hear in every one of them.

Seeing was another matter. "From the uppermost rows, known as the 'peanut gallery' in common jargon," wrote Robert Goelet in his memoirs, "only about one-quarter of the seats had a view of the stage. The writer

15

can vouch for this fact, having had to sit in them on various occasions when he served on committees to see if the situation could not be ameliorated." But the opera house, of course, had not been designed for occupants of the peanut gallery. Essentially it was a semicircle of boxes with an opera house built around them, a private club to which the general public was somewhat grudgingly admitted.

As originally constructed, the Metropolitan had four rows of boxes. On the ground-floor Orchestra Circle there were twelve *baignoire* boxes, so called because of their resemblance to bathtubs. Above these were the thirty-eight parterre boxes. The First Tier and Second Tier (later renamed Grand Tier and Dress Circle) had thirty-six boxes each. Only the seventy-four boxes of the parterre and Grand Tier were allotted to shareholders of the Metropolitan Opera House Company; the others were rented for $12,000 a season.

The *baignoire* and Dress Circle boxes soon disappeared; not even New York in the Cleveland Administration could support 122 boxes at the opera, with seats for 732 persons. The Grand Tier boxes were removed when the house was remodeled in 1940. Only the parterre boxes remained to the very end.

Even with a last semicircle of boxes, the house had a quality of grandeur felt by everyone who ever attended a performance there. The opulent red-and-gold splendor of its interior was all the more impressive because of the rather modest entrance through which it was reached; it was almost as if one had entered through a labyrinth of narrow tunnels that opened on a sumptuous *palazzo*.

Its sunburst chandelier, waffle-grid ceiling embellished with paintings and gold leaf, and ornately carved box fronts belonged to the elegance of a bygone age; in our severely functional times, no architect would have the nerve to design them. The names carved across the top of the six-story gold proscenium — Gluck, Mozart, Beethoven, Verdi, Wagner, Gounod — struck some observers as incongruous, considering the erratic manner in which the first three had figured in Metropolitan history. But the Metropolitan honored Gluck, Mozart and Beethoven, even if it did not always perform them.

The Metropolitan's interior had grandeur — and something more. It reflected an era, somewhat as that era was reflected in the short stories of

O. Henry. It mirrored New York in its Augustan Age — urbane, prosperous and self-assured, undisputed leader of the nation in every aspect of business, finance, science, industry and the arts, wanting nothing but the best and willing to pay to get it. Like the Fifth Avenue Public Library and the Pennsylvania Station, it was part of what Lewis Mumford called "the Imperial Façade."

A Metropolitan performance has just ended. The asbestos curtain is down, the musicians' heads are barely visible as they file out of the orchestra pit, the boxes and the first rows of orchestra seats are already empty and Ward McAllister (extreme right), social arbiter of the "Four Hundred," is helping Mrs. Albert Stevens with her ermine wrap.

At McAllister's right elbow is the somewhat dour-looking "Mrs. Logan," probably the wife of General John A. Logan of Illinois, unsuccessful Republican candidate for Vice-President on the Blaine-Logan ticket of 1884.

Next to Mrs. Logan is bearded Benjamin Harrison, the President of the United States. At his right is Chauncey M. Depew, noted as a businessman and after-dinner speaker.

At Depew's right, with a flower in his lapel, wearing pince-nez glasses and looking remarkably like Gustav Mahler, is Vice-President Levi P. Morton. At Morton's right is white-bearded James G. Blaine, other half of the Blaine-Logan ticket. Peering over Blaine's shoulder is John Wanamaker, New York–Philadelphia merchant and Postmaster General in Harrison's cabinet.

Speaker of the House Thomas B. Reed, at Morton's left, gestures with his fore-finger to emphasize a point, but Morton appears more interested (as are Blaine and

Wanamaker) in the pretty brunette at his right. She is Mrs. Grover Cleveland, wife of the former and future President. Her mustached husband is at her elbow.

Half hidden behind President Cleveland is the Rasputin-like figure of black-bearded, slope-browed Jay Gould. Next to Gould are white-bearded Charles A. Dana of the New York sun and black-bearded, curly-haired former Secretary of the Interior Carl Schurz.

The trio of beauties at the extreme left are Mrs. Herman Oelrichs, Mrs. Samuel Colgate and the Duchess of Marlborough.

The fifty-nine clearly recognizable portraits in this drawing also include business-men Andrew Carnegie, Collis P. Huntington, Russell Sage, Darius Ogden Mills and Henry Clews; theatrical producers Augustine Daly and Dan Frohman; actress Lillian Russell and actors Joseph Jefferson, Edwin Booth and John Drew; publishers Joseph Pulitzer and James Gordon Bennett; authors Bret Harte and William Dean Howells; socialite F. Gray Griswold and a generous sprinkling of Vanderbilts and Astors.

Visible at ground level are the "bathtub" boxes and the doors in the proscenium arch, on either side of the stage, through which the performers emerged to take their curtain calls. Calvé used to look through the peep-hole to count the house. All these features disappeared when the interior was rebuilt after the fire of August 27, 1892.

3

Opening Night

THERE WAS ALWAYS SOMETHING SPECIAL about an opening night at the Metropolitan; no other social event was quite like it. To begin with, there was the wine-sparkling air of October in New York. A stranger could sense it the moment he stepped off the train. Almost involuntarily his shoulders would go back and his step would quicken. Much-traveled Edna Ferber said she would rather be in New York in October than anywhere in the world.

There was stimulation in the air and anticipation in the opera house. An audience that would be jaded enough by April looked forward eagerly to the new season. New works to be performed, old ones to be revived, new voices to be discovered, familiar favorites to be heard again — if the season wasn't quite to live up to its promise, that fact wouldn't be apparent on opening night.

That particular evening always had a strange heady quality that made people do all sorts of curious things. In a later season, Richard A. Knight, whose career had included disbarment from the law and kidnaping a child from his own wife to stop a divorce action, would turn cartwheels through Sherry's Restaurant with full-dress tails flying, and stand on his head for the benefit of photographers. Dowager Mrs. Frank Henderson, also for the sake of photographers, would place her leg on a table at Sherry's, observing: "What's Marlene got that I haven't got?"

Part of the headiness undoubtedly was due to the alcoholic refreshments that were always consumed in generous quantities. But people drank elsewhere with less picturesque results; nor was the same genial madness evident at other performances of the season. Opening night was special.

There is no reason to suppose it was greatly different on October 22, 1883, when the new opera house came to life for the first time. As the sun sank over the Hudson River, a few blocks away, gaslights fluttered on to illuminate the foyer and marquee. Windows glowed one after another as lamplighters made their way from room to room, until the whole building was alight. The auditorium chandelier came on in a brilliant ring of flame. The Metropolitan was open.

Across the street, clerks and stenographers lingered for opening-night office parties. Lumberyard workers in the next block headed for a saloon to watch the excitement. At the hotels St. Cloud and Metropole, two blocks up Broadway, elegant bars hosted merry groups in evening dress, opera-bound. At the Normandie, a block down Broadway, vocalises filled the air as singers did their final warming up for the performance.

In his backstage office, manager Henry E. Abbey busied himself with final preparations for the performance. Abbey, a well-known theatrical producer and concert manager, had been chosen to present opera at the Metropolitan much as Colonel Mapleson presented it at the Academy of Music. Abbey was to offer a season of sixty-one performances, for which the boxholders posted a guarantee of $60,000 against possible losses.

As a boy in Akron, Ohio, Abbey had acquired a taste for music by playing the cornet in the high-school band; but he had had no actual experience in producing opera. He therefore intended to take no chances with his opening-night production. He had scheduled the most surefire opera imaginable — *Faust*, with a cast headed by Christine Nilsson and Italo Campanini.

Abbey had cause for concern. Colonel Mapleson, who did not intend to give up without a fight, had audaciously scheduled his Academy of Music opening for the same night. His opera was *La Sonnambula*, with the phenomenal coloratura Etelka Gerster in the title role. And to complicate Abbey's situation still further, the socially obligatory National Horse Show was also scheduled.

As the curtain time of 6:45 approached, Abbey observed the house. It was well filled; many ticketholders had come early to admire the decor and stare at the boxholders. Newspapers that day had printed diagrams showing whose box was where. But the boxes were mostly empty. Prudently, Abbey delayed his curtain half an hour.

Finally they began arriving, driving up in polished broughams, victorias and cabriolets, with liveried coachmen and footmen, high-stepping horses clop-clopping on the Broadway cobblestones. They passed through the sidewalk crowds, the men in top hats, opera capes lined with red satin, white-tie formals and pearl shirt studs; the ladies sparkling with emeralds and diamonds, satin-gowned, wrapped in sable or chinchilla. The audience itself was part of the show.

Abbey's first production was not an especially remarkable one. It was a familiar cast in a familiar opera: *Faust,* much as everyone was accustomed to hearing it at the Academy of Music. Three of the male principals — Campanini, Giuseppe Del Puente and Franco Novara (an Englishman whose real name was Frank Nash) — had in fact been lured by Abbey from the Academy of Music. Both Campanini and Nilsson, although popular favorites, were a little past their prime. And the playing of the orchestra recruited by conductor Auguste Vianesi in Venice, Naples, Leipzig and London left much to be desired.

But the house magnificently performed the social function which was its chief *raison d'être.* In those days *Faust* was given in five acts. Four long intermissions gave people plenty of time to visit one another's boxes, to see and be seen. Champagne corks popped and glasses clinked throughout the performance.

When Nilsson sang the Jewel Song, according to H. E. Krehbiel in the New York *Tribune,* "an avalanche of plaudits overwhelmed the fair singer. Bouquets rained from the boxes, and baskets of flowers were piled over the footlights as if there was to be no end. In the midst of the floral gifts there was also handed up a magnificent velvet casket inclosing a wreath of gold bay leaves and berries, ingeniously contrived to be extended into a girdle to be worn in the classic style, and two gold brooch medallions, bearing the profiles of Tragedy and Comedy, with which the girdle was to be fastened. The donor was not mentioned, but an inscription told that the gift was in 'commemoration of the opening of the Metropolitan Opera House.' "

It was past midnight when the last of the shining carriages pulled away from the gaslit marquee. Meanwhile, twenty-five blocks downtown, an equally brilliant performance had been taking place at the Academy of Music. Besides the Knickerbocker aristocrats, the audience included J. N. A. Griswold, first president of the Metropolitan, who by now had rejoined the Academy fold. Also at the Academy were New York's two most famous musicians, Theodore Thomas and Leopold Damrosch.

And at the old Madison Square Garden, the glittering National Horse Show further compounded the dilemma of those who wished to be where the fashion was. Some hostesses solved the dilemma by spending part of the evening at one attraction, part at another. Mrs. Paran Stevens, it is said, managed to attend all three.

With the histrionics of opening night out of the way, the Metropolitan settled down to producing its first season of opera. Colonel Mapleson was formidable competition. In addition to Gerster, he still had under contract the inimitable Patti, who would be returning early in November. And when the Colonel staged his own *Faust*, he introduced another drawing card, Lillian Norton Gower. She was from the small town of Farmington, Maine, then as now one of the unlikeliest spots for the appearance of a prima donna who would become world-famous as Lillian Nordica.

Henry T. Finck, the critic of the *Evening Post*, wrote of Nordica: "Her voice was huge; the biggest orchestra could not submerge it in its tidal wave of sound. It was also as beautiful, as smooth, mellow, velvety and luscious as the voice of any prima donna I have ever heard.

"Patti, Gerster, Tetrazzini, Calvé, Sembrich, Melba had to keep strictly in their field if they wanted to escape trouble, as we saw in the case of Melba. Nordica could roam and rove wherever she pleased.

"Her voice easily rose above the mighty surge of sound produced by a hundred fortissimo players. In the soaring melodies of the last scene of *Siegfried*, the superbly complicated and sonorous orchestra was as a mere guitar accompaniment to her voluminous emotion-laden voice. And when she came to that thrilling high C, she rose to it as easily as if her voice had had wings — unlike some other Brünnhildes who always filled me with dire apprehensions when that climax drew near."

Unlike Patti and Melba, Nordica was not born with a perfect vocal technique. She had had to work hard to achieve vocal mastery. She was a "slow study" but a stubborn and industrious student, and when she learned a part it was for good. Before venturing to sing Isolde, she underwent

Lillian Nordica as Brünnhilde in DIE WALKÜRE

the drudgery of more than a year's piano rehearsals. At the final rehearsal, her accompanist was so moved by her singing that he attempted to kiss her. Nordica slipped from his embrace and, after a chase around the studio, escaped.

Later someone asked why she had made such a fuss over so relatively trifling a matter.

"He had been eating garlic," Nordica replied.

Nordica had a corpulent but devoted suitor in Willie Schutz, the brother of the soprano Félia Litvinne. Willie was said to have proposed to Nordica at least twice a week. Once he invited her to go to Paris. Nordica refused but allowed Willie to take her white poodle, Toutou. In Paris, Willie received the news that Nordica had married Zoltan Doeme, a Hungarian tenor whose real name was Solomon Teitelbaum.

"He sang *Parsifal* at Bayreuth only once," James G. Huneker recalled of Doeme. "I was present. So was Nordica. Yet she married him."

The news was almost fatal to Willie Schutz. When next he appeared in public, the poodle had been dyed mourning black and wore around its neck a huge crepe bow. The tenderhearted *cocottes* on the terrace of the Cafe Monferino set up a wail of commiseration: *"Oh! Le pauvre Toutou, il a perdu sa maman."*

The Metropolitan unveiled a discovery of its own at the second 1893 performance, a *Lucia di Lammermoor* in which the title role was sung by Bohemian-born Marcella Sembrich.

Aside from the performers, there was little to choose between the Metropolitan's season and Colonel Mapleson's. The Metropolitan, it is true, had scheduled one work not previously heard in New York, *La Gioconda.* Otherwise its repertoire was chosen from the same Rossini, Bellini, Donizetti, Gounod and Verdi standbys as Colonel Mapleson's. In either company's prospectus, Krehbiel observed, "there was little to interest a public supposedly weary of the barrel-organ list."

Where the Metropolitan *did* shine was in the lavishness of its productions. Abbey was an open-handed spender. The sets he provided for the enormous Metropolitan stage were without precedent in any American theatre. In the sumptuous wardrobe, every costume, every shoe and stocking was supplied by Worth of Paris, then the most famous dressmaker in the world. Abbey paid his stars a thousand dollars a performance, an

27

astronomical fee in those days. The sums of money tossed about by Abbey were staggering to Lilli Lehmann, the frugal prima donna who rode horsecars to the Metropolitan to save the expense of a hack.

The Metropolitan had its first Wagnerian production on November 7, with *Lohengrin*. Campanini sang the title role, and Lohengrin's famous aria, *Nun sei bedankt, mein lieber Schwan*, was heard as *Addio, addio, cigno caro*. Like all the operas of the opening season, *Lohengrin* was sung in Italian.

Four days later there occurred the first of the Sunday evening concerts, featuring members of the company and prominent guest artists, that became a Metropolitan tradition until the arrival of Rudolf Bing.

After a Christmas Eve performance of *Rigoletto*, Abbey took his company to Boston for a two-week stand. The New York season was resumed with *Carmen* on January 9, Zelia Trebelli making a much-praised appearance in the title role. In mid-January the company set off on a tour that took them as far as Chicago. Altogether, there were fifty-four out-of-town performances during the opening season.

Abbey's forces returned to the Metropolitan for a spring season that lasted from March 10 to April 11. Then Abbey and his accountants sat down to go over the books. Presently, shareholders of the Metropolitan Opera House Company, Ltd were staggered to learn that in his opening season their general manager had run up a deficit of $600,000.

It was a formidable sum, more than one-third of what it had cost to build the house. When Krehbiel heard the size of the deficit, he asked to have it confirmed in writing. Abbey's deficit established a long-standing record; so great a loss was not again incurred until after World War II.

Part of Abbey's losses, of course, was the result of what would be termed in a modern corporation "heavy start-up expenses." At least a part of the deficit was actually an investment in sets and costumes, which had to be paid for at once but whose cost could be amortized over a number of seasons. Abbey in fact had had to stage nearly a score of operas from scratch, which would strain the resources of any company, even today. In the following season, however, the company would be that many operas ahead of the game.

Abbey appears to have been unable to get the boxholders to take that view of the matter. They were preoccupied with the Worth gowns, the expensive out-of-town engagements and the operating loss of $600,000. Under the terms of their agreement, of course, the boxholders were liable for only one-tenth of that amount. It was up to Abbey to find the remaining $540,000.

Abbey offered to manage the following season without fee if the shareholders would assume the deficit. This unbusinesslike suggestion so shocked the shareholders that they dismissed him. They did, however, permit him the use of the opera house for a benefit on his own behalf.

Abbey's theatrical ventures had given him valuable contacts on both sides of the Atlantic, and the benefit performance he presented at the Metropolitan on April 21, 1884, was memorable. It included overtures by Rossini and Meyerbeer; scenes from *Lucrezia Borgia, Il Trovatore, Aida* and *Les Huguenots*, performed by leading members of the company; the Trial Scene from *The Merchant of Venice*, with a cast headed by Henry Irving and Ellen Terry, and a concluding "Grand Ballet Divertissement."

The bright star of the performance, however, was Marcella Sembrich. In the Lesson Scene from *Il Barbiere di Siviglia*, she sang a brilliant coloratura showpiece, the Proch Variations. Later she appeared onstage with a violin to play the slow movement and concluding Rondo of the de Bériot Concerto no. 7. When she had concluded a remarkably polished and musicianly performance, the house could scarcely restrain its enthusiasm. As an encore, Sembrich sat down at the piano to play a Chopin mazurka. For good measure, she played the violin obbligato to Nilsson's singing of the Bach-Gounod "Ave Maria."

It was a *tour de force* of musicianship perhaps unmatched in the history of music. Mozart performed publicly both as pianist and violinist, but in singing he seems to have had a "composer's voice." As a youthful student of piano, voice and violin, Sembrich had shown such extraordinary gifts in all three directions that her perplexed teachers had finally taken her to Franz Liszt for an opinion. It was Liszt who advised her to choose a singing career.

The concert netted Abbey $16,000 — a respectable sum but hardly a drop in the bucket in terms of his total liability. He was obliged to use the profits of three other theatrical ventures to pay off his Metropolitan liabilities. Having done so, he disappeared temporarily from the Metropolitan's history.

The boxholders now had to look for another general manager. Ernest Gye, the impresario of Covent Garden, had been considered before Abbey was engaged, and negotiations with him were now resumed. But Gye was married to a soprano from upstate New York who had honored her home-town by taking the stage name of Emma Albani. In those days "prima donna" meant what it said, and no company could have more than one. The Metropolitan's "first lady" was Nilsson. If Albani came, it would have to be as Nilsson's associate. Gye decided to remain at Covent Garden.

By now the boxholders were becoming alarmed. It was August; the negotiations with Gye had consumed most of the summer. There was talk of having to cancel the season. At that moment, like the *deux ex machina* of a baroque opera, unexpected help arrived in the person of Leopold Damrosch.

Damrosch needed little in the way of introduction. His bearded, frock-coated figure had long been a familiar sight in the New York concert halls. A native of Silesia, Damrosch had been trained as a physician and had actually practiced medicine in his native Breslau. But his musical bent was too powerful to be denied. Emigrating to New York, he had quickly taken a leading part in the city's musical life. He was the founder-conductor of the still-flourishing New York Oratorio Society and of the New York Symphony, which merged with the Philharmonic in 1929.

Damrosch placed before the Metropolitan's directors a revolutionary proposal — a season of opera in German. It would be supported by the city's German population, at that time estimated at a quarter of a million. It would emphasize Wagner, the coming man of opera; partic-ularly those Wagnerian works that New York had not seen before. Abbey's highly paid stars would be replaced by capable but lower-priced artists recruited from the opera houses of Central Europe.

The directors appear to have accepted Damrosch's offer on the spot, which tells something about his reputation and his power of persuasion. And Damrosch showed his expertise and his intimate knowledge of the European musical scene by sailing in August (at which time an impre-sario normally would be planning the season after next), recruiting his company and being ready to open with *Tannhäuser* on November 17.

Singing the title role was Anton Schott, whose explosive style led con-ductor-pianist Hans von Bülow to dub him the "military tenor."

"He is an artilleryman," Bülow told Krehbiel. "When he sings flat, he *des*tonates, when he sings sharp, he *dis*tonates, and when he sings in tune, as he sometimes does, he *de*tonates." (In German, *des*, *dis* and *de* mean, respectively, D flat, D sharp and D natural.)

The opening night was an immense success and augured well for Damrosch's season. A highlight was the first New York performance of *Die Walküre*, with Amalia Materna in her world-famous interpretation of Brünnhilde. The sets and costumes were faithful copies of those at Bayreuth, and the Bayreuth staging that had been supervised by Wagner himself was carefully imitated.

By mid-January of 1885, it was clear that Damrosch's policy was succeeding. Although his admission prices were barely half what Abbey had charged, twice as much money had come into the box office as in the first two months of the preceding season. His performances had been critical and popular successes. And they had proved murderous competition for Colonel Mapleson, presenting the same old *Lucia*s and *Barber*s at the Academy of Music.

Physically, the Academy was as rundown as its repertoire. More than once, said Krehbiel, a dramatic climax on the stage had been spoiled by the collapse of a seat in the auditorium. By Christmas, Colonel Mapleson's season was finished. Soon he would leave New York for good, exclaiming: "I cannot fight Wall Street." His nephew Lionel would remain as the Metropolitan librarian, to make, with primitive recording equipment on a catwalk six stories above the stage, the famous "Mapleson cylinders," which include the only known recording of Jean de Reszke.

In mid-January, Damrosch's contract was renewed for another year. His fee for the first season had been $10,000; for the second he was to receive $8,000 and a share of the profits. But he did not live to get it.

All season Damrosch had been carrying a tremendous artistic and administrative burden. In addition to the hundreds of details an impresario must supervise, he had rehearsed and conducted every performance. One February afternoon he came home from a rehearsal and lay down in a cold bedroom, too exhausted to turn up the heat or reach for a blanket. An attack of pneumonia resulted.

On February 11, twenty-three-year-old Walter Damrosch took his father's place in the orchestra pit. The elder Damrosch died four days later, after going over the scores of the remaining operas with his son and exhorting him to finish out the season. All of musical New York turned out for Damrosch's funeral, held on the stage of the Metropolitan with the Reverend Henry Ward Beecher as principal speaker.

The remaining performances of the season were conducted by Walter Damrosch and chorus master John Lund. The younger Damrosch, however, was obviously too young and inexperienced to be his father's successor. Once again the boxholders were faced with a dilemma. Schott, the "military tenor," asserted his qualifications to be the new director, but nobody took them very seriously. Eventually a decision was made: Walter Damrosch would be sent to Germany to offer the post to Anton Seidl.

4

The German Seasons

ANTON SEIDL, OF THE BREMEN STADTTHEATER, was a thirty-five-year-old Hungarian who had been Wagner's assistant and protégé at Bayreuth. He brought to the Metropolitan immense learning, a thorough understanding of the Bayreuth traditions and selfless devotion to Wagner's works. A stern taskmaster, he would brook no nonsense from performers, however celebrated. He won respect for his knowledge and musicianship, during rehearsals for the *Lohengrin* that opened the 1885–1886 season, by correcting from memory 186 errors in the printed score.

The critic Henry T. Finck knew most of the Metropolitan singers intimately and found that while they squabbled over many things, on one point they agreed: Seidl's conducting was incomparable. "We feel that things *can't* go wrong when he is in the pit," one artist said, "so we're at ease, which is half the battle."

"If I forget a line," said Jean de Reszke, "I look at Seidl and read it on his lips."

"He never drowns our voices with his enormous orchestra," was another compliment.

The public was grateful for the dexterity with which Seidl reduced the duration of *Siegfried* from four and a half hours to three hours and forty minutes.

Seidl worked hard at conducting. After every act, he was obliged to go to his dressing room and change clothes from the skin out. But his dedication got results. Finck was present at a *Fidelio* performance during which the *Leonore* Overture no. 3, interpolated then as now into the last act of

33

the opera, won the highest possible praise: Even the boxholders were applauding.

Seidl was to be responsible solely for artistic matters. Administrative details were in the hands of Edmond C. Stanton, who had been executive secretary of the Metropolitan's board of directors and who now assumed the title of manager.

The choice of *Lohengrin* for opening night on November 23, 1885, was not a particularly adventurous one. The score was familiar to New York listeners and most of the principals had been heard in the same roles before. But it was a well-prepared performance that showed Seidl knew what he was about, and augured well for things to come.

Seidl lost no time in bringing out works by Wagner that were less familiar to the New York public — the first United States performances of *Die Meistersinger von Nürnberg, Rienzi, Tristan und Isolde.* Eventually the Metropolitan for the first time presented *Der Ring des Nibelungen* in its entirety. Illustrated weeklies took their readers backstage at the Metropolitan to see the concealed staircase by which the Gods crossed the rainbow bridge to Valhalla and the two-story movable towers on wheels atop which the Rhine Maidens lay prone, waving arms and legs to create the illusion of swimming.

The capstone of the Wagnerian edifice was *Parsifal*, produced in a pirated version over the strenuous objections of Bayreuth. It had been Wagner's wish, which his widow endeavored to carry out, to have the work performed nowhere but at his own *Festspielhaus*. George Bernard Shaw, then a London music critic, observed that the widow Cosima's efforts to suppress non-Bayreuth *Parsifals* would almost reconcile him to the custom of suttee.

The big commercial success of Seidl's first season was Goldmark's *Die Königen von Saba (The Queen of Sheba)*. It had a run of fifteen performances, a record unmatched at the Metropolitan until the nineteen *Fledermaus* performances of 1950–1951. After a decade in the repertoire, the opera disappeared and today, in this country, at least, the name of Goldmark* is hardly more than a listing in reference books.

The German repertoire was further enlarged with *Fidelio, Euryanthe*

---

* Goldmark was both helped and hindered by the fact that his father was an influential critic in Vienna. One musician is supposed to have asked another whether "the Goldmark

and *Der Freischütz*. French and Italian operas, however, were not neglected, although all performances were sung in German. Presentations of *Faust* were so numerous in the early seasons that the critic W. J. Henderson gave the Metropolitan the ironic nickname of *"Das Faustspielhaus."* One *Faust* took place during Seidl's first season: a virtually uncut performance of the monster score, in seven acts. It was believed to have been the longest opera performance ever seen in New York.

The Metropolitan heard its first *Aida* in German, with Theresa Herbert-Förster singing the title role. She had told Walter Damrosch she would come if he would find a place for her intended husband, a cellist with aspirations as a composer. Victor Herbert became a cellist in the Metropolitan orchestra.

A Seidl importation was Max Alvary, a "matinee idol of enormous conceit" but redeemed by his "splendid vigor and freedom." Seidl also presented the tenor Albert Niemann. At fifty-seven, Niemann was no longer in his vocal prime, but his Tristan had flashes of its onetime greatness. "Musical and dignified" Emil Fischer became one of the great performers of Hans Sachs in *Die Meistersinger*; interpretations were still being compared to Fischer's in the Twenties, when Friedrich Schorr joined the Metropolitan.

What was one to make of an artist who sang her debut in the mezzo-soprano role of Carmen and followed with the high C's of Brünnhilde in *Die Walküre*, the equally taxing dramatic soprano part of Isolde and the florid title role in Bellini's *Norma*? Lilli Lehmann had come to the Metropolitan partly because she wished to appear in a wider variety of roles than she was allowed to sing in Europe.

Lehmann, as hardworking as she was versatile, had polished her natural gifts by diligent study. In her memoirs she told how, despairing of the voice-teaching profession, she had learned breath control from a horn player in the Berlin Philharmonic Orchestra.

(For all her gifts, Lehmann was not always fortunate in her relationships with colleagues. Once, at a *Fidelio* performance, as the soprano Marianne Brandt was about to begin the aria *O namenlose Freude*, a woman's

---

was grateful." In the special sense in which it is used by musicians, the word "grateful" refers to a piece that goes well for the voice or lies well under the fingers.
"The music, no," was the reply, "the father, very."

voice in one of the boxes was heard in a burst of sardonic laughter. Brandt was so unnerved that Seidl, conducting, had to begin the aria again. Brandt always maintained that the offender had been Lehmann.

Another time, during an intermission, Nordica — by then an established artist — approached Lehmann deferentially to ask when she might call to pay her respects. In a voice that could be heard for yards, Lehmann replied: "I am not taking pupils this season.")

An interesting fact about the performers of Seidl's early seasons was that most of them had given up pension rights and other court-theatre prerogatives to appear at the Metropolitan. Thus, from the beginning, the prestige of a Metropolitan performance was one of the attractions that enabled the company to lure great artists from all over the world.

At the end of Seidl's first season, the company took stock of its condition. The deficit had been reduced to $25,000, and much of that had been incurred by a two-week stand in Philadelphia during the Christmas holidays. Advance sales were so gratifying that the board of directors voted to continue its opera-in-German policy for three additional seasons.

"Opera in German" of course meant Italian opera in German, too. But Seidl, who appears to have had the earnestness of a thoroughgoing German musician, disapproved of the frivolous strain that, for lovers of Italian opera, is one of its special delights. Victor Herbert once recalled the time when a group of musicians, including Seidl, were discussing the philosophical differences between German and Italian opera. In the property room of the Metropolitan, said Seidl, was a white helmet that had been worn by the tenor Italo Campanini in *Lohengrin*. The helmet, with its swan's-knight emblem, was authentic in every respect, except that Campanini had added to it a blue plume three feet long. "That, my dear gentlemen," Seidl concluded, "is Italian opera."

Walter Damrosch, who had remained as Seidl's assistant, also at times left something to be desired as an interpreter of Italian opera. Once, after an oddly paced performance of *Il Trovatore*, the critic W. J. Henderson asked: "For goodness' sake, Walter, where did you get those tempi?"

"I don't know," was Damrosch's disarming reply. "I never conducted it before."

As time passed, it gradually became evident that the Metropolitan was attempting to please two distinct publics — a predominantly German-speaking audience (seventy-five percent, the *Times* estimated), and box-holders who were bored with the murky world of Wagner's Nibelungen. The boxholders passed the time with conversation, to the annoyance of those who had come to hear the music. The *Times* described "the admonitory hisses of the three-dollar men and women who sit in the orchestra stalls and grow weary under the constant down-dropping upon their heads of diamonds of speech from the thirty-two-hundred-dollar ladies and gentlemen in the boxes."

Eventually the management was forced to post a small printed card in the boxes:

Many complaints having been made to the directors of the Opera House of the annoyance produced by the talking in the boxes during the performances, the Board requests that it be discontinued.

By order of the Board of Directors.

Henry C. Clews and Elbridge T. Gerry retorted that the stockholders were tired of being rebuked by the ticket-buyers and would conduct themselves as they pleased. Henderson's ironic suggestion was that the stockholders bar ticketholders from future performances. "It will cost them only seven thousand dollars each," said Henderson, "to enjoy their conversations without the interruption of hissing."

The manager, Edmond C. Stanton, in frantic efforts to placate the boxholders, went to such lengths as not lowering the lights for the Dungeon Scene in *Fidelio* — which made ludicrous Florestan's exclamation: "God, what darkness here!" New works were presented as an offset to those the boxholders found heavy going.

One of the novelties hopefully brought forward during the 1890–1891 season was *Diana von Solange*, a work composed thirty years earlier by Ernest II, Duke of Saxe-Coburg Gotha. At its second performance, the opera had already been nicknamed *Diana von So-Langweilich*. A third performance had been scheduled but did not take place. The opera was withdrawn after a petition signed by three hundred opera-lovers was presented to the management.

Soon rumor was circulating that a ducal decoration had influenced Stanton to produce the ill-starred *Diana*. Whether or not that was the final straw, Stanton's contract was not renewed for the following season. Instead, Abbey returned. The wounds of his first managerial season having healed, he was directing a touring opera company headed by Adelina Patti, making one of the "farewell tours" that occupied the last twenty years of her career. ("It is certain that this public will never again hear her in the roles with which her name and fame are identified," read an advertisement for one of the early tours.)

Abbey's associate was Maurice Grau, a shrewd impresario who made many of the day-to-day artistic and managerial decisions. John B. Schoeffel, though he took little part in Metropolitan affairs, was also, nominally at least, a member of the managing triumvirate. Their engagement marked an about-face in Metropolitan policy — abandonment of opera in German in favor of French and Italian opera, sung by all-star casts.

The Metropolitan's German era came to an end with a performance of *Die Meistersinger* on March 21, 1891. As Fischer delivered Hans Sachs's concluding apostrophe to "sacred German art," operagoers pelted the baritone with flowers until he was obliged to make a speech of acknowledgment — in English.

The seven German seasons left their permanent mark on the Metropolitan. They were pioneering years that introduced Wagner's later works not only to New York audiences but also, through the tours conducted by Walter Damrosch, to other cities as well. During one season (1889–1890), the company staged ten of Wagner's thirteen operas in a period of three months — a *tour de force* not duplicated even at Bayreuth. Henceforth, Wagner would be a staple of Metropolitan fare. His star might sometimes be in eclipse, but never for long.

5

Fire!

ABBEY, GRAU AND JOHN B. SCHOEFFEL lost no time in making good their promise to present all-star casts. Their opening-night production on December 14, 1891, offered the first American appearances of Jean and Edouard de Reszke, and the debut in her native country of Emma Eames, at twenty-four internationally famous through her Parisian successes. Also in the opening-night cast was Jean Martapoura, the *nom de chant* of a Belgian nobleman, Baron van Heeckeren. The opera was Gounod's *Roméo et Juliette*, the first French-language performance that had ever taken place at the Metropolitan.*

It was the beginning of an era on which old-timers would look back with fond nostalgia. Of a performance of Meyerbeer's *L'Africaine* with the de Reszkes and the great baritone Jean Lassalle in principal roles, H. E. Krehbiel wrote: "To see three such splendid representations of physical and artistic manhood on the stage was in itself a unique sensation." Jean de Reszke was also Walther in *I maestri cantori* (from the absurdity of presenting Verdi in German, the Metropolitan had now gone to the opposite absurdity of staging Wagner in Italian). And he sang the title role in *Otello*, with Emma Albani as Desdemona. The opera was staged by the de Reszkes and Albani; not one of the Metropolitan stage directors was familiar with the work.

Nordica appeared in *L'Africaine* and *Les Huguenots*, and the incredibly versatile Lilli Lehmann made her first venture into Italian, singing Leonora in *Il Trovatore*.

* *Faust* had been done in Italian.

Patriotic pride, gratified by Nordica's success, was heightened by the debut of another native, Marie Van Zandt. Old-timers could remember Italian opera companies headed by her mother, Jennie Van Zandt, performing in New York a generation earlier. Marie Van Zandt, a petite and attractive coloratura, had been singing in Europe for ten years and, said Krehbiel, "had won as much favor as any American artist ever enjoyed in Paris." She had been Delibes's favorite interpreter of the title role in his *Lakmé,* and introduced it to Metropolitan audiences in her first season. Abbey used his engagement of Van Zandt (and of a rising new star named Melba) as strong selling points with the Metropolitan's directors.

Eames sang Santuzza when *Cavalleria rusticana* had its first Metropolitan performance; it was preceded by Gluck's *Orfeo* as a curtain-raiser.

The glittering season was concluded by two weeks of extra performances, during which Patti made "farewell" appearances in *La Traviata, Martha, Lucia di Lammermoor* and *Il Barbiere di Siviglia.* The Lesson Scene in the Rossini work was surely one of the longest on record. For her interpolated number, Patti sang Eckert's "Swiss Echo Song." It was cordially received, and she sang "Home, Sweet Home" as an encore. (Patti, critic George Bernard Shaw had sourly noted, would spoil the most tragic scene that ever was by taking a bow if someone dropped his walking stick.) Still the applause went on; Patti obliged with "The Last Rose of Summer," then "Comin' Through the Rye."

The stockholders obviously were pleased by the first season under the Metropolitan's new management. Early in April, it was announced that Abbey and Grau had signed a contract to produce opera at the Metropolitan for the next two seasons. Singers and conductors, glamorous operatic birds of passage, scattered to their various summer destinations, while Abbey, Grau and Schoeffel turned their attention to their other, nonoperatic theatrical ventures.

Since the Metropolitan was unused during the summer months and had by far the largest stage of any of the Abbey-Grau-Schoeffel theatres, it was the logical place for painting scenery, not only for the opera house but for the other theatres as well. On the hot, humid morning of Saturday, August 27, 1892, great quantities of painted canvas littered the Metropolitan stage and still more scenery was stored beneath it. A workman's carelessly dropped cigarette was all that was needed for disaster. By the time the horse-drawn fire engines could get there, the entire stage was aflame.

The fire was discovered at nine o'clock, shortly after it began. It was extinguished by noon; but in that time it had done damage to the opera house estimated at $300,000.

In Newport and Bar Harbor, Saratoga and Southampton, Metropolitan stockholders received the news with stunned disbelief. Was not the building fireproof? Many of them made for the first time the painful discovery that in risk-taking circles, "fireproof" is a relative term. It means that something is left standing — walls and a roof — when a fire occurs.

Moreover, several of architect Cady's fire precautions had been modified. The metal supports beneath the stage had been replaced by wooden beams that gave more space for storing scenery. The primitive but ingenious sprinkler system had been drained; its rooftop tank froze in winter unless heated, an expensive nuisance. Cady's asbestos curtain might have prevented the fire from spreading to the auditorium, but it had been chained up to allow paint fumes to escape.

The most discouraging news of all was that because of its supposed invulnerability to fire, the building had only been insured for $60,000.

The fire was the death knell of the Metropolitan Opera House Company, Ltd. Of its seventy stockholders, fifty-one wanted no further part of opera at the Metropolitan. Among those who withdrew from sponsorship were James Gordon Bennett, William Rockefeller, Cyrus Field, James Harriman, James A. Roosevelt and Jay Gould.

Nineteen tenacious opera-lovers, however, voted to rebuild the theatre. They included the two Goelets, two Vanderbilts, George F. Baker, D. Ogden Mills, W. C. Whitney, J. P. Morgan, Adrian Iselin and Henry C. Clews.

"The opera house property is a good investment," said Clews. "The original cost, building and all, was about two million dollars. Now the ground alone is worth that much and the enhancement of values has been so great that I am sure that it has increased more than three times the original cost."

The nineteen were joined by sixteen newcomers, among them Augustus D. Juilliard, whose Juilliard Foundation was to be a financial mainstay of the company in later years. They formed a new organization, the Metropolitan Opera and Real Estate Company. Each of the thirty-five founders subscribed to three hundred shares of stock at $100 a share. In addition, each founder subscribed a further $30,000 for the reconstruction of the house.

With the money in hand — $2,100,000 — the Metropolitan Opera and Real Estate Company proceeded to acquire the house from the Metropolitan Opera House Company, Ltd, at a cost of $1,425,000. Membership in the new company was limited to thirty-five, the number of boxes planned for the parterre of the rebuilt theatre. In addition, the bylaws provided that "no transfer of stock shall be made except to a person or persons previously approved by the directorate."

The 1892 reorganization was the basis on which the Metropolitan functioned for nearly half a century. The Metropolitan Opera and Real Estate Company owned the building and paid for taxes, maintenance and repairs. To cover these expenses, each boxholder was assessed up to $4,500 a year. In return, he received the use of a box for every performance of the season. The Metropolitan Opera Company — the actual producing organization — had the use of the opera house rent-free. It kept all money taken in at the box office, and its only obligation was to produce a different opera each weekday night, and two on Saturdays.* While it lasted, and while the boxholders kept their assessments paid, this made the Metropolitan one of the most prosperous theatres in operatic history.

The rebuilding of the fire-gutted Metropolitan began on April 14, 1893. The house reopened on November 27, with a brilliant *Faust* that offered Eames, Lassalle and both de Reszkes. Operagoers were dazzled alike by the stage spectacle and the cream, red and gold interior of the renovated house. The most spectacular change was the installation of electric lights, which, glittering on the jewels in the parterre boxes, soon gave the parterre the nickname "Diamond Horseshoe."

There was another semicircle of boxes on the Grand Tier, just above the parterre. These, however, were merely rented for the season. They conferred on their occupants a markedly lower social standing than that of the Diamond Horseshoe. The real inner circle consisted of the men and women who sat in the parterre, owning their boxes and, for that matter, the opera house itself.

---

* It was an arrangement, not dissimilar in principle from that by which Fredric R. Mann was to rescue Philadelphia's faltering Robin Hood Dell concerts sixty years later.

Diamond Horseshoe people fell into three main groups. One consisted of Vanderbilts and Vanderbilt in-laws; two boxes alone were in the name of Cornelius Vanderbilt III. Next was the Morgan group. J. P. Morgan himself, when lots were drawn for box locations, had had the luck of the draw and occupied Box 35, squarely in the center of the magic circle. Near him sat Morgan partners J. Hood Wright and G. S. Bowdoin; former partners Levi P. Morton and Cornelius Bliss; business associates like George F. Baker and C. T. Barney, president of the Knickerbocker Trust Company. Then there were the Astors, Cuttings and Van Nests, of the "Knickerbocker aristocracy" who had moved uptown from the Academy of Music. (Not quite fitting any category was Augustus Juilliard, who must be classified as fundamentally a music-lover.)

Unhappily, some boxholders were fundamentally not music-lovers. During opera season, New York's social leader — in the Nineties it was Mrs. William B. Astor — would appear in her box at nine o'clock, regardless of what opera was playing or when it had started. At intermission she would receive, rarely leaving her box to visit another. By the next intermission she would often be gone. When the arbiter had departed, others would drift away, too. The opera was somewhere to go after dinner and before appearing at a ten o'clock ball.

The Old Guard Ball, which from the Eighties until the turn of the century occupied a place in New York social life comparable to that of Philadelphia's still-flourishing Assembly Ball, or the St. Cecelia Ball in Charleston, was held at the Metropolitan. A temporary floor, in portable sections, was installed above the orchestra seats at the level of the stage, thus converting the opera house into a ballroom nearly the size of a city block. It was around this ballroom that the Grand March took place, ladies magnificent in evening dress, officers and members of the Guard in full-dress uniforms topped by bearskin shakos.

From the reopening in 1893 to the period of the First World War, the Metropolitan was the focal point around which the winter social season revolved. In the days of Ward McAllister's Four Hundred, as many of the Four Hundred as possible sought to be seen in or near the Diamond Horseshoe. Monday night became, and remained to the end, the fashionable night. The opera was regarded as a social function pure and simple, which everyone with any claim to social standing attended. Opening night at the opera marked the official beginning of the season. Mothers with eligible daughters presented them to society at the opera. A well-connected young man with evening dress and a dollar to buy standing room was almost certain of a welcome in the Diamond Horseshoe in exchange for making himself agreeable during intermission. Henry James, reporting on his native land in 1907, was astonished by "the general extravagant insistence on the Opera, which plays its part as the great vessel of social salvation."

Gradually, over the years, there were changes in the faces to be seen in the Diamond Horseshoe. The changes, however, were not extensive; between 1892 and the reorganization of the company in 1940, boxes changed hands only about twenty times. Box 21, the Morgan box, was bought and sold only within the firm.

One reason sales were slow was the scarcity of would-be buyers who were acceptable to the board of directors. Another was the sheer cost of a box at the opera. By 1903, a box that represented an original investment of $60,000* was selling for $100,000; such, at least, was the reported price of a sale that took place that year. The first publicly recorded transaction, in 1913, was for $120,000. During the opulent Twenties, there were sales nearly every year and the going rate was $200,000. The clouds of 1929 had not yet begun to darken the financial skies.

---

* Only $40,000 if the buyer had been a stockholder of the older Metropolitan Opera House Company, Ltd. In that case, he had put up $60,000 but had received back $20,000 as his share of the proceeds from the sale of the house to the Metropolitan Opera and Real Estate Company in 1892.

6

Melba

Helen Porter Mitchell Armstrong, born into a comfortable household in Melbourne, honored her native city by taking the stage name of Nellie Melba. To escape an unhappy marriage, she went to Paris to study with Mathilde Marchesi, who in the Eighties, aside from Manuel Garcia in London and the Lampertis in Milan, was the most famous singing teacher in the world. Five years later, Melba too was famous. In Russia, she recalled, a student had seized the pencil with which she signed an autograph, bitten it with "strong white teeth," as Melba put it, and distributed the fragments to his less fortunate friends. The scene made Melba think of medieval peasants scrambling for the relics of a saint.

In Paris, Melba learned from Abbey and Grau that because of the Metropolitan fire, the season for which she was engaged would not take place. They added that since her contract contained no "escape clause," she would be legally justified in demanding her entire salary. Grandly Melba replied that if she didn't sing, she didn't expect to be paid. "They looked relieved," she recalled.

Then Melba realized that because of the heavy expenses of a long tour, she had only two hundred pounds in the bank and no prospects of an immediate engagement. Melba decided to trust to Providence. With two maids instead of one, and with no idea of how she was going to pay the bill, she engaged the best rooms in the best hotel at Nice.

Providence did not fail her. Grau was there for a holiday and offered to get her engagements at four thousand francs a performance. Loftily Melba

45

replied that she wouldn't think of singing for less than five thousand francs. She got her fee.

Melba arrived in New York after a stormy crossing in early December, 1893. During her first night at the old Waldorf-Astoria, she awoke with a feeling of suffocation. It was her first experience with American steam heating. After opening all the windows, wrote Melba, she and her secretary went back to sleep "in healthy English fashion."

Although one would scarcely guess it from reading her memoirs, Melba's first season at the Metropolitan was by no means a heady triumph. She made her debut as Lucia, a role in which any newcomer was bound to be compared to Patti. She had a formidable rival in Eames, Shanghai-born of American parents, brought up in Bath, Maine, and sent to study with Marchesi at the same time as Melba. The two hated each other as only two divas can who are having comparable success in similar roles in the same opera house. In her memoirs Melba did not mention Eames; Eames referred only to "the soprano who prevented my debut at Brussels."

During all this time, Melba had gradually become the star of the Sunday evening concerts, which were setting new attendance records. Her appearances at regular performances, too, were arousing greater and greater enthusiasm. After one magnificent rendition, with the de Reszkes, of the final trio in *Faust*, the applause went on and on. Finally the de Reszkes gallantly pushed a piano onstage — the orchestra had already left the pit — and "Darling Jean" sat down to play the accompaniment while Melba sang "Home, Sweet Home."

In her memoirs Melba noted that an artist sensed a "subtle difference between her and the rest of society." Specifically, this meant that Eames was invited to dinner by the Four Hundred, while Melba was not. Melba, who had mingled socially with grand dukes in Moscow and with the Royal Family in London, felt left out. But in due time the invitations began to come. One was from Mrs. Paran Stevens, who had managed to attend all three opening nights in 1883. When Melba arrived for dinner, she found herself being delivered to a vacant house. Eventually the mystery was unraveled. Mrs. Stevens, who was absent-minded, had moved the year before but had forgotten to change the address on her calling cards.

Melba dined with the William K. Vanderbilts, admiring the placidity of Fifth Avenue and Fifty-second Street. It reminded her of some secluded

Nellie Melba as Marguerite in FAUST

neighborhood in London. She wondered if the area would ever be covered with skyscrapers, like downtown Manhattan. Vanderbilt said he didn't think so; "we grow fast in New York, but we don't grow as fast as all that."

"Side by side with American millionaires, I was having a good taste of American democracy," Melba recalled. Once, as she was going to the Metropolitan for a Sunday evening concert, it was snowing heavily. To save herself a dozen steps across the pavement, Melba entered not by the stage door but under the marquee of the Thirty-ninth Street carriage entrance. Naturally, she had no ticket. The ticket taker would not let her pass.

"Surely you know who I am?" said the astonished diva. "I am Madame Melba."

"I don't care who you are," he replied. "You're not going to pass without a ticket."

A man behind her immediately offered his. "No, thank you," said Melba. "If I can't get in without a ticket, I shan't get in at all."

Disaster was averted by the arrival of Abbey, whom someone on recognizing Melba had hastily summoned to the scene. The fuming prima donna demanded that the doorman be sent to her dressing room to apologize. He refused.

"I was only doing my duty," he said. "I might have got fired if I hadn't."

Melba couldn't help smiling. But if it ever happened again, she said, he would have to go down on his knees and beg her pardon.

"However, it never did happen again, and after that he was one of my most loyal servants."

At the beginning of the 1896–1897 season, the Metropolitan was rocked by scandal. Nordica was not returning to the company. The Maine-born soprano had won high favor with the public and her absence was widely and sincerely deplored. Then Nordica came forward with a public accusation. She was not returning, she said, because of "intrigues" by Melba and Jean de Reszke.

Actually, "intrigues" was perhaps too strong a word. The story went back to Covent Garden days, when George Bernard Shaw, one of the most outspoken of Wagnerites, was publicly scolding Jean de Reszke in the London *Star* for not lending his voice and prestige to the cause of Wagnerism. As the leading tenor of the day, Shaw maintained, it was incumbent on de Reszke to sing the Wagnerian roles — in German.

De Reszke was drawn to the idea. If the Wagner operas seem a little old-fashioned to us today, they were a new and exciting discovery for music-lovers of the Eighties and Nineties. Also, de Reszke may have viewed the Wagnerian roles, with their less demanding *tessitura*, as insurance against the days when he could no longer cope with the high notes of *Faust* and *Les Huguenots*.

De Reszke made meticulous preparations. For a year and a half before his first German-language performance, he and his brother Edouard spoke only German at home. On November 27, 1895, de Reszke had a magnificent success at the Metropolitan, singing Tristan to Nordica's Isolde. For the following season he planned to sing the title role in *Siegfried*.

Melba throughout her career had an unrequited affection for the music of Wagner. Her lovely light voice was totally unsuited to Wagnerian roles, as an unsuccessful Metropolitan appearance in *Tannhäuser* had shown. But now she conceived the mad idea of singing Brünnhilde in "darling Jean's" first *Siegfried*.

Melba said that when she sounded out de Reszke, he said she would be a splendid Brünnhilde. De Reszke said he had suggested she sing the more lyric role of the Forest Bird. If de Reszke made the suggestion, he must have put it forward with tongue in cheek; an artist like Melba would never sing a minor part in which the performer does not even appear on stage.

In Paris, Marchesi would have nothing to do with the *Siegfried* project. She greeted it "with a horrified expression and a great fluttering of hands, as if I had threatened to cut my throat." Melba then got Herr Kniese of the Metropolitan staff to coach her in the part.

Also, she extracted from Abbey and Grau exclusive rights to the *Siegfried* Brünnhilde for the 1896–1897 season. Since it was a "Nordica role," Nordica's nose was thereby put out of joint. She left the company, although Abbey and Grau, knowing her value to the dramatic soprano repertoire, tried to dissuade her. But Melba got her exclusive; by then her leverage at the box office was too powerful to resist.

As the *Siegfried* performance date — December 30, 1896 — drew nearer, Melba, usually self-possessed, grew more and more nervous. Although Brünnhilde appears only in the last act of *Siegfried*, she amply earns her fee. To the other strains of performance are added that of waiting until nearly eleven o'clock before going on the stage.

The moment Melba began to sing, she realized that Marchesi had been right and she was wrong. The music was too much for her. "I felt as though I were struggling with something beyond my strength. I had a sensation almost of suffocation, of battling with some immense monster. . . ."

Krehbiel recalled that Melba drove her fragile voice to its limit in an effort to produce Wagnerian-scale tone. As the performance continued, she began to tire visibly. The two climactic high C's in which the act culminates were utterly beyond her. When the performance ended, the exhausted diva threw on a dressing gown and summoned her personal manager. "Tell the critics that I am never going to do that again," Melba said. "It is beyond me. I have been a fool."

To her alarm, Melba found the performance had done a good deal of damage to her voice. Her physicians told her that if she attempted to continue without a rest, her voice might be harmed beyond repair. In mid-January she sailed for Paris and three months' enforced silence.

The Melba fiasco was only one of the events that made the 1896–1897 season one long disaster. Katherina Klafsky, engaged for Wagnerian roles, died, following brain surgery in September, without reaching the Metropolitan at all. Abbey died a month later, leaving Grau to carry on alone. Nordica, after her tiff with the management, had taken other engagements and thus was unavailable as a replacement in dramatic soprano roles. Melba was lost to the company after January. In February another blow fell; Emma Eames underwent surgery and a scheduled *Figaro* had to be withdrawn.

In its place, *Martha* was performed, with Armand Castelmary as Tristano. The stage action at the end of Act II calls for Tristano to run about the stage and stumble. The exertion was too much for the sixty-three-year-old baritone. He collapsed of a heart attack and died in the arms of Jean de Reszke, while viewers applauded what they took to be a masterly bit of pantomime.

In one way or another, the season limped to a close on April 20, with a gala performance for the benefit of Henry Abbey's daughter, Kitty K. Abbey.

All season, though attendance had been excellent, there had been persistent reports that there might not be opera at the Metropolitan next year. The newspapers proved to be good prophets. What with the death of his partner, the consequent dissolution of Abbey, Schoeffel and Grau, and the somewhat chaotic financial condition of the opera company, Grau felt it necessary to pause and regroup his forces.

Grau's lease on the building was renewed for three years, with the understanding that during 1897–1898 he was free to rent the opera house to whomever he could. Events of the season included five weeks of performances by a company under the direction of Walter Damrosch, with many of the Metropolitan's regular artists in its ranks.

At one of the performances, Melba, still not having learned her lesson, sang Aida with results almost as disastrous as those of her Brünnhilde the year before.

In her memoirs, Melba said she gave up singing Aida because she disliked the dark makeup and ropy black wig that the role required.

7

Otello and Iago

DURING HER FIRST METROPOLITAN SEASON, Melba was overshadowed, like nearly everyone else, by the spectacular success of Emma Calvé's Carmen. New York had never seen anything like it. Calvé's portrayal brought Prosper Mérimée's gypsy to life in vivid flashes. For operagoers old enough to remember, it was the standard by which all later Carmens were judged.

."What a night it was, that first Carmen of hers!" said James G. Huneker. "She chucked tradition to the winds, also her lingerie. Some of the elder critics are still blushing." The twelve *Carmen* performances that season broke all box-office records. Krehbiel complained that Calvé's Carmen had become a "mere fad," overshadowing her much finer performance of other roles.

Old recordings give some idea of how extraordinary Calvé's singing must have been. With the full-textured chest-voice of a mezzo-soprano, she could go up and up in head-voice, and in addition had mastered the trick of the "flute voice" by which coloratura sopranos attain their highest notes. Although she did not use it in performance, specially favored listeners were sometimes invited to hear a demonstration of her *"troisième voix."*

Oddly, Calvé's Carmen was more admired in New York and London than in Paris. She had interpolated bits of fresh "business" not in the characterization of Galli-Mariée, the original Carmen. (French opera-goers set great store by tradition. When Lassalle sang the title role in Ambroise Thomas's *Hamlet*, he was criticized for omitting a gesture used by Jean-Baptiste Fauré, who created the role. In the scene between Hamlet and his mother, Fauré had turned to face the wings, as if he could not bear to confront the turn events were taking. Even though it had the sanction of tradition, Lassalle thought the gesture absurd. He asked Fauré why he had adopted it. Fauré had a ready explanation. "At the first perform-ance," he said, "I had to spit.")

During Melba's second Metropolitan season, there was fresh competition. Francesco Tamagno, for whose trumpet voice Verdi had written the title role in *Otello*, created a sensation in that part. Great things were also expected of a young Italian soprano, Libia Drog. Her debut, however, was dis-astrous. Substituting at short notice as Matilda in *William Tell*, a role she had never sung before, she forgot the words of Matilda's great aria, *Selva opaca*. In vain she appealed to conductor Luigi Mancinelli for help.

Mancinelli, said Krehbiel, "seemed to have lost his head as completely as the lady had her memory. So had the prompter, who pulled his noodle into his shell like a snail and remained as mute.

"Signor Tamagno entered in character, and indulged in dumbshow to a few detached phrases from the orchestra. Then the awfulness of the situa-tion overwhelmed him, and he fairly ran off the stage, leaving Matilda alone. That lady made a final appeal to the conductor, switched her dress nervously with her riding-whip, went to the wings, got a glass of water and then disappeared. The audience, which had good-humoredly ap-plauded until now, began to laugh, and the demoralization was complete."

Tamagno, baritone Mario Ancona and Edouard de Reszke saved the day by a magnificent performance of the trio *Troncar suoi di*. In fact, said Krehbiel, had not Tamagno stopped to bow and to pick up a bunch of violets thrown to him from a box, the effect would have been "dramatically electrifying." As for Drog, she redeemed herself two evenings later with a splendid performance of Aida.

Sybil Sanderson, a native of Sacramento, had had a great success in Paris, where rumor said she had been the mistress of Jules Massenet. It was for her that Massenet created the role of Thaïs. In her Metropolitan debut as another Massenet heroine, Manon, she disclosed a somewhat un-steady voice and an almost total lack of acting ability. Old photographs, however, leave no doubt of her striking good looks, and the reviews had the sorrowful tinge that creeps into the writing of middle-aged critics

Emma Calvé as Carmen

when they are forced to say unkind things about a young woman with an attractive figure.

Melba was amused by the foibles of her colleagues. Tamagno, who made great sums of money, endeavored to keep as much of it as possible. When he was invited to dinner he would fill his pockets with hors d'oeuvres enough to make a meal next day. Once, at the conclusion of a formal dinner, Melba watched, fascinated, while Tamagno spread a napkin in his lap and calmly filled it with crystallized fruits, salted almonds and chocolates. Then he asked if he might have the orchid centerpiece to take to his daughter, who was ill at the hotel. Melba guessed that if he had begun to fill his pockets with table silver, the stunned hostess would have raised no objection.

Once Mancinelli invited Melba, Tamagno and several Metropolitan colleagues to lunch at an Italian restaurant in New York. The main course was veal cutlet *alla Milanese*. When Tamagno saw that there were several cutlets left over, he sent the waiter for a newspaper and began to wrap them. "For my dog," Tamagno explained. "He loves veal cutlets."

Next day Mancinelli invented an excuse to call at Tamagno's hotel at noon. Tamagno and his daughter were lunching on veal cutlet *alla Milanese*.

When Tamagno had sailed for his first season at the Metropolitan, impresario Maurice Grau had sent him the money for a first-class stateroom. Tamagno bought steerage and pocketed the difference. Grau, who was crossing at the same time, assumed Tamagno had missed the boat, until he spotted his famous tenor among the shawled and cloth-capped immigrants. Tamagno explained that he was a man of democratic principles. Since Grau had done so thorough a job in publicizing Tamagno that he could not afford to have him arrive otherwise than in first class, the long-suffering impresario was again obliged to lay out the money for Tamagno's fare.

On December 3, 1894, with Eames as Desdemona, Francesco Tamagno and Victor Maurel offered the characterizations of Otello and Iago which they had created at La Scala under the supervision of Verdi himself. Old recordings give a faint idea of what Tamagno's trumpet voice must have been. Maurel's singing was rather dry, with the curious sepulchral quality that French voices sometimes have. It was because of his superb acting that Verdi entrusted Maurel with the roles of both Iago and Falstaff.

Tall, handsome, a skilled boxer, Maurel was an imposing figure on and off the stage. A photograph of him in boxing trunks shows the torso of a Greek statue. Women found him irresistible, even those who most vehemently criticized his philandering. His conquests ranged from the opera house to the Social Register. Women in society had been known to desert hearths and husbands for the handsome Frenchman.

Once, in St. Louis, the tables were turned. Maurel received several ardent letters, each making an appointment for the same hour but in a different part of town. Maurel hurried all over St. Louis, to no avail. The Merry Wives were in hiding, and their laughs were longer than the one at Herne's Oak. "Had Eames, Scalchi, Melba or Calvé hatched the plot against his happiness?" asked Huneker. "I'll never tell."

In his best years, said Huneker, "Maurel was an inspiring swell. On Fifth Avenue, of a fine day, he was to be seen with his retinue. He swaggered. He was the Great Lover to the life. Surrounded by his secretaries, his pugilist, his fencing-master and a lot of singers, he was an event on the Avenue. One could have said some fantastic Italian Prince of the Renaissance had strayed into the nineteenth century."

A painter once saw Maurel at the Metropolitan, wearing evening clothes topped by a Byronic turndown collar fastened by two gold pins. It created an effect of such bizarre, audacious elegance that the painter determined to match it. He tried every shirtmaker in New York but couldn't quite capture Maurel's flair. He went to London, then to Paris, where he was nicknamed "Monsieur Collar." Finally he found what he wanted, and hurried back to watch for Maurel. When the baritone appeared, his collar was a high-standing monstrosity with flaring points. It was Maurel's habit to ease the psychic stress that resulted from the end of a love affair by changing the style of his collars.

8

Opera for Profit

MAURICE GRAU, born in Brünn, Austria, in 1849, was brought to New York by his parents when he was five years old. He was educated in the New York City public schools and at the Free Academy, now the City College of New York. After graduation, he entered Columbia Law School and read law in the offices of Morrison, Lauterback and Spingarn.

But Grau also had had intimate contact with the entertainment world ever since he had sold opera librettos, as a boy, for his uncle, the operatic and theatrical manager Jacob Grau. Young Grau found his legal studies dull, compared to the world of opera, theatre and concerts. He gave up law without seeking admission to the bar, and with a capital of $1,500 launched himself as a concert manager.

Grau's first attraction was Aimée, a French *opéra bouffe* singer who had had a success at the Paris Opéra. Grau's first week, in Bridgeport, Connecticut, paid the expenses of the entire engagement. Thereafter, Aimée was to tour America repeatedly and profitably under the management of Grau.

In his first season, Grau also managed tours by Henri Wieniawski and Anton Rubinstein.* He cleared $60,000 on Rubinstein alone. By 1874, when he was twenty-five, Grau was managing three operetta companies and had leased the Lyceum Theatre on Fourteenth Street.

---

* It was the heyday of blackface entertainment. Rubinstein told Sir George Henschel with relish of one Western town in which the local manager asked nervously, as concert time approached: "Say, Mr. Rubinstein, hadn't you better start putting your burnt cork on?"

Like most impresarios, Grau had his ups and downs. After several periods of bad luck, he formed a partnership with Abbey and Schoeffel in 1883. Abbey's death in the fall of 1896 plunged the partnership into bankruptcy. Schoeffel, who was not greatly interested in the Metropolitan and had never played an active part in its management, withdrew, taking with him the partnership's only tangible asset, the Tremont Theatre in Boston.

It was Grau who averted ruin by assuming the liabilities of the defunct organization. With the aid of poker-playing cronies like Frederick Rullman, publisher of the Metropolitan's librettos, he raised $150,000 capital to form a new organization, the Maurice Grau Opera Company. (The Metropolitan Opera and Real Estate Company subscribed $25,000 to the new venture.)

Grau spent his "sabbatical" season of 1897–1898 in London, recruiting talent. He also, through the influence of Jean de Reszke, took over the direction of the opera at Covent Garden. The double leverage of New York and London made Grau better able to command the finest singers of the world than any impresario before or since. When he announced his plans for the 1898–1899 season, of the major celebrities of the day only Calvé was not on the Metropolitan's roster.

It was with the Grau seasons that the Metropolitan's "Golden Age" began. He understood what the public wanted, and supplied it: performers with international reputations, like the famous all-star cast of *Les Huguenots* — Melba and Nordica (their differences reconciled), Scalchi, the de Reszkes, Pol Plançon and Victor Maurel. And the stars packed the house, drawing, in a day of easygoing fire regulations, as many as a thousand standees.

Micaela, in *Carmen*, is a relatively brief role and virtually singer-proof; accordingly, it is sometimes assigned to a young soprano who has not made her mark. But Grau gave his subscribers, as Micaela, Emma Eames. After one performance, Eames remarked: "You must be a very rich man, Mr. Grau, to pay me eight hundred dollars to sing Micaela."

If Grau paid his top stars lavishly, he made up for it by skimping elsewhere. Players in his orchestra received fifty dollars a week, choristers fifteen dollars a week. When the chorus went on strike, their salaries were raised to twenty dollars a week. By cutting corners wherever possible, Grau was able to hold admission prices to a five-dollar top.

The critic Henderson, who was familiar with the fine, state-subsidized court operas of Dresden, Munich, Vienna and Berlin, compared their standards of performance with those prevailing at the Metropolitan. Grau, he said, managed very nicely by "omitting factors usually found in the subsidized opera houses — namely, fine chorus, orchestra, ballet and *mise-en-scène* — and providing what the kindly aid of Government never secures — namely, the services of the world's greatest singers."

Grau's subscribers realized and valued what they were getting. In his first season, a memorable *Lohengrin* on January 9, 1899, offered Jean de Reszke in the title role, Nordica as Elsa, David Bispham as Telramund, and Ernestine Schumann-Heink in her Metropolitan debut as Ortrud. Next day the *Tribune* exclaimed: "Fortunate public, destined to be the envy of future generations!" It was a prophetic comment.

Grau balanced one element of his productions against another with the same astuteness with which he speculated on the New York Stock Exchange. It was said of him that he "knew where to spend a dollar and where to save a nickel." And Jean de Reszke observed: "Grau will give you a good cigar, but not the match to light it with."

David Bispham, the Quaker baritone from Philadelphia who joined the Metropolitan in 1896, regarded Grau with awed admiration. The impresario, said Bispham, "reveled in difficulties and delighted in fitting together engagements for his artists in concert and opera. He was a great card player, expert at chess, an inveterate operator on the Stock Exchange, and viewed the profession of an impresario in the light of a complicated and highly interesting game in which, when his partners did not upset his calculations, he was usually successful.

"I remember that I came into Mr. Grau's private office one day and found him in the midst of a discussion of the most intricate nature, arising out of the illness of several of his principals and the need for filling their places in compliance with their contracts, taking into further account the probable effect upon the public of the changes in the casts. At the same time he was hearing a complicated report from the managers of the company; discussing the terms of his written agreement with an artist without referring to the document, except to prove the artist wrong; speaking as many as three foreign languages in rotation with men of as many nationalities about him; calling up his broker in Wall Street and giving him orders to buy and sell, and evidently calculating the possible gains and losses mentally as he spoke. He had indeed a photographic mind, the absorptive and retentive power of which I have never seen equalled."

Grau once met his match, however, in a baritone named Giuseppe Campanari, who among other things sang the role of Kothner in *Die Meistersinger*. Since Kothner in the opera has nothing to do after the first act except to appear in the parade of Mastersingers in the opera's closing scene, Campanari proposed to leave as soon as Act I was over, lending his costume for a member of the chorus to wear in the Mastersinger parade.

As the same thing was true of the eight other Mastersingers in the cast, Grau did not want Campanari to establish such a precedent. In vain Grau appealed to the spirit of Bayreuth, where world-famous artists often sang minor roles to have a more complete ensemble. What would the Meister have thought? Campanari shrugged his shoulders.

Then Grau remembered that Campanari was a gourmet who took with him the paraphernalia for preparing his favorite foods whenever the Metropolitan went on tour. Grau told the baritone that if he would return to his dressing room after Act I, he would find a hot bird, a cold bottle and a box of cigars.

As the time approached for Act III, Grau went backstage. He found that Campanari had eaten the supper, drunk the wine, filled his pockets with cigars and departed.

Grau's tastes were eclectic. He offered his subscribers two new operas by Puccini, *La Bohème* and *Tosca*. He also presented as much Wagner as circumstances permitted. His contract with the Metropolitan Opera and Real Estate Company sharply limited the number of Wagnerian performances to be presented on Monday evenings, and stipulated that operas by Wagner should not constitute more than forty percent of the season's repertoire. Nevertheless, his first season offered the Metropolitan its first uncut *Ring* cycle. After the Grau era, an uncut *Ring* would not be heard again at the Metropolitan until 1929.

Grau gave the Metropolitan its first *Magic Flute*, and presented new contemporary works, most of them long since forgotten — Luigi Mancinelli's *Ero e Leandro*, with the composer conducting; Louis-Étienne-Ernest Reyer's *Salammbô*; Isidore de Lara's *Messaline*; Paderewski's *Manru*.

Der Wald was composed to a German text by an Englishwoman, Dame Ethel Smyth. It was a negligible work, but for opera-lovers Dame Ethel's memory is green because of a line in her memoirs, concerning an English country gentleman who lent her horses at fox-hunting time: "He always mounted me in hunting season."

Grau was bearded, multilingual and urbane. He knew his patrons as well as he knew his performers and was perfectly content to let the tastes of the former determine the latter. When Krehbiel wondered why a certain artist was not engaged, Grau replied that his admiration for the artist was equal to Krehbiel's own; but she did not draw at the box office. "I've never made money with her," he said.

Throughout Grau's management, Krehbiel's *Tribune* seats were directly behind those of the impresario. Never once, said Krehbiel, did he fail to receive a pleasant greeting, no matter what the *Tribune* had had to say about last night's performance. Grau accepted congratulations with a cordial "Thank you!" and let the matter drop. Condolences were received in the same unperturbed manner. Grau was always calm and aloof, neither volunteering information nor withholding it. Only once, Krehbiel recalled, did the impresario make a comment that came close to betraying emotion. Looking about the theatre, he observed ironically: "Encouraging, isn't it? Some say the public want novelties." He had spent a fortune to produce *Salammbô* and the house was half empty.

During the season of 1899–1900, Jean de Reszke did not return. Paris and London, he decided, were more convenient to his summer estate in Poland. That season, singing at Covent Garden, he had a harassing bout with influenza that gave rise to rumors that he had lost his voice. Grau, knowing the rumors to be false, prevailed on de Reszke to sing at the Metropolitan once more.

For the record-breaking fee of $2,500 a performance, de Reszke sang thirty times during the 1900–1901 season. The diversity of the roles in which he appeared was astonishing; his versatility equaled Lilli Lehmann's. His first appearance was as Lohengrin. He followed that role by singing Faust, Radames in *Aida*, Roderigo in Massenet's *Le Cid*, Tristan, Siegfried in *Götterdämmerung*, Raoul in *Les Huguenots*, Vasco da Gama in

L'Africaine, Siegfried in *Siegfried*, and Walther in *Die Meistersinger*. French, German, Italian; dramatic roles and lyric roles — de Reszke sang them all and sang them, according to contemporary witnesses, superbly.*

De Reszke made one final Metropolitan appearance, at a gala performance following the regular season. The great tenor was heard on April 29, 1901, in the second act of *Tristan*, with Nordica, Schumann-Heink and his brother Edouard. It was common knowledge that the performance, his last of the season, might also be his last at the Metropolitan, and the house was packed. The combination of heat and excitement caused sixteen women to faint, setting a new record for the theatre. The demonstration for the de Reszkes also set a record; it lasted for a full half hour.

De Reszke long had a consuming ambition: to sing Parsifal. He thought of going to Bayreuth to do so. One of his dearest friends, however, the Princess of Wales, asked why he should give pleasure to the German Kaiser, whom she described as a "horrid old man." The German Crown Prince and the future Edward VII were brothers-in-law. De Reszke was too gentlemanly to pursue the matter further.

He gave up singing entirely after 1903, finding it increasingly difficult to control his weight and consequent shortness of breath. He made his home in Nice, where he taught singing as much as suited him and received admirers from all over the world. He died in Paris in 1925, virtually forgotten by the public but mourned by friends and colleagues such as Melba. In her memoirs, Melba described de Reszke's swan song. On his deathbed, his voice suddenly returned. For three days the house rang with the music of his great roles — Faust, Raoul, Tristan, Lohengrin, Siegfried — as de Reszke lay dying.

Among gala performances of the Grau regime, none was more so than the special tribute to Prince Henry of Prussia, brother of the German Kaiser, on February 25, 1902. For the occasion, programs were printed on silk and the house was festooned with Southern smilax. Wreaths of the evergreen covered walls, pillars and fronts of balconies and boxes. Wreaths of smilax covered the proscenium arch, topped by a standard of American and German flags and shields. The chandelier was festooned like a Christ-

---

* The lone "Mapleson cylinder" is acoustically wretched, but in the midst of the grinding and scratching it is possible to hear the faint echo of a fine tenor voice, resonating brilliantly *dans le masque* in the final phrases of *O paradiso*!

The brothers Jean and Edouard de Reszke

mas tree. In the center of the lower tier, partitions separating five boxes had been removed to form one large "royal box," canopied in crimson velvet and white satin, and decorated with American Beauty roses. Orchestra seats cost thirty dollars, with other seats in proportion. "Persons who could pay such sums," said Krehbiel, "could also afford to dress well, and at no public affair in my time has New York seen such a display of gowns and jewels."

The Prince arrived late and therefore missed the evening's first German-language production, an act of *Lohengrin*, with Johanna Gadski, Schumann-Heink, Andreas Dippel and Bispham. It was followed by an act of *Carmen*, with Calvé, Albert Alvarez and Antonio Scotti; an act of *Aida*, with Eames, Louise Homer, Emilio de Marchi and Giuseppe Campanari; and an act of *Tannhäuser*, with Milka Ternina, Ernst Van Dyck and Anton Van Rooy.

When the curtain fell on *Tannhäuser*, with two acts of opera still to go, it was 12:16 A.M. The Prince and his party had long since departed, and with them most of the audience. A scheduled act of *La Traviata* was canceled — because of the lateness of the hour, the official explanation went. Gossip soon buzzed, however, that Sembrich, the scheduled Violetta, refused to face the half-empty house. Lucienne Breval and Alvarez completed the gargantuan evening with a scene from *Le Cid*.

Grau was to continue only one more season as director of the Metropolitan. The recurrent heart condition that finally compelled him to retire suggests that the outward calm which so impressed Krehbiel masked a normal amount of the agitation to which an impresario is subject.

Grau's immediate problem was to fill the void — there could be no question of finding a successor — left by the departure of Jean de Reszke. One of the replacements engaged by Grau was an ill-starred tenor named Georg Anthes. At a performance of *Lohengrin* on January 10, 1903, as he stepped into the swan boat to take leave of his too-inquisitive bride, Anthes leaned back too far. The boat capsized, plunging the hapless Grail Knight into the River Scheldt. No harm was done, except to Anthes's dignity and dramatic illusion. Ten days later, in the Forging Scene in *Siegfried*, Anthes's sword failed to split the anvil until the third blow. These mishaps possibly unnerved the tenor; he did not return for the following season.

He did, however, sing excerpts from *Lohengrin* at the gala farewell performance on April 27, 1903, with which Grau formally took leave of the Metropolitan. Heard on the same program were Fritzi Scheff, Gadski, Schumann-Heink, Alois Burgstaller, Van Rooy, Sembrich, de Marchi, Eames, Alvarez, Edouard de Reszke, Marcel Journet, Scotti and Bispham. Of the company's leading artists, only Nordica, indisposed in Pittsburgh, was missing. The enormous program, consisting of acts from six different operas, lasted until long past midnight. At its conclusion there were calls for Grau, but he had left the theatre.

Grau's last years were spent in his beautiful home at Croissy-Chatou, on the Seine, about ten miles from Paris. He died in Paris on March 14, 1907, two years short of sixty.

According to Henry B. Dazian, the theatrical costumer who was Grau's executor, the impresario left an estate of over $600,000. Some of this came from well-advised investments, but the greater part represented Grau's share of Metropolitan earnings in the five seasons that followed the dissolution of the Abbey-Schoeffel-Grau partnership. The Metropolitan under Grau never had a losing season. Its earnings topped $100,000 in every season except 1900–1901, when the company netted only $15,290. That was the year of the expensive *Salammbô* production and a financially disastrous Western tour. As the homeward-bound Metropolitan train rolled through the picturesque hills of New York State, Grau addressed his artists philosophically: "Look well, my children. You will not enjoy this view again at my expense."

Ernestine Schumann-Heink
(left) as Magdalene, and
Johanna Gadski (right) as
Eva in DIE MEISTERSINGER

Fritzi Scheff

9)

Opera Without Profit

GRAU'S SUCCESSOR, HEINRICH CONRIED, had been born Heinrich Cohn, the son of a weaver in Silesia. As a young man he had become an actor at the Burgtheater in Vienna. At twenty-three he had come to New York to help manage one of the German-language theatres then flourishing in the city. He was so successful that he soon opened a theatre of his own. He obtained American rights for various operettas by Strauss and Millöcker, and produced the dramas of Sudermann, Fulda and Hauptmann years before they reached the Broadway stage.

As a profitable sideline, Conried supplied steamer chairs to the Hamburg-American Line. And to the end of his career he augmented his income by giving private acting lessons in his office.

Since it was well known that the Maurice Grau Opera Company had paid handsome dividends to its shareholders, Conried had no difficulty in organizing a similar group, the Conried Metropolitan Opera Company. The new company purchased the costumes, scenery and other assets of the Maurice Grau Opera Company and negotiated a new lease with the Metropolitan Opera and Real Estate Company.

One of the directors of the new Conried company was Otto H. Kahn, a partner in the investment-banking firm of Kuhn, Loeb & Company. He had been proposed by the firm's senior partner, Jacob Schiff. The latter himself had first been invited to serve on the board of directors but did not feel he could spare the time.

Kahn was drawn to the idea — he was a music-lover and had studied three instruments as a boy — but he wondered whether it was wise to risk his banking reputation in anything so frivolous as producing opera. He asked his friend E. H. Harriman for an opinion. Harriman advised him to go ahead, so long as he treated the opera seriously and thoughtfully, as he would any other business.

Thereafter, the affairs of the Metropolitan Opera had high priority in Kahn's eighteen-hour working day. Over a period of thirty years he contributed an average of $100,000 a year of his own money to the running of the opera. Gradually he became the most influential voice on the Metropolitan's board of directors.

All that was in the future, however, when Conried was preparing to open his first season on November 23, 1903. Unlike his predecessor, Conried was concerned with what would nowadays be called his "image" and that of his opera house. To lend tone to the establishment, he had his ushers wear evening dress, with silver badges to distinguish them from patrons. The house itself had had its interior done over by John M. Carrère and Thomas Hastings, who later were to create the New York Public Library, the New Theatre on Central Park West and the Frick mansion on upper Fifth Avenue.

Carrère and Hastings changed the interior to resplendent red and gold. Four oval paintings of music-making cherubs, clearly visible only to patrons of the topmost balcony, the Family Circle, ornamented the waffle-grid ceiling. Rosettes of lights on the balconies culminated in a magnificent sunburst chandelier. Six names on the redesigned proscenium symbolized the eclecticism of the Metropolitan's repertoire — Gluck, Mozart, Beethoven, Verdi, Wagner, Gounod. The house had the look it would retain for the rest of its sixty-year life-span, except for one detail: The gold curtain was not added until 1905.

There were other changes in the business and administrative offices. Old-style high bookkeeper's desks, before which one sat on a tall stool, were banished as "inartistic." Instead, Conried's assistants were supplied with rolltop desks. Conried also chose the massive Spanish-mission-style furniture with which the Opera Club on the Grand Tier was furnished until its face-lifting for the 1946–1947 season.

In Conried's time, the general manager's office was on the second floor. By means of a spiral staircase, it communicated directly with the office of the business manager, on the ground floor just below. When Grau had

The opera house as most people remember it

business to discuss with business manager Ernest Goerlitz, he would often simply lean over the winding balustrade and shout: "Goerlitz!" Conried had the stairway sealed off; nothing must be allowed to intrude on his privacy. He scrapped Grau's four-foot-square worktable, replacing it with a fine mahogany desk. And a bare anteroom became Conried's study, artistically furnished with portieres, curtains, couches, easy chairs and a washstand camouflaged as a rolltop desk. It was in this study that Conried gave lessons in acting and elocution.

Conried began his season auspiciously by realizing an impresario's dream, that of presenting a sensational new tenor. A story fostered by Conried in interviews, and reported in the more trusting sections of the press, was that the impresario had gone down to Mulberry Street to ask Italian immigrants there the name of the greatest singer in the world. The answer he received was Enrico Caruso. When his bootblack confirmed the opinion, Conried cabled to Italy for Caruso.

The prosaic fact was that Grau had been negotiating with Caruso, whom he had heard at Covent Garden, for two years, and in one of his last official acts had signed the tenor to a contract for forty performances. Conried was at first disinclined to honor the contract, reducing the performances to twenty. Caruso cabled back that it was hardly worth his while to make the voyage for fewer than twenty-five appearances, and that was the number finally agreed upon.

The reviews of Caruso's debut in *Rigoletto* have often been quoted as evidence that critics do not always know a good thing when they hear it. Actually, Caruso sang badly at his debut. He was extremely nervous, as he always was before a performance, and was perhaps thrown off by the tricky acoustics of the house. After the performance he was in such low spirits that Conried offered to manage his engagements, worldwide, on a five-year sliding scale eventually reaching two thousand dollars a performance. Caruso declined; he was depressed, but not that depressed.

Caruso quickly recovered himself, however, and before the end of the season it was usual for operagoers to inquire at the box office what was available for Caruso's next performance.

Conried's first season began auspiciously, along familiar lines — a good deal of Italian opera, a bit of French opera and no Wagner on Monday nights. Although not a trained musician, Conried had taste and imagination. He realized the shortcomings of the orchestra, chorus and ballet in the Grau regime, and set about making the needed improvements.

Conried's own shortcoming, however, was that he lacked Grau's suave aplomb. He could be stubborn and tactless. He was, as an associate put it, "lacking in those small courtesies which people like."

An incident of the first season strained his relations with the newspapers. When Caruso appeared in his first *Tosca*, critics left after the second act to begin writing their reviews. In those days the space on the Grand Tier that later became the Opera Guild Room was set aside for the use of the press. Reviews written in hot haste were rushed by waiting copyboys down to Park Row. (No newspaper had yet ventured as far uptown as Forty-second Street.)

Conried suddenly appeared in the press room. He threatened the assembled reviewers that unless they returned for the third act and Caruso's singing of *E lucevan le stelle*, he would bar them from future performances at the Metropolitan.

Let no one who has not met a newspaper deadline raise his eyebrows at the critical habit of leaving before the end of a performance. It is not necessary, as critics are fond of pointing out, to eat a whole pie in order to judge its flavor. And it is highly improbable that *E lucevan le stelle* will reveal facets of a tenor's art that have not already been disclosed by *Recondita armonia* and the ensembles of the first two acts. It is less conspicuous to leave after the death of Scarpia, and that accordingly is the time-honored critical point of departure. In any case, Conried could no more have made his banishment stick than could the Shuberts in later years. It was an ill-tempered outburst that merely ruffled tempers all around.

Aside from Caruso's debut, the great event of Conried's first season was *Parsifal*. His announcement that he intended to produce the work created a furor. Wagner's will had stipulated that *Parsifal* not be performed outside Bayreuth for fifty years after his death. Cosima Wagner, the composer's widow, brought suit for an injunction in the federal courts. The decision, however, was in favor of Conried; since no agreement on copyrights and performing rights existed between the United States and Germany, it was ruled that grounds for a writ of injunction did not exist.

Conried next found himself in hot water with the clergy. A number of ministers, some "of unquestioned sincerity, others mere seekers after notoriety," according to Krehbiel, attacked the opera as "sacrilegious." To make matters worse, Conried had scheduled his first performance for Christmas Eve.

A petition was addressed to Mayor Seth Low, begging him to revoke the license of the Metropolitan Opera House so far as performances of *Parsifal* were concerned. The petition was not granted, but the furor lasted up to the very day of the performance. It provided Conried with invaluable free advertising.

Excitement mounted as Christmas Eve approached. Operagoers wrote letters to the editor, asking whether they should wear evening dress to a performance that began at five o'clock in the afternoon. Pianist Fanny Bloomfield-Zeisler chartered a special train, the *"Parsifal* Limited," to bring Chicago opera-lovers to the performance. Special trains ran from other cities also.

On the day of the performance the *Evening Telegram* brought out a *"Parsifal* Extra." The *Times* published a cartoon depicting the strange mania that had overcome New York, *Parsifal*-itis. It showed a bewildered Father Knickerbocker watching newsboys hawk papers headlined: HOW TO DRESS FOR PARSIFAL. An organ-grinder carries a sign: *"Parsifal* Selections Only." The biggest sign reads: "Sermon Morning and Evening Denouncing *Parsifal* as sacrilegious by Rev. Warn 'em." But a crowd is streaming into a lecture: "What *Parsifal* Means, With Maps and Diagrams." There are advertisements for *Parsifal* hats, *Parsifal* Cough Drops, a *Parsifal* five-cent cigar, a breakfast food called Par-see-fall, a "New Historical Novel, *Parsifal, Jr.*," and a Signor Parsifal, Fortune Teller and Mind Reader. A handsome new skyscraper offers *"Parsifal* flats," and smoke from a factory chimney forms itself into the letters "PARSIFAL."

The five scheduled performances of *Parsifal*, at doubled prices (ten dollars top), sold out so quickly that Conried quickly scheduled five more. After an added eleventh performance, Conried announced that *Parsifal* had earned $186,308, or an average of nearly $17,000 a performance. It was guessed that after subtracting production costs and singers' fees, about $100,000 of the total was profit.

With receipts of $1,100,000, Conried's first season netted $60,000. Earnings would have been higher except for Conried's practice of charging off the cost of new productions during the season they were introduced, rather than amortizing them over several years. The second season's profit was even better — $111,000. The third season, however, was marred by disaster. On a Western tour, the company had the misfortune to be in San Francisco at the time of the earthquake. Many of the artists escaped with nothing but the clothes on their backs. Caruso had been able to save only an autographed photograph of President Theodore Roosevelt.*

Advance subscription sales had been brisk, and there had been time to give only two performances. By the time scheduled for the third performance, the San Francisco opera house was a heap of ruins. When word of the disaster got back to New York, there was consternation in the business office; the San Francisco stand would result in a deficit of monumental proportions.

"Deficit be damned!" cried Conried. "The company is in danger!"

Conried ordered the Metropolitan's telephone switchboard closed to all incoming and outgoing calls except those to or from Western Union, long distance, and the railway companies. During the fifty-six hours that the switchboard remained open on this emergency basis, Conried himself sat in at the board from time to time while weary operators catnapped or ate a hasty sandwich. As the little stagedoor lobby on Thirty-ninth Street began to fill with wives, mothers, children and sweethearts of the touring performers, all apprehensive and clamoring for news, Conried sent out for food. Many relatives remained in the lobby all night, seizing on each scrap of information as it came over the wires.

Finally came the long-awaited telegram from Nahan Franko, concertmaster of the Metropolitan orchestra: Every member of the company was accounted for, and unharmed.

---

* Caruso, according to Aimé Gerber, longtime paymaster of the Metropolitan, loved to tell at his own expense the story of the Roosevelt photograph. During one of his earliest seasons, the company had reached Washington, D.C., on its annual spring tour. It was a warm evening, and between the acts of *Pagliacci*, Caruso had stepped out to get a breath of air and gossip with the stagehands. A doorman brought word that the President was backstage and wished to see him.

Suspecting a practical joke of the sort he was not above playing himself, Caruso replied that he would see "the President" as soon as he finished his cigarette. When he reentered the theatre, he found a beaming Theodore Roosevelt.

"Hello, Mr. Caruso," said the President. "They told me you were busy out in the alley, so I waited here."

President Roosevelt was so amused by the tenor's obvious surprise and embarrassment that the autographed photograph arrived next day.

Although the Metropolitan might have evaded responsibility by pleading a natural calamity, Conried sent Goerlitz to San Francisco with instructions to refund the advance subscriptions dollar for dollar. In some cases proof was difficult to establish, since virtually every house in the disaster area had been damaged either by the earthquake or the fire that followed. Some subscribers could show tickets — or the charred remnants of tickets; others could give nothing but their bare word that they had purchased tickets for such and such a location.

Goerlitz listened to every claim, and paid. When the books for the tour were balanced, it was found that the amount refunded matched the amount taken in as advance subscriptions virtually to the penny.

It remained one of Conried's most cherished memories that the people of San Francisco had not taken advantage of Metropolitan generosity. But there was little else to show for the Western tour. From the company's trainload of costumes and scenery, scarcely a dozen trunks remained.

Hardest hit were the orchestra, most of whose instruments were damaged beyond repair. When the company returned to New York, Sembrich further endeared herself to the public and her colleagues by singing a benefit recital for the orchestra players at Carnegie Hall. The event raised nine thousand dollars for the hapless musicians.

Storm clouds were gathering as Conried prepared for his 1906–1907 season. The veteran theatre manager Oscar Hammerstein was building an opera house on West Thirty-fourth Street, where he planned to present opera in competition with the Metropolitan.

Hammerstein had made a million dollars from a cigar-cutting machine and from a trade journal devoted to the tobacco industry. He was now able to indulge his passion for music and the theatre.

Hammerstein loved to mingle with people from the world of theatre and opera. Once he was at the bar of the old Gilsey House with Gustave Kerker, composer of *The Belles of New York, Castles in the Air* and other operettas, and several drama critics. After the third drink, Hammerstein offered to bet that he could compose an operetta — words and music — in forty-eight hours. Kerker took him up, promising to arrange and orchestrate the finished product.

Rooms were engaged at the Gilsey House, a piano was moved in and Hammerstein began picking out tunes. Producer Louis Harrison tried to distract the composer by engaging relays of organ-grinders to play outside his window; but Hammerstein never faltered. Complaints began pouring in to the management that a madman was howling, stamping the floor and pounding the piano. Hammerstein, however, had barricaded his door and refused to give up.

In forty-eight hours, exhausted but still smiling, Hammerstein emerged with his finished score. As expected, it was a hodgepodge of reminiscences, but done with such cleverness and humor that Kerker had to confess himself beaten. *The Kohinoor* was produced, to the side-splitting laughter of Hammerstein's cronies, at the New York Theatre with considerable success.

Hammerstein's hat was the barometer of his temperament. When it was pulled low over his eyebrows, members of his companies learned to stay out of the way. When his hatbrim was on an even keel, all was serene; and when it was pushed back expansively on his forehead, that was the time to ask for a raise. It was believed that stenciled inside the headband in gold letters were the words with which Voltaire's *Candide* ends: "*Il faut cultiver nos jardins.*" The story could not be verified, because nobody ever saw Hammerstein without his hat. He was said to wear it even to bed.

Krehbiel said that in the beginning many people did not take Hammerstein seriously as an opera impresario; "he did not seem illogical enough." But skepticism gave way to anticipation when it became known that he had assembled a company headed by Melba, the tenor Alessandro Bonci, baritone Maurice Renaud and Luisa Tetrazzini, a phenomenal coloratura whom Conried had had under option but hadn't gotten around to engaging.

Melba told how Hammerstein had persuaded her to return to New York — by sheer persistence. Once he pursued her to the door of her Paris bathroom, offering successively higher fees. Between splashes Melba told him to go away. When she had dressed, she found her drawing room literally carpeted with banknotes — 100,000 francs' worth.

Melba couldn't resist the lavish gesture. She signed.

By luck or design, Hammerstein had hit on the idea of presenting the then-modern French operas, which for some reason the Metropolitan had been backward in bringing out. Giulio Gatti-Casazza, Conried's successor, felt Conried had been remiss in not buying up the rights to the works with which Hammerstein scored his greatest successes — Massenet's *Thaïs*, Charpentier's *Louise*, Debussy's *Pelléas et Mélisande*. Rights to all of them, and the artists who performed in them, had been offered to him by the Parisian agent Gabriel Astruc.

"It would have paid Conried," said Gatti, "even if he had not intended to produce them, at least to buy them up and throw them into his desk drawer."

Conried, however, had dismissed the idea "with a contemptuous wave of his hand," said Astruc. He would not even talk about Hammerstein.

Besides, Conried had plans of his own. He intended to produce Strauss' *Salome*, with which he hoped to create a furor as great as that of *Parsifal*.

Hammerstein had hoped to open on the same night as the Metropolitan but neither his theatre nor his singers were ready. The Metropolitan had the field to itself on November 26, 1906, when it opened with *Roméo et Juliette*.

One week before the opening, Caruso had been arrested in the monkey house of the Central Park Zoo, charged with making improper advances to a passerby, Mrs. Hannah Stanhope. Caruso protested that it was a misunderstanding caused by his faulty command of English. The lady said he had pinched her. Although Mrs. Stanhope did not appear in court, Caruso was fined.

The event might well have had disastrous consequences both to Caruso's career and at the Metropolitan box office. Conried fretted to see how Caruso would be received at his first appearance, which came in *La Bohème* two nights after the opening. The roar of applause that followed Rodolfo's narrative lifted a heavy burden from the shoulders of both tenor and manager.

On opening night, Conried had again scored by presenting a brilliant new star — Boston-born Geraldine Farrar, who had achieved sensational triumphs in Berlin and whose name had been linked romantically with that of the young Crown Prince. On December 5, Conried presented both a new star and a new opera — the American premiere of Giordano's *Fedora*, with Lina Cavalieri in the title role.

She was a strikingly beautiful Italian brunette who, gossip said, had started her career as a flower-seller in the streets of Rome. An elderly marquis had discerned the beauty under her shabby clothes and had helped to launch her career. It had taken her to the Folies Bergère in Paris, where she had been billed as "The World's Most Beautiful Woman," and finally to the opera house.

"Miss Cavalieri justified her reputation as a beauty," wrote Henderson appreciatively. "Her figure is exquisite and her face a delight to see."

Others thought so, too. Among them were young "Willie" Vanderbilt, whose father was a director of the Metropolitan. Willie Vanderbilt's romance with Cavalieri caused so much gossip that the elder Vanderbilt saw to it that she was not reengaged.

Another Willie who lost his heart to Cavalieri was Robert Winthrop Chanler, a member of the Astor clan, who in later years became a sculptor of sorts with a studio on East Nineteenth Street. He married Cavalieri in Paris after complying with her demand that he sign over his entire fortune to her. According to one story, Cavalieri then abandoned him, saying she had agreed to marry him but not to consummate the marriage. Another version is that the marriage lasted for "one week of joy and terror."

A friend lent Willie money to return to America, where he was relieved to find that his older brothers, who were also his trustees, refused to validate the transaction with Cavalieri. Willie escaped with most of his fortune intact.

At the height of the uproar Willie received a telegram from another brother, who was confined in a mental institution. The message, which quickly became a byword of the day, read: "WHO'S LOONY NOW?"

On January 18, 1907, Puccini was on hand to hear the first Metropolitan performance of his *Manon Lescaut*. He slipped into the director's box during the first act. At intermission he was recognized and greeted with a fanfare by the orchestra. The audience applauded him so long and enthusiastically that he ended by withdrawing to the rear of the box, out of sight, so the performance might go on. After the second act he sent a gracious note in French to the press. It said in part: "I consider myself happy to be able to say that I am among my friends, to whom I can speak in music with a certainty of being understood."

Two days later came the dress rehearsal of *Salome*. Conried had perhaps been unwise to schedule it for a Sunday, before an invited audience many of whom had just come from church. The work left hearers a bit stunned, both at the dress rehearsal and at the performance the following Tuesday.

Lina Cavalieri onstage, February, 1932

Walter Prichard Eaton, then a reporter for the *Tribune,* described the scene:

"Many voices were hushed as the crowd passed out into the night, many faces were white almost as those at the rail of a ship. Many women were silent, and men spoke as if a bad dream were on them. The grip of a strange horror or disgust was on the majority. It was significant that the usual applause was lacking. It was scattered and brief."

The Metropolitan's board of directors promptly met and adopted a resolution which was communicated to Conried: "The directors of the Metropolitan Opera and Real Estate Company consider that the performance of *Salome* is objectionable and detrimental to the best interest of the Metropolitan Opera House. They therefore protest against any repetition of this opera."

Conried was aghast. The performance, sold out at advanced prices, had brought in nearly $20,000, and three more performances were scheduled. He pleaded with the directors to reconsider.

A stormy meeting was held on January 30, in J. P. Morgan's library on Madison Avenue. Arguing on behalf of Conried were Kahn, Robert Goelet, James Speyer, H. R. Winthrop and Rawlins H. Cottenet. Opposed were J. P. Morgan, William K. Vanderbilt, Augustus D. Juilliard, August Belmont and a majority of the other directors. The Morgan group prevailed, and *Salome* was banished from the Metropolitan.

Krehbiel, though revolted by the morbidity and decadence of the Oscar Wilde drama, was fascinated by Strauss' score. He was especially struck by the throat-slitting music that depicts the decapitation of John the Baptist. While the double basses sustain a low E flat *tremolando,* one of the basses plays B flat by pinching the highest string of his instrument and sounding the note with a short quick stroke of the bow. Strauss found this device for imitating a human groan, said Krehbiel, in Berlioz's great treatise on instrumentation. Berlioz, as a young winner of the Prix de Rome, had learned the trick from a double-bass player in the Piedmont.

On the whole, Krehbiel regretted the decision to ban the opera: "It would have been better and conduced more to artistic righteousness if the public had been permitted to kill the work by refusing to witness it. In my opinion there is no doubt but that this would have been the result. . . ."

He was probably right. In later seasons *Salome* never attained lasting popularity at the Metropolitan. It is a somewhat awkward work to stage. It is a bit too short for a whole evening and for some reason doesn't go well on a double bill. It demands a performer of extraordinary dramatic as well as vocal gifts in the title role. And people who go to the opera to hear fine singing find little in the score to engage their interest.

The disastrous *Salome* was the last straw so far as Conried's tenure at the Metropolitan was concerned. Season by season, receipts had gone up but profits had gone down. The 1906–1907 season ended with a deficit of $84,039. In vain Conried pleaded the increasing cost and difficulty of producing opera. The directors of his company could not see how the difficulties could be greater, since there was so much more money to solve them with.

Conried was in poor health; he was afflicted with neuritis that hampered his walking and made him unable to go to his office for days at a time. There were scandalous tales of mismanagement, or worse, in the business office.

And there was the growing threat of Hammerstein. Although he had begun his season late, he had carried it through successfully, ending with a profit of $100,000. In March he announced that subscriptions for the next season already amounted to $200,000, of which $100,000 had come from the four principal ticket speculators of New York. Clearly Hammerstein was a dangerous rival, to cope with whom a new, vigorous, younger man was needed at the Metropolitan.

Conried performed one final service for the Metropolitan: In Berlin he met Gustav Mahler and engaged him as a conductor.

10

New Faces

ALTHOUGH HE RECEIVED HIS DIPLOMA as a naval engineer, Giulio Gatti-Casazza had a typically Italian love for opera. He attended his first performance, Rossini's *Semiramide*, at Mantua, when he was not quite four years old. Sixty years later he recalled vividly the great Temple Scene, with the choristers dressed as priests in long red cloaks.

During his student days in Genoa, Gatti went to the opera almost nightly. Since his school was across the street from Verdi's apartment, he saw the great man going in and out, and once followed him at a distance until Verdi froze him in his tracks with a glare. Years later, when Gatti recalled the incident, the Maestro laughed and said:

"What a pity! At that age, with a good pair of legs under you, you should have been following some pretty girl."

As a graduation present, his father gave Gatti the money for a trip to Bayreuth. He saw *Parsifal* and became a lifelong Wagnerite. In later years, Metropolitan subscribers seated near the director's box would be disconcerted to hear Gatti absent-mindedly singing with the orchestra whenever *Die Meistersinger* was performed.

In 1893, Gatti's father, having been elected to Parliament, felt obliged to resign the directorship of the opera at Ferrara. The job was offered to his son. Young Gatti hesitated; he was only twenty-four.

"If you have no other excuse," said Count Cosimo Masi, the mayor of Ferrara, "nothing remains but to accept immediately. And find yourself some youthful colleagues who are also devoted to the theatre."

Gatti plunged into his work with enthusiasm and flair. He inaugurated a highly successful spring season and presented works that were new to Ferrara — Puccini's *Manon Lescaut,* Verdi's *Otello* and *Falstaff.* When Gatti wired congratulations to Verdi on the triumphant success of *Falstaff,* the composer replied laconically: MANY THANKS BUT PLEASE INFORM SIZE OF BOX-OFFICE RECEIPTS AT FOLLOWING PERFORMANCES.

In his Ferrara years, Gatti was already developing the qualities of a successful impresario. He was tactful, resilient and resourceful. He could deal with a temperamental soprano and coax the annual subsidy out of a recalcitrant city council. He had taste and imagination, and never hesitated to try new ideas.

Gatti's qualities were being noted elsewhere. In 1898, after five years at Ferrara, he was offered the direction of Italy's most famous theatre, La Scala in Milan.

"Bravo!" said Verdi when he heard the news. "You've caught a famous cat to skin." He added a piece of advice that Gatti never forgot. "Read the newspapers as little as possible. Journalists are good fellows, to be sure, but never in accord. Instead, read most at-ten-tive-ly" (*"at-ten-tiv-a-men-te,"* accentuating each syllable) "the reports of the box-office. These are the only documents that measure success or failure, and they represent not mere opinions but facts. The theatre is intended to be full and not empty."

At La Scala, Gatti found his work cut out for him. Through a series of mishaps, the theatre had been dark for sixteen months — the first season it had omitted in its century-long history. Finances were inadequate. There was no record of salaries, expenses and receipts from previous seasons; the former impresarios had left not a scrap of written information behind. There was no scenery, chorus, ballet, orchestra or stage crew. Everything was gone, everything needed to be reorganized. Publishers were in a bad humor, the press was hostile, the Scala public was notoriously capricious and unpredictable.

Gatti stroked his long beard thoughtfully and went to work. It was all very much like Ferrara.

Gatti had one priceless advantage: His new musical director was Arturo Toscanini. The two men hit it off immediately and worked together with mutual esteem and respect. It was Toscanini's brilliant Wagnerian performances, played to sold-out houses at La Scala, that first began to make him internationally famous.

Another asset was Caruso, then just beginning to become known, who saved a faltering *Elisir d'amore* and scored a personal triumph in his Scala debut. And Feodor Chaliapin's brilliant portrayal of the title role in Boito's *Mefistofele* was further proof that the new Scala director had a knack for discovering talent.

In his third season at La Scala, Gatti felt secure enough in his position to stage *Siegfried* and *Tristan* without a ballet.

In the summer of 1907, Gatti received a note from a friend in Rome. A "very important person who, for the moment, does not wish to be named" wanted to know whether Gatti would consider becoming director of the Metropolitan Opera. Because of Conried's illness, the Metropolitan's directors were searching for a successor.

Gatti's feelings were mixed. He had just signed a new nine-year contract at La Scala, where he was well situated in every respect. On the other hand, the offer pleased and tempted him. Despite its relatively brief life-span, the Metropolitan had acquired a *cachet* exceeded by no opera house in the world.

Toscanini urged Gatti to accept. During the previous season, Toscanini had declined an invitation to the Metropolitan from Conried, whom he did not know. With Gatti at the Metropolitan, however, it would be a different story. And Toscanini was tired of La Scala and its fickle public. He had already resigned once and it had taken all Gatti's powers of persuasion to get him back.

The "very important person" was Otto Kahn. Having business in Paris, Gatti called on Kahn at his apartment there. He found the banker charming and his offer generous. Gatti would be given a three-year contract, with complete authority and all possible support. An invitation would also be extended to Toscanini. Kahn wondered, however, how Toscanini would feel about conducting at the Metropolitan with Mahler there. Toscanini's reply was that he admired Mahler and would infinitely prefer him as a colleague to any mediocrity.

Eventually, by letter and private cablegram, the details of the agreement were worked out. Meanwhile, in time-honored fashion, Kahn in New

York and Gatti-Casazza in Milan denied that any negotiations were going on.

Announcement of Gatti's appointment put an end to the rumors that had been buzzing about Conried's successor. Names put forward, and objected to, were those of Jean de Reszke (he might fill the house with his pupils), Tito Ricordi (he might load the repertoire with Puccini scores), Anton Fuchs (too German) and André Messager (too French). The name of Gatti-Casazza, however, had scarcely been mentioned; few New Yorkers had ever heard of him.

In mid-April, Gatti sailed aboard the later-to-be famous *Lusitania* for his first Metropolitan season. On the pier in New York, he received his first shock. Awaiting him was Andreas Dippel, whose title was administrative manager of the Metropolitan. In practice, Gatti soon discovered, he and Dippel were expected to serve as co-directors of the company. Gatti was thunderstruck; not once during the negotiations with Kahn and, later, with Rawlins Cottenet, secretary of the board of directors, had Dippel's name been mentioned.

Much later, Gatti discovered what had happened. Kahn, as board chairman of the reorganized Metropolitan Opera Company formed after Conried's resignation, had made his offer in good faith. When Gatti accepted, Kahn and his colleagues met with directors of the Metropolitan Opera and Real Estate Company to tell them the news.

An influential member of the Metropolitan Opera and Real Estate Company — rumor said it was J. P. Morgan — looked surprised and asked: "But why go to Europe to get a director when you have the very man you need right here?"

"Who is this person?" Kahn asked.

"Andreas Dippel."

Dippel was a tenor who had sung with the Metropolitan since the 1898–1899 season. His singing appears to have left little impression; but, of course, he was placed at a disadvantage — what tenor wasn't? — by being in the same company with Caruso. He seems to have been one of those versatile, dependable singers whom it is always good to have around. During one season he sang sixteen different roles, in three languages, ranging from the lyricism of Count Almaviva in *Il Barbiere di Siviglia* to the heroics of Siegmund in *Die Walküre*. He was noted for his ability to substitute for an indisposed colleague at short notice. And he knew everybody — as Gatti, to his sorrow, was shortly to discover.

The nomination of Dippel placed Kahn in an embarrassing position. Actually, the choice of a director did not concern the Metropolitan Opera and Real Estate Company; the Metropolitan Opera Company had responsibility for performances and should have been free to choose the director it thought best qualified. But the Metropolitan Opera and Real Estate Company did, after all, own the building; and Kahn, as a member of the Wall Street community, had no desire to antagonize J. P. Morgan. Hence, as a compromise, the two-headed Gatti-Dippel regime.

Gatti found that Dippel had already made most of the arrangements regarding finances and organization. His plans included two choruses, each of a hundred voices. One chorus, to sing the French and Italian repertoire, was to be chosen by Toscanini; the German-language chorus, by Dippel. As a latecomer to the scene, Gatti had no choice but to acquiesce, though he let it be known that he considered the double chorus an absurd extravagance and was not to be held accountable if it did not work. After fifteen years in Italian opera houses, Gatti knew a thing or two about intrigue himself.

More shocks were in store for Gatti when it came time to choose performers and repertoire for the season. Compared to La Scala, there was little system or discipline at the Metropolitan. At La Scala, the principal features of the repertoire and principal members of the casts were charted weeks and months in advance. At the Metropolitan, there was a meeting every Monday to choose artists and repertoire for the following week. The Monday meetings were attended by the principals themselves. Gatti once found himself surrounded by three prima donnas — one with her secretary, another with her mother, the third with her husband — all waiting for him to decide which of the three was to sing Mimi in *La Bohème*.

Despite problems and vexations of all kinds, the first Gatti-Dippel season opened on November 16, 1908, with a magnificent *Aida*. Everyone who heard that performance talked about it to the end of his days. The sets, costumes and props had been borrowed from La Scala. Singing the title role was a superb new Bohemian soprano, Emmy Destinn. Louise Homer was Amneris, Caruso was Radames, and Scotti, Amonasro. Toscanini's conducting of the familiar score was a revelation. At the end of the second act there was such an ovation that not only performers and con-ductor, but finally the managers, had to come before the curtain for a bow.

Next day the press, which had been following with relish the backstage skirmishing at the Metropolitan, predicted that, as Gatti-Casazza had taken the first curtain call, he would eventually win out over Dippel.

Dippel by now was no longer concealing his hostility toward Gatti-Casazza. Gatti, on the other hand, had made such an impression on the Metropolitan's board of directors that they informed him that his contract and Toscanini's were to be renewed. Dippel was, in effect, on probation.

Word got around, as such things always do. Dippel was well known and liked by most of his colleagues, whereas Gatti was an aloof, reserved newcomer. Alarmed by the thought of having Gatti in sole command, a group of artists addressed a petition to the directors. The signers included Farrar, Scotti, Sembrich, Eames and, of all people, Caruso. The tenor had no reason to dislike Gatti; in fact, his engagement at La Scala had been an important upward step in his career. It has been guessed that he good-naturedly signed when pressed to do so by his colleagues.

The directors responded with an open letter that said in effect: "Dear artists, continue to sing, which is your job, and do not trouble yourselves about things that do not concern you."

Gatti had a personal disappointment in his first season. Frances Alda, the Australian soprano whom he was shortly to marry, was coolly received at her first performances. Henderson, reviewing Alda unfavorably in *Faust*, underscored what was generally known about Alda's relationship with Gatti by adding that it was pointless to dwell on her shortcomings "for the next three years at least." Three years was the term of Gatti's contract.

All this time, Hammerstein's Manhattan Opera House was providing mur-derous competition for the Metropolitan. Hammerstein was a fighter. He delighted in such direct confrontations as scheduling an opera on the same evening it was to be done at the Metropolitan. Once, when *Aida* was being performed at both houses, word came to the packed Manhattan that the Metropolitan was half empty. The news arrived at intermission and the curtain was down. The jubilant cast, led by the conductor, did a triumphant snake dance around the stage.

Hammerstein scored one of his biggest hits with a new singer and a new opera: Mary Garden in the title role in *Thaïs*. In her memoirs, Garden noted candidly that a feature of the role was a costume of flesh-colored *crêpe de chine* that left piquant uncertainty of how much that was showing was Garden.

Garden was Mélisande when Hammerstein gave New Yorkers their first *Pelléas et Mélisande*. Krehbiel found Debussy's score unmelodious and turned up his nose at "M. Maeterlinck's infantile plays." *Pelléas et Mélisande*, he said, was "on the border-line between the marionette drama and that designed for the consumption of mature minds." But the work's novelty and Garden's acting carried the day. *Pelléas* played to sold-out houses.

Another personal triumph for Garden was in the title role in *Salome*, presented by Hammerstein in French rather than the original German. Krehbiel noted that "in the climax of the dance the utmost limit of disrobing ever reached by an actress within a long memory was attained." Henderson admired "the pearly surface of her flesh" but found it added up to "a dance with commentary," since "Miss Garden cannot sing a phrase of Strauss' music."

Salome was done in Philadelphia over the protests of the city's clergy. Boston wouldn't have it.

Not all of Hammerstein's novelties were successful. Feodor Chaliapin made his appearance, but audiences were put off by his mannerisms and his habit of blowing his nose through his fingers. And in view of Willie Chanler's unfortunate experience, New York society felt Hammerstein showed poor taste in reimporting the beautiful Lina Cavalieri. There were even murmurs of "reprisals."

Hammerstein scored a triumph, however, with a brilliant new coloratura, Luisa Tetrazzini. Her vocal acrobatics drew cheers in *Il Barbiere* and *I Puritani*. Later, although he disliked coloraturas, Tetrazzini's demonstrated box-office power left Gatti no alternative but to engage her for the Metropolitan.

"Coloratura sopranos are almost in a class by themselves in their pull on the public," said Gatti. "It is always the same story with them, and I, for one, do not know any reasonable explanation. I, for example, am left cold by the florid, high voices."

A ready explanation, however, was put forward by Robert A. Simon, longtime music critic of the *New Yorker*. Of the climactic moment when the orchestra pauses on the chord of the dominant while the soprano executes her turn, takes a deep breath and goes for the high note, Simon said: "Essentially, it's no different from a trapeze act. What thrills the public is seeing a woman triumph against heavy odds."

(Many years after her New York triumphs, the story goes, Tetrazzini, retired and living in Italy, received a visitor from America who told her about the sensational new coloratura who was then appearing at the Metropolitan.

"Lily Pons!" sniffed Tetrazzini. She turned on a phonograph and played the Mad Scene from *Lucia*. "There, you see," she said, "*I* had the high E flat — with balls.") *

Hammerstein, not content with providing formidable competition for the Metropolitan, never lost an opportunity to poke fun at the rival opera house and its two-headed management. "I haven't two heads on me," a typical public statement began, "but what is worse, I enjoy a triple capacity. This afternoon, serving as my own board of directors, I called a meeting. The board decided to re-engage me as general manager and administrative manager, but at a reduced salary. I shall accept."

For the second season of dual management, Dippel proposed an audacious plan for outdoing Hammerstein. Concurrently with its regular season, the Metropolitan would offer performances at the recently built New Theatre at Central Park West and Sixty-first Street. New Theatre productions would be of works like *Der Freischütz*, *The Bartered Bride* and *Werther*, which would benefit from an intimate setting. Whatever else might be said about the Metropolitan, it wasn't an intimate house.

Dippel's ambitious program would be rounded out by performances at the Brooklyn Academy of Music, the Academy of Music in Philadelphia and the Lyric Theatre in Baltimore.

Gatti proposed a much simpler program, adding his opinion that Dippel's was absurd. Gatti especially resisted the New Theatre series. As if the competition from Hammerstein were not enough, the Metropolitan would in effect be competing with itself.

Dippel would not budge, and a showdown ensued. The board of direc-

---

* *Con coglioni* — the highest possible form of praise in operatic circles. Its opposite, *senza coglioni*, is used to characterize a limp, lifeless performance.

Mary Garden as Salome

Luisa Tetrazzini

tors accepted Dippel's proposal, with the understanding that if it succeeded, he was to have all the credit; if it failed, all the blame.

Gatti must have had some uneasy moments as the opening of the 1909–1910 season approached. Soon, however, it became apparent that things were not going well for Dippel. The New Theatre had not achieved the hoped-for quality of intimacy (too many boxes), and its acoustics were spotty. In some places one could hear the voices but not the orchestra; elsewhere, the other way around. The New Theatre productions were a mixed assortment of uneven quality, and they were not well attended. Between the New Theatre productions, the out-of-town performances and Hammerstein, the Metropolitan ended its season with a deficit of $248,-795. Hammerstein publicly twitted the Metropolitan for losing more money than he had.

Dippel withdrew, with a formal resolution of thanks from the company "in whose services you have been since twenty years," a Germanicism that caused some people to wonder whether Dippel himself drafted the resolution.

Dippel went to Chicago, to become manager of a new organization formed from the remnants of Hammerstein's company. The Metropolitan's directors had quietly made a deal with Hammerstein (publicly, of course, denying that any such deal was contemplated) whereby, in return for a payment of $1,200,000, he undertook not to produce opera in New York for a period of ten years.

Not every aspect of the Metropolitan-Hammerstein deal is fully understood or is ever likely to be. Hammerstein could not have continued much longer in any case; in addition to producing opera, he had become involved in several real estate projects and, like most real estate operators, was chronically short of cash. In taking over his assets, the Metropolitan's directors were buying an organization that was virtually bankrupt.

Most of the $1,200,000 is said to have been put up by William K. Vanderbilt. When his son had become involved with Cavalieri, he had seen to it that she left the Metropolitan.* When Hammerstein had the temerity to bring her back, Vanderbilt vowed to oust Hammerstein from New York.

---

* Cavalieri's final years were spent in Italy. In 1944, still beautiful at seventy, she was living in Florence when the sirens signaled an Allied air raid. Cavalieri started for the bomb shelter, then turned back to get her jewels. She didn't make it.

Hammerstein was in London when the final arrangements were made at Kahn's house on East Sixty-eighth Street. His son Arthur, with the down payment — a certified check for $100,000 — in his pocket, went to the Knickerbocker Hotel bar and bought champagne for everyone in sight. Then he sent his father a 750-word cablegram to inform him the deal was closed.

Hammerstein, after using $900,000 of the money to pay off outstanding debts, invested the remainder in an opera house he was building in London. The venture went into bankruptcy two years later.

With Dippel and Hammerstein gone, Gatti was in sole command. He was now in a position to begin setting his artistic house in order. The next prima donna who arrived with an entourage for the Monday casting conference would be due for a rude surprise.

11

On Guard

WITH DIPPEL AND HAMMERSTEIN both disposed of, Gatti-Casazza for the first time was free to plan a season on a rational basis. The double chorus and orchestra were reduced to more usual, and economical, size. Performances in Brooklyn and Philadelphia were restricted to Tuesdays, when the company was not playing at the Metropolitan. The season, for the first time, was extended to twenty weeks. And the operating surpluses which Gatti hoped to achieve would no longer be distributed to shareholders as dividends; they would be kept as a reserve to draw on in case of need.

One of Gatti's moves was to engage Hammerstein's press agent, William J. Guard. During the Hammerstein-Metropolitan rivalry, Guard had shown great skill in stoking the journalistic fires. As one writer put it: "Hammerstein was a man of daring and imagination. So was Guard, his indispensable propagandist, whose creative temperament matched Hammerstein's in its quicksilver responsiveness and understanding."

Guard showed his resourcefulness during World War I, when for a time it appeared that Viennese conductor Artur Bodanzky would not be able to get to New York. French and English warships, patrolling the North Atlantic shipping routes, were inspecting all steamers and refusing to let German nationals or their allies proceed. At Gatti's request, Guard went to London and Paris to see what could be done. After several conferences at the American embassies, he succeeded in getting a special permit to let Bodanzky through.

Guard in his later years was a Dickensian figure with a straggly mustache and horn-rimmed glasses that gave him the look of an amiable, slightly inebriated owl. He worked in an office cluttered with odds and ends that had been accumulating for years — old press releases, programs, letters, souvenirs, stacks of newspapers. Guard never cleaned up his desk and no one else dared try. His office went unpainted for years; it wasn't possible for painters to get at the walls. Nobody could sit down in his office except a few special, close friends who pushed the papers off a chair in order to do so.

Although Guard was a prodigious drinker, that fact was seldom apparent except to a few colleagues who could determine by certain signs just how far gone he was. Sometimes, however, his condition was obvious to all. One such occasion was the night he came to the opera in full dress, wearing two Windsor neckties. It was surmised that having seen two images in his mirror, he had decided on a separate necktie for each.

"In all his twenty-two years with the Metropolitan," Gatti said of Guard, "there was never the least misunderstanding. I felt a special esteem for this man. I never heard anyone make a complaint against him. Everyone loved him."

Gatti may not have spoken to the leading soprano who called at Guard's office one evening when Guard was even deeper than usual in his cups. At sight of her, he burst into a tirade:

"My God! You think you can *sing!* You have the goddamnedest lousiest voice I ever heard here. You do nothing but bust your guts and yell!"

The soprano was outraged; but seeing that nothing was to be done with Guard in his condition, she had no choice but to make her exit with as much dignity as possible.

The painful part was that Guard was perfectly right. The singer owed her position not so much to vocal skill as to friendship with a person having considerable influence at the Metropolitan.

The story was told of the soprano that she had once sung Micaela in *Carmen* with even less finesse than usual. In the Smugglers' Scene in Act III, after Micaela has finished her big aria, *Je dis que rien ne m'épouvante,* a shot is fired offstage and Micaela, frightened, runs out. The shot was fired on cue, Micaela hurried offstage and from one of the balconies a weary voice exclaimed: "Oh, hell — he *missed* her!"

Guard's colleagues wondered nervously what the repercussions of the

100

Guard tirade would be. There weren't any, except that Madame shortly appeared in a magnificent new fur coat. The influential person had decided not to use his influence.

How did Guard keep his job? Helen Noble, in *Life with the Met*, supplied the answer: "He had so many contacts he was invaluable. He knew too much about too many people. He knew every concert manager, newspaperman, society editor, every top socialite in town. He did favors for them and never needed to be repaid."

As the years passed, Guard had various successors, among them Margaret Carson, an alumna of Toledo journalism. As a newcomer, and a young, attractive one at that, Miss Carson was reminded in various subtle ways that she was among old-timers, custodians of the Metropolitan's hallowed traditions.

One evening she saw one of America's most distinguished critics and musicologists looking at her quizzically from the doorway.

"I suppose you're going to tell me," said Miss Carson, "that you remember William J. Guard sitting at this very desk."

"I knew Billy Guard very well," Alfred Frankenstein replied. "He was a no-good son of a bitch."

Edward Ziegler, with his silver hair parted in the middle and his rimless pince-nez, looked the part of an uncommonly astute investment banker. Few, on meeting him, would have taken him for an opera impresario's assistant or would have guessed that he had been music critic of the New York *Herald* and was fluent in four languages. On Gatti-Casazza's first day in New York, Ziegler had interviewed him for the *Herald*. It was Ziegler who, before going to the *Herald*, originated the "Mephisto's Musings" column that still appears in *Musical America*.

Otto Kahn showed himself a shrewd judge of men by persuading Ziegler to join the Metropolitan staff. Ziegler quickly made himself indispensable. He was self-effacing, meticulous and a quick learner. He was soon negotiating all union contracts — a relief to Gatti, who never became adept at English — and lending a hand in making contracts with the artists. Gradually he took over administration of the company's business affairs, from artists' fees to scenery-warehouse leases. In his first season he more than earned his salary by selling the Metropolitan's endorsement of the Knabe piano. He kept a sharp eye on the scheduling of rehearsals; all union members received overtime, and if rehearsals were carelessly planned, the cost could be staggering. Ziegler believed, and demonstrated, that such things could be watched and controlled.

Ziegler concerned himself with an astonishing range of details. He approved — and often rewrote — Guard's press releases. When the "Save-the-Met" campaign was launched in the Thirties, he wrote Lucrezia Bori's speeches. He prepared the financial statements for meetings of the board of directors. And, with Gatti, he attended the auditions that took place during the afternoons of the regular season. It was Ziegler's custom, no matter how poor the performer, to hear him to the end and thank him for coming.

Ziegler could break off an important contract negotiation to give, in any one of four languages, the complete musical background of the lady who sang the Second Flower Maiden in the *Parsifal* of April 10, 1914; the difference in curtain times between the cut and uncut versions of *Die Meistersinger*; the cue for the big tenor aria in Act I of *La Fanciulla del West*; the demands made by the choristers' union for the 1920 contract; the full text of any of the standard Schubert-Schumann-Brahms-Strauss *lieder*; the New York City ordinance relating to fire hazards; the number of times a certain child appeared as the Baby in *Madama Butterfly*; the principal themes of the Brahms First Symphony, or the condition of the locks on the doors of the ladies' room.

Ziegler's office, next to Gatti's at the Seventh Avenue–Thirty-ninth Street corner of the building, was nicknamed the "Torture Chamber." There contracts with artists, initiated by Gatti, were discussed, fought over and finally signed. Contracts with the unions, often preceded by violent debates, were hammered out. The daily squabbles among conductors, assistant conductors, stage managers and heads of departments were settled. Whatever the problem, Ziegler's decision was final.

The walls of the "Torture Chamber" were covered with charts and diagrams — rehearsal schedules, dates of performances, lists of casts, assignments of conductors, chorus masters and stage managers. On a blackboard, in a secret code known only to Ziegler and one trusted assistant, was

The Hanging Scene in LA FANCIULLA DEL WEST. *The heroine Minnie (Emmy Destinn) arrives just in time to save the outlaw Dick Johnson (Enrico Caruso). The Sheriff (Pasquale Amato) is incongruously dressed for outdoors*

charted the menstrual cycle of every leading soprano in the Metropolitan Opera Company.*

Gatti came to lean heavily on his capable lieutenant. He welcomed Ziegler's fluency in Italian no less than his selfless devotion to the Metropolitan. Often after a performance the two men would drive in a cab for hours, discussing the shortcomings of the evening's opera, the troubles they were having with a temperamental prima donna, or plans for future productions.

In the morning, as soon as he had gone through his mail, Gatti would enter Ziegler's office, take the only comfortable chair and throw a leg over the arm of the chair. The movement caused the top button of his trousers to pop open. The first time this happened, Helen Noble, Ziegler's secretary, was appalled. Ziegler, who had been chatting with Gatti in Italian, grinned and said in English: "Don't worry, it never goes any farther."

"And sure enough, it never did," Miss Noble said. "Morning after morning, year after year, that first button always popped, but never the second."

Between four and five each afternoon, said Miss Noble, "Gatti would come in to fling himself into the armchair and sit silently. We might be in the midst of dictation but he would pay no attention to us or we to him. He seemed to need this relaxation, to feel safe from the prima donnas who were eternally after him; here was his sanctuary and we respected it.

"Gatti had a personal secretary, but he used to ask me to do odd jobs of typing for him. I remember that I typed out his list of stocks and bonds for tax purposes each year, and that it was pages long. After his divorce, though, it was shorter and much easier to do."

As time passed, it became more and more Ziegler's function to soothe the ruffled feelings of prima donnas who felt their artistic dignity had been affronted. Gatti would sometimes pretend not to understand what was going on. Accordingly, if a star was assigned a dressing room other than the one she preferred, it was Ziegler's telephone that would ring.

Ziegler would be ready with a dozen reasons why the assigned room was really preferable. It had just been cleaned, he would point out. And hadn't she noticed how much better the air circulation was?

Ziegler's manner was somewhat frosty, and his gimlet eyes practically

* Vocalists with cramps are miserable, like everyone else, and often sing badly in consequence.

bored holes into one. He looked like a banker on the point of refusing a loan. For this reason, many people thought him cold and humorless. For cronies, however, such as Otto Kahn, who kept in daily touch with the opera house and often had a picnic supper in Ziegler's office before a performance, Ziegler had a plentiful supply of smoking-room stories.

The Metropolitan often had difficulty with a soprano who could never be pinned down to a direct answer to any question. When he learned she was married and expecting a baby, Ziegler commented:

"Well, she finally said Yes to somebody."

As soon as he learned the baby's name, Ziegler dictated a telegram:

CONGRATULATIONS, THOMAS. DOES YOUR MOTHER KNOW YOU'RE OUT?

Soon after Gatti's arrival, a youngster named Earle R. Lewis joined the Metropolitan's box-office staff. The boy, still in knickerbockers, was given what was possibly the most thankless job the company had to offer, that of selling tickets to the Family Circle.

The Family Circle, better known as the "peanut gallery," was the topmost of the Metropolitan's six levels of seats. It offered two advantages; it was unrivaled as a place to hear the music, and it afforded patrons a fine close-up view of the paintings of music-making angels that ornamented the gold waffle-grid ceiling. Otherwise it was as uncomfortable and as unfashionable as operagoing could get.

The Family Circle had its own entrance; its own staircase, entailing, until the humane installation of elevators during the Gatti regime, a five-story climb; and its own box office, a drafty cubicle in the Fortieth Street lobby.

In this cheerless *cul-de-sac*, young Lewis chatted with patrons as he dealt out tickets and made change. He was soon greeting regulars by name and questioning them about their likes and dislikes in the way of repertoire and performers. Why did they want seats for this performance but not that? The replies, carefully tabulated, formed a series of reports that began finding their way to the General Manager's office.

Gatti was impressed. Here was a young man who sensed the importance of Verdi's admonition, "The theatre exists to be full and not empty," all up and down his spinal column. When veteran box-office treasurer Max Hirsch retired, Lewis was named to succeed him and to apply his marketing research technique to the subscription list as a whole. Eventually he would become one of the managing triumvirate that guided the Metropolitan through the shoals and breakwaters of the depression.

During the season, Lewis devoted six hours out of the twenty-four to sleeping, one to eating and the rest to business. He arrived at the Metropolitan before nine A.M. and stayed until the performance ended.

Lewis's respite from the rigors of a Metropolitan season was golf, which he played with better than average skill. His favorite partner was the tenor Richard Crooks. The two men once golfed their way across the country, motoring from one famous course to another, and often sneaked away for golfing weekends. At the close of more than one Friday evening performance, the backstage crew were amused to see Lewis, impatient to get started, standing in the wings with a golf bag over each shoulder and calling out, as the tenor went out again and again to bow: "Come on, Dick — hurry up with those curtain calls."

12

Toscanini

"As simple, savage and selfish as a child."

Charles O'Connell, longtime musical director for RCA Victor, doubtless wrote with searing memories of Toscanini recording sessions. Moreover, O'Connell, a devout Catholic, was offended by Toscanini's outspoken anticlericalism.

Nevertheless, many an opera singer, orchestral musician and hostess must have concurred with O'Connell's opinion of Toscanini. At rehearsals and in performance, there was no room for conflicting ideas; only one interpretation was possible, the Toscanini interpretation, and he shouted, swore and splintered batons until he got it. At parties he was capable of sulking in a corner all evening, or of walking out altogether, leaving behind a roomful of embarrassed guests and a hostess in tears. A trifling mishap in performance would cause him to go berserk with rage and smash everything in his dressing room.

Toscanini, in fact, would have been utterly impossible except for the selfless artistic integrity that burnt in him. He was indifferent to applause. When he felt it had gone on long enough, he would pinch the concertmaster's arm, a signal for the musicians to begin filing out. He cared nothing for personal publicity. He never granted interviews and would go to extreme lengths to avoid being photographed. His only goal, to attain which he drove himself as mercilessly as he did the performers under his baton, was to realize a composer's intentions in performance as fully and perfectly as possible. And he lavished the same zeal and devotion on every

108

score, whether it was an authentic masterpiece or the third-rate work of an untalented beginner.

At one rehearsal, the composer made such a pest of himself by stopping the orchestra at every other bar that an aide finally whispered: "Maestro, shall I throw this jerk out?"

Toscanini was shocked. "Oh, no!" he said. "It helps me to have the composer's ideas."

His brilliant debut in Rio de Janeiro, at the age of nineteen, might have turned another man's head. Toscanini took it as a matter of course. He had been the only man in the touring opera company's orchestra who knew the score of *Aida* by heart. *Ma che!* He went back to playing second cello at La Scala.

Verdi once reprimanded him for playing too loudly. Half a century later, the memory still rankled.

"It was not I who was playing too loudly," Toscanini recalled. "The first cellist was playing too softly."

Toscanini's first encounter with the Metropolitan orchestra, at a rehearsal of *Götterdämmerung*, was characteristic. He made a short speech (at Gatti's insistence; Toscanini hated speeches), then began the rehearsal with no score before him. After a few measures, he stopped the orchestra and said to the first cellist: "That note should have been B flat."

"No," the cellist replied, "that's not what I have here. I have always played that note as A natural."

"Then," said Toscanini, "you have always played it wrong." Seeing by his face that the musician was not convinced, Toscanini had the full orchestral score brought in for verification. Toscanini was right. The red-faced cellist corrected the error in his part and Toscanini received an ovation at the end of the rehearsal.

Toscanini's phenomenal memory was already a legend when he went to the Metropolitan. At rehearsals as well as performances, he always conducted without a score, for two reasons. One was his near-sightedness. Although he could distinguish a pretty girl a block away, he could not make out the notes of a score on the conductor's music stand. The second reason was his firm belief in the maxim that a conductor should have the score in his head, not his head in the score.

Musicians told many stories about the Toscanini memory. One of the most famous concerned the bassoon player who came to the Maestro in consternation just before a performance. His instrument had been damaged and would not produce the low E flat.

After a few moments' reflection, Toscanini said: "That's all right. The low E flat does not occur in the bassoon part in any of the music we are playing today."

Toscanini had extraordinary sensitivity, not only to the notes being played by every instrument, but also to the failings, potentialities and even the momentary emotional states of the players. And men who played under him say he was able to convey his intentions to an orchestra with almost startling clarity. A brass player about to execute a *fortissimo* passage, for example, might find himself held back by Toscanini's beat. It was as if Toscanini, sensing what a player of that particular temperament, with that amount of air in his lungs, would be likely to do, caused his baton to signal: "I do not like the way you are about to play that passage. Please make the following alteration in your plans."

Toscanini never tyrannized over a nervous player. A mistake, unless it was the result of carelessness or downright stupidity, met with encouragement and patient drilling until the phrase came out right. It was another story, however, when a prima donna tried to assert her primacy.

"As an operatic conductor he left much to be desired," Emma Eames said tartly. "His conducting was a stone wall of resistance to any personality but his own."

At one rehearsal Toscanini had a difference of opinion with Geraldine Farrar, at that time the only female singer in the company with a dressing room assigned for her own exclusive use. "You seem to forget, Maestro," said Farrar coldly, "that I am a star."

"The only stars I know are in the heavens," Toscanini retorted. "Once more, if you please."*

A contralto loved to cling to the high note in her big aria, *Che farò senza Euridice*, from Gluck's *Orfeo ed Euridice*. Since no *fermata* is written in the music, Toscanini would not have it. Despite repeated warnings by

---

* This story is so widely circulated that there is a German version, in which Toscanini says *"Ein Star ist für mich ein Vogel"* ("A star for me is a bird."). *Star* is the German word for starling.

the conductor, at the performance the contralto sustained the high note. Toscanini brought in the orchestra with the chord of resolution, leaving the hapless contralto dangling from her high F.

Once at a *Meistersinger* performance, tenor Leo Slezak was absent-minded and made a number of mistakes. At intermission Toscanini rushed backstage, beating his head against the wall and exclaiming: "This tenor is an animal!" For the rest of the performance, although Slezak sang his best, he got not a glance from Toscanini.

At the Hotel Ansonia, where they both lived, Slezak was waiting for the elevator when Toscanini came in, scowling, with his hat jammed over his eyes. Slezak stammered an apology, promising it would not happen again. Somewhat mollified, Toscanini said: "My dear, you were terrible!"

For seven years Toscanini led great performances at the Metropolitan. The range of his art was as broad as the music itself. He excelled in works of all styles and nationalities. He was already becoming one of the great Wagnerian conductors of his time; indeed, of all time. He was, naturally, at home in the Italian repertoire and had known Verdi, Puccini, Leoncavallo, Mascagni and their contemporaries.* He brought Gallic verve to Massenet, classic elegance to Gluck.

It was at the Metropolitan that Toscanini made his American debut as a symphonic conductor, leading a performance of Beethoven's Ninth Symphony at a Sunday night concert.

Toscanini's principal reason for leaving the Metropolitan, wrote Gatti tactfully in his memoirs, was the outbreak of World War I, "during which War he did not want to leave his own country."

A more widely held belief, however, is that Toscanini walked out for the same reason he had walked out at La Scala and was later to leave the New York Philharmonic and (temporarily) the NBC Symphony Orchestra: because he could not get what he wanted, artistically speaking.

A galling feature of a repertory opera house is the constant rotation of casts caused by illness, previous commitments elsewhere and so on. A conductor who has labored to bring a work to a lofty plane of excellence

---

* Toscanini came from Parma, and that fact was the basis for a sly dig at the Maestro by Leopoldo Mugnone, a contemporary who could never understand why Toscanini was world-famous and he wasn't. Whenever he appeared before an orchestra which had just been conducted by Toscanini, Mugnone would take out his handkerchief, fan the air and exclaim: *"Che puzza di Parmegiana!"* ("What a stench of Parmesan!")

can hardly be blamed for annoyance if, at the next performance, half the cast consists of new faces.

Toscanini once refused to conduct *Tristan* because he had not had an opportunity to rehearse with two members of the cast. Since there was no time to schedule a rehearsal before the performance, it was announced that Toscanini was "indisposed" and *Götterdämmerung*, with Alfred Hertz conducting, was performed instead.

Toscanini also had his troubles with operagoers. The incorrigible Metropolitan audience insisted on talking during performances. When Toscanini conducted *Tristan*, he insisted that the doors be closed and latecomers kept outside until the Prelude was finished. At an *Euryanthe* performance in his final season, there was audible whispering during the interlude between the first and second scenes. Toscanini stopped the orchestra and rapped with his baton until the house grew quiet. Then he resumed the performance.

During his last three seasons at the Metropolitan, Toscanini made numerous threats to resign. In the spring of 1914, he stated flatly that when his contract came up for renewal the following year he would not sign. What may have been the last straw, however, was a *Carmen* performance that Toscanini conducted on April 13, 1915, with Farrar in the title role, Giovanni Martinelli as Don José, Alda as Micaela and Pasquale Amato as Escamillo.

Just before the performance, Toscanini learned that Tullio Serafin, his successor at La Scala, was in the house. Serafin was passing through New York on his way to an engagement in Havana.

The news put Toscanini on his mettle. He would show Serafin what a first-rate opera house was capable of achieving. Calling the performers together, he told them to watch his stick even more closely than usual. For this performance, he expected the utmost cooperation.

Unfortunately, things immediately began to go wrong. Farrar was in poor voice. Amato was indisposed and had been replaced by a mediocre baritone (he lasted only three seasons) named Riccardo Tegani, who was singing Escamillo for the first time. There were a number of conspicuous errors in the orchestra, and the stage band started playing ten measures before its cue.

Arturo Toscanini

One can imagine what the Maestro's dressing room looked like after that performance. The next night he conducted Mascagni's now-forgotten *Iris* and left the Metropolitan for good. His remaining performances of the season were taken over by Giorgio Polacco. It was announced that Toscanini was "indisposed," although he was seen in public on nights when Polacco was conducting in his place.

Gatti did his utmost to persuade Toscanini not to resign. He offered Toscanini virtually unlimited rehearsal time, plus the title of artistic director. His offer was seconded by a graceful cablegram from Otto Kahn that concluded: YOU MAY REST ASSURED THAT ANYTHING IN MY POWER TO MAKE YOUR WORK SYMPATHETIC AND SATISFACTORY TO YOU WILL BE CHEERFULLY DONE.

It was too late. Perhaps Toscanini was already drawn to the symphonic repertoire, in which he won his greatest fame, as a more rational *métier* than opera. At any rate, New York did not see him again until he returned as conductor of the Philharmonic in 1926.

Late in his career Toscanini returned to opera, conducting *La Bohème, La Traviata, Otello* and other works with the NBC Symphony Orchestra, in concert form. The recordings give an idea of what performances must have been like in Toscanini's great days at the Metropolitan.

13

Caruso

HE NEVER SHATTERED A MIRROR or a wineglass with his voice.

He did not make his debut as a baritone. His first appearance was in the leading tenor role in *L'Amico Francesco*, a long-forgotten work by a wealthy dilettante named Mario Morelli. It was staged at the Teatro Nuovo, a small opera house in Naples that is now a movie theatre. A photograph taken on the day of the performance shows Caruso draped in a bedspread; when the photographer arrived unexpectedly, his only shirt was being laundered.

His first season of opera was at the Cimarosa Theatre in Caserta, where he made his debut as Turiddu in *Cavalleria rusticana*. At Caserta his fee was ten lire (about $2.50) per performance. When the season was unexpectedly cut short, he arrived back in Naples with the equivalent of twelve cents in his pocket.

During his first season at the Metropolitan he sang for $1,000 a performance. Thereafter the fee was gradually increased to $2,500. Caruso would not go beyond that; the responsibility and consequent nervous strain, he said, would be too great. Outside the Metropolitan, however, he earned much larger fees — as much as $15,000 a performance.

In eighteen seasons at the Metropolitan, Caruso sang 607 times in thirty-seven different operas. His earnings at the Metropolitan were a million and a half dollars. During the same period, the Victor Company paid him $1,825,000 in record royalties.

His generosity matched his income. At Christmas he gave a gold coin to every member of the Metropolitan's backstage staff. As Christmas presents he gave jewels to people who disliked antiques, and antiques to people who disliked jewelry. At one time he was supporting nearly a hundred persons. He received daily appeals for money, often from people he didn't know. His wife never knew him to refuse anyone. "But surely all these people can't be deserving?" she protested.

"You are right, Doro," Caruso replied, "but can you tell me which is and which is not?"

Yet, with all his spending, Caruso was meticulous in recording the daily outgo to the last penny. On the day he was married, he recorded in his account book: "$50.00 for my wedding."

He was an avid collector. He collected stamps, antique furniture, velvets, brocades, marbles, bronzes, tear bottles, snuffboxes and jeweled watches. Eventually his collections overflowed his fourteen-room apartment at the Hotel Knickerbocker. To house them, he rented his own art gallery on Fiftieth Street near Fifth Avenue. He had an extraordinary, instinctive knowledge of art and was rarely cheated.

He was not a musical illiterate, although he played no instrument. As a youngster he added a few lire to his income by copying songs for other students. A facsimile of his manuscript would do credit to a professional copyist. It shows Caruso's method of studying a song. Between the vocal line and the piano accompaniment is written the Italian text, the English translation and a phonetic rendering of the English in a system devised by Caruso. His phonetic version of "The Star-Spangled Banner," using Italian vowel sounds, began: "O seiken iu sii bai dhi dons erli lait huat so praudli ui heild at dhi twailaits last glimmin."

He composed songs and made recordings of two: "Tiempo antico" and "Dreams of Long Ago." The latter, with an English text by Earl Carroll, was composed for Henry W. Savage's 1907 Broadway production, *The Million*.

His cartoons were almost as famous as his singing. They poked good-humored but never malicious fun at Presidents, people in the news, his colleagues at the Metropolitan and himself. The cartoons were published regularly by Marziale Sisca in his Italian-language New York newspaper, *La Follia*. Once, when Mark Twain gave a dinner party for all the leading cartoonists of New York, Caruso was deeply hurt at not being invited to attend. "It seems," said Caruso, "that he knows me only as a tenor."

One day, seeing one of his caricatures in a shop window, Caruso made his wife go in to inquire about the price. When he learned it was seventy-five dollars, Caruso beamed. "Better we stop singing and draw," he said.

A closet in his apartment held eighty pairs of shoes. Another contained fifty suits. Each time he came in from the street, Caruso changed all his clothes. At home, unless guests were expected, he never wore a conventional suit. Instead, he wore red, green or blue brocaded coats with sashes, gray silk trousers and soft shirts.

His concern for personal cleanliness was almost fanatical. He took two baths daily. If he wore a shirt even for an hour he never put it on again until it had been laundered. During a performance he changed his clothes after every act, having himself sprayed with *eau de cologne* as he put on each fresh garment. He found it almost impossible to make convincing stage love to unwashed sopranos who had eaten garlic.

He traveled with his own blankets, sheets and pillowcases. He could sleep only on linen and whether at home or in hotels, trains or steamers, it had to be changed daily. He had special down-filled pillows, and two wedge-shaped mattresses precluded all possibility of his falling out of bed.

His body was firm but not muscular. He did not care for sports and took no exercise beyond that required by rehearsals and performances. His chest was enormous and he could expand it nine inches. His mouth was so large that he could put an egg in it, close his lips and no one would guess the egg was there.

He was always nervous before a performance and didn't try to conceal it. On the day of a performance he rarely spoke. He played solitaire, drew cartoons, pasted clippings in his scrapbooks or sorted the gold coins he kept in a safe in his apartment "for emergencies." At six-thirty he sang vocalises, mainly simple scales and arpeggios, for half an hour. At seven he left for the theatre. When his makeup was completed, he smoked a final cigarette, then gargled with salt water. His valet held out a box of Swedish snuff, from which he took a pinch to clear his nostrils. Next he took a wineglass of whiskey, a glass of soda water and a quarter of an apple. Finally his valet handed him his amulets — holy medals and old coins on a thick gold chain — and Caruso was ready to sing.

At the end of a typical performance, he had lost three pounds.

He made 266 recordings, not one of them uninteresting. Some of the early discs are extremely rare and valuable collector's items, but those one is likeliest to find in the attic are of works like *O sole mio* and *Celeste Aida*, which sold millions of copies and therefore have little value. Caruso's voice communicated, as it communicates to a generation that never heard him, despite the limitations of the early "acoustical" method by which it was recorded.

Noel Straus, who heard Caruso many times and once interviewed him for the New Orleans *Times-Picayune*, said that what was most notably absent from the recordings was the *mellow* quality of Caruso's singing. As discs that most faithfully represented the voice as it actually sounded, he named Tchaikovsky's "Pourquoi" and the duet *O terra addio* from *Aida*, sung with Johanna Gadski. Mrs. Caruso's favorite was a song by P. Mario Costa, "Sei morta nella vita mia." "It's as if Rico were in the next room," she said.

An amusing touch is found in the duet *O quanti occhi fisi* from *Madama Butterfly*, made with Geraldine Farrar. Caruso, the story goes, lunching with congenial friends, kept Farrar waiting nearly an hour at the Victor recording studio on Twenty-fourth Street. He arrived penitent and full of apologies. Farrar smiled sweetly and said it didn't matter.

Toward the end of the duet, the tenor sings: *"Io t'ho ghermito, ti serro palpitante, sei mia!"* The soprano's reply is: *"Sì, per la vita!"* Instead, Farrar interpolated a line not found in Puccini's score: "He's had a highball!" Victor officials either didn't notice the substitution or were too amused to mind. The record remained in the Victor catalogue for years.

He made one recording not intended for release: the bass aria *Vecchia zimarra*, from *La Bohème*. It was a consequence of a madcap *Bohème* performance in Philadelphia for which each of the principals was fined a hundred dollars. "But wasn't it worth it?" said Caruso.

When the four Bohemians made their first appearance, each was wearing a fake monocle. As Alda, playing Mimi, bent to warm herself at the fire, Andrès de Segurola, the evening's Colline, squirted her from the wings with a seltzer bottle. Later, when de Segurola put on his top hat, his wig and shoulders were powdered. Alda had retaliated by filling his hat with flour. A glass supposed to hold water turned out to be filled with ink. In the third act, in which it is supposed to be snowing, along with the stage snowflakes Alda felt her bonnet being pelted with nails, buttons, paper and bits of string.

The fun turned serious after Act III. De Segurola stood backstage, pale, shaking and hoarse as a crow. He had lost his voice. And his big aria was coming up in the final act.

When Caruso sang an opera, he knew it by heart — not only his own words and music but everyone else's, too. "Just go through the pantomime," he told de Segurola. "I'll sing it for you."

And, with his back to the audience, he did. Vocally, the feat wasn't remarkable; the touching aria in which Colline, in the opera, bids farewell to the beloved coat he is about to pawn is as simple as a hymn tune, and its lowest note is within any tenor's range. But Caruso, the dependable performer, was prepared to sing it at a moment's notice.

Next day, Caruso went to the Victor studio in Camden to record the aria. Four copies of the recording were pressed: one each for Caruso, de Segurola and conductor Giorgio Polacco, and one which was kept by Victor. Many years later, a collector obtained Polacco's record, from which he made a limited-edition pressing. Once in a great while, a copy comes on the market. It is a polished, beautifully nuanced performance and a wonderful item with which to baffle people in the collectors' favorite game of "Guess Who?"

Caruso was essentially a man of the theatre. At first he was ill at ease in recital, and did not make a concert tour until 1917. Thereafter, during the three remaining seasons of his career, he sang regularly to enormous audiences in auditoriums, hockey arenas, bullrings and National Guard armories, at fees from seven thousand dollars up. A typical advertisement said — quite truthfully, as it turned out: "Posterity will envy you the privilege of hearing the most glorious voice of this generation."

He sang all over the world, but he loved America best. For eight months of the year, New York was home. During World War I he raised $21,-000,000 by singing at benefits, and gave enormous sums to Allied relief organizations and the American Red Cross. He converted all his prewar

Enrico Caruso as Canio in I PAGLIACCI

securities to United States government bonds and invested thereafter only in Liberty bonds.

He received the Legion of Honor from France and decorations from England, Belgium, Spain, Germany and Italy; but the decoration he valued most highly was the gold badge of an honorary captain in the New York Police Department. The new captain's first official act, on being sworn in, was to go to the Metropolitan and place Gatti under arrest.

Early in his career, he was hissed at Naples's famous theatre, the San Carlo. The incident was blamed on the rivalry between a pro-Caruso and an anti-Caruso faction, a characteristic feature of Neapolitan operatic life. Caruso, however, was cut to the heart. He never sang in his native city again. But he went back, at forty-eight, to die.

Mawkish, yet touching, was the ballad composed by a songwriter named Jack Stanley: "They Needed a Songbird in Heaven (So God Took Caruso Away)."

14

"My Broken Promise"

LEO SLEZAK WAS A BURLY CZECH GIANT more than six feet tall. A shipboard photo shows him towering head and shoulders above the slender Toscanini. When Slezak made his Metropolitan debut as Otello, on November 17, 1909, Krehbiel wrote that "it seemed as if a section of the proscenium arch had stepped on the stage." He had nothing but praise for the performance, however, finding Slezak "superb in his wrath and final broken-hearted despair."

What Krehbiel might also have noted was that Frances Alda, the evening's Desdemona, had had some difficulty in being a convincing stage corpse. During the death scene, it was Slezak's custom to tickle the soprano.

Slezak was Renaud in a performance of Gluck's *Armide*, which Toscanini introduced to the Metropolitan during the 1910–1911 season, at the Brooklyn Academy of Music. The stage manager of the Academy at that time was a distinguished-looking, white-bearded man who always appeared backstage in evening dress. Going out for a curtain call, Slezak impulsively dragged the stage manager with him. Reporters rushed backstage to find out who he was.

"That was Gluck," said Slezak, adding, "He said that in all his experience he had never heard a tenor sing the role as I did."

The Brooklyn newspapers that published this story soon began to receive letters from readers, pointing out that Gluck had died in 1787. The Brooklyn editors in turn let Gatti hear from them and the wrathful impresario imposed a hundred-dollar fine on Slezak. Putting on a black mourning veil, Slezak went downtown to Otto Kahn's office and got the fine rescinded.

At one performance of *Salome*, the role of Jokaanan was sung by a hypochondriac baritone who in cold weather put plugs of cotton in his ears, believing that by doing so he warded off colds. Slezak had a word with the property crew and when the severed *papier maché* head of Jokaanan was served up on its platter, there was a piece of cotton projecting from each ear. Everyone was amused but the soprano, who had difficulty in completing the performance with a straight face.

Slezak was responsible for one of the most famous of all operatic stories. The event took place, according to his son Walter Slezak, at a *Lohengrin* performance in Vienna. In the last act, having taken his farewell from Elsa, Slezak had reached the point at which he was about to step into the swan boat and be drawn offstage. There was a mixup backstage, however, and the boat glided into the wings without him.

Turning to the audience, Slezak asked the German equivalent of: "When does the next swan leave?"

Slezak sang at the Metropolitan for six seasons, from 1909 to 1915. Walter Slezak remembers, as a boy, roller-skating in the vast corridors of the Hotel Ansonia. He also recalls disrupting a *Magic Flute* performance by calling out from a box: "Look out, Papa! The snake!"

After World War I, Slezak remained in Europe, singing at the Vienna State Opera and other European theatres. One evening in Vienna, he sang a performance of *Pagliacci* in which, as he put it, he "felt eighteen again." After *Vesti la giubba*, applause roared straight through the intermission until the curtain rose on Act II. Next day Slezak was summoned to the opera house, where officials told him his contract had been extended for three years. Slezak told them to keep the contract; the performance he had just sung would be his last.

Having finished his operatic career, Slezak went on to have another career, singing operetta, and still a third, in the movies. He lost a fortune in the Austrian currency inflation of the Twenties but amassed another later on.

Slezak published a volume of memoirs and reflections, entitled *My Collected Works*. Among other things, it purported to be a guide to the world of Wagnerian opera. A sample comment is on *Lohengrin*: "When the curtain rises on Act II, it is obvious that, since the only furniture on stage is a wooden bench, it is going to be a somewhat uncomfortable bridal night."

The book was so popular that Slezak was forced to bring out another. Its title was *My Broken Promise*.

In the summer of 1938, shortly before his death, Slezak paid a visit to New York, where his son was now a rising star on Broadway. Although opera was out of season, the Metropolitan was opened for them. Slezak showed his son the exact spot where Toscanini had beaten his head against the wall when he missed a cue in the *Meistersinger* quintet, and the dressing room he had used.

Although it was now on the women's side of the house, Walter Slezak insisted on having the same dressing room when he made his own Metropolitan debut, in a nonsinging role in *The Gypsy Baron*. The younger Slezak inherited his father's build but not, to his great disappointment, his father's larynx. As a young man, whenever he tried out his voice, a maid would presently arrive with a message: "Mr. Walter, your father says you're to stop singing."

At Sherry's Restaurant on the Metropolitan's Grand Tier, there was a magnificently Moorish-looking portrait of Slezak in costume as Otello. The portrait showed the tenor wearing a kinky black wig, coffee-colored makeup, a black beard, gold earrings and a richly embroidered doublet. It had formerly hung in the dining room of Walter Slezak's house in Larchmont.

One day the Slezaks' daughter brought a school friend home for lunch. Noticing the portrait, the friend asked who it was.

"That," said Miss Slezak, "was my grandfather."

"Oh, *really*?" said the friend.

Not long afterward, the portrait turned up at Sherry's.

15

The Search for the Great American Opera

WHEN GATTI-CASAZZA arrived at the Metropolitan, he hoped "to discover some good American operas which I could produce and maintain in the repertoire." In the Italian theatres where he had been trained, new works were brought forward as a matter of course. It was sometimes a condition of the state or municipal subsidy that a certain number of new works be produced each season.

"No national school of opera has ever developed without the incentive of performance," said Gatti. "In America the conditions are harder for the native composer than in any other country, chiefly because there are so few stages upon which his works can be presented."

Besides wanting to perform what he regarded as one of the essential duties of any impresario, Gatti also was shrewdly aware that, as an Italian, he would be open to criticism if he appeared to favor the works of his countrymen over the native product. The thing to do, he decided, was to make it known that the Metropolitan was hospitably disposed toward American composers. He proposed to the Metropolitan's board of directors a contest open only to American composers, the winner to receive a $10,000 prize and a Metropolitan performance of his opera.

The directors approved. Even before the contest could get under way, however, Gatti learned that *The Pipe of Desire*, an opera by the American composer F. S. Converse, had been given a semiprofessional performance in Boston. Gatti hurried to Boston to sign Converse to a Metropolitan contract.

Frederick Shepherd Converse was a suburban Boston Brahmin who gave up a business career for music. Trained at Harvard in banking and finance, he also studied composition with John Knowles Paine. Later he graduated from the Royal Academy in Munich and for many years taught at the New England Conservatory. In the Twenties his style become more and more avant-garde, though eventually he became disillusioned with "the extravagant elements of modern music."

All that was in the future, however, when he wrote *The Pipe of Desire*, an old-fashioned romantic opera full of sylphs, mermaids, salamanders and gnomes.

The first performance of *The Pipe of Desire* took place on March 18, 1910. Pittsburgh-born Louise Homer and Kentuckian Riccardo Martin headed the cast, all of whom were American except the Englishwoman Leonora Sparkes. It was the first opera by an American to be performed at the Metropolitan. It was also an immediate and decisive failure from which Gatti derived little except the satisfaction of having done his duty. "Nevertheless," he said, "I felt that we were on the right path."

Meanwhile, the contest had inspired more than thirty scores by American composers. They were examined by a jury consisting of conductor Alfred Hertz, composer-conductor Walter Damrosch and composers George W. Chadwick and Charles M. Loeffler. The work they chose was *Mona*, by Horatio Parker.

Parker was an experienced composer with a demonstrated ability to write well for voices. His *Hora Novissima* remains perhaps the most successful large-scale choral work ever written by an American composer. The church music he turned out in large quantities showed technical assurance, facile melodic invention and skill in setting English texts to music. There was curiosity to see what he had done with Brian Hooker's libretto.

At many points, Parker did extremely well. There are moments of great beauty in the score. But it is not a successful opera; the characters never come to life.

Mona is almost a parody of Bellini's *Norma*. Mona, like Norma, is a British druid in love with a soldier of the Roman occupation. Her lover, known to the Britons as Gwynn, is in reality Quintus, son of the Roman governor.

The action begins with quasi-Masonic symbolism. Opening her robe, Mona shows Quintus the Tetragrammaton, or Ineffable Name, in Runic

*Giulio Gatti-Casazza with composer Richard Strauss (left)
and Metropolitan conductor Alfred Hertz (right)*

symbols on her breast. Her quaintly worded explanation: "I was born therewith."

Because of the birthmark and because she is the last of the line of Queen Boadicea, Mona is obsessed by the idea that she was born for some high purpose. She determines to drive the Romans out of Britain, neglecting her romance with Quintus to rouse the Britons to arms. The call to arms is a temple scene which Parker works up into a tremendous second-act curtain.

But the Romans are waiting, and drive off the Britons with great slaughter. Mona, assuming Quintus has betrayed their plan, kills him with a captured Roman sword. It turns out, however, that the Roman governor has known about the uprising all along and has refrained from crushing it only at the entreaty of his son.

Cause lost, lover dead, Mona stands among the Roman soldiers and bids them, in the circumspect language of 1912, "take their will of her."

Mona was performed on March 14, 1912, with Homer in the title role and a predominantly American cast. There was great enthusiasm at the first performance and a half-empty house at the second. Would Parker have done better with a stronger libretto? Gatti was inclined to doubt it. "Parker was a learned musician, but not a man of the theatre," Gatti said. "And from conversations I had with him I could not help being convinced that he believed himself right and considered the public mistaken."

For theatre-wise Gatti, this was heresy. As Verdi said, the theatre exists to be full, not empty.

It was to a composer almost as much a man of the theatre as himself that Gatti next turned. Walter Damrosch had practically grown up in the opera house. As the subject of his opera he had chosen a universal favorite, Rostand's *Cyrano de Bergerac*. His librettist, the critic W. J. Henderson, was an operagoer of long experience. Damrosch's *Cyrano de Bergerac* was performed on February 27, 1913, with a cast headed by two of the Metropolitan's best artists, Frances Alda and Pasquale Amato.

But a fine cast, theatrical experience, a popular subject and critical erudition did not add up to a winning combination, and *Cyrano* went to join *Mona* in the warehouse.

Even more disappointing was the failure of Victor Herbert, alumnus of the Metropolitan's cello section and brilliantly successful composer of

Broadway musical comedies, to produce a viable opera for the Metropolitan. His one-act work, *Madelaine*, is hardly more than an anecdote set to music.

Madelaine, favorite of the Paris Opéra, is receiving presents on New Year's Day, 1770. The Chevalier de Mauprat brings her a jeweled bracelet but declines her invitation to dine. He is having dinner with his mother. Next the Duc d'Esterre arrives with a present of four English horses but can't stay. Madelaine, vexed, says he doesn't love her. The Duc replies that last night the Baron de Fontanges said her high C was flat, and they are fighting a duel at dawn; but today he is dining with his mother. Madelaine then invites the Baron de Fontanges, the other party to the duel. Back comes an apologetic note; he is dining with his mother.

Growing desperate, Madelaine invites her maid, Nichette, to dine. Nichette reminds her that she has been promised the afternoon off; she is dining with her mother.

Next the painter Didier arrives, bringing a portrait of Madelaine's mother which Madelaine has commissioned. He, too, is dining with his mother but invites Madelaine to join them. Madelaine, however, has a better idea. She places the portrait on an easel. Now she, like the rest, is having dinner with her mother.

Madelaine, with Alda in the title role, had its first performance on January 24, 1914. According to Gatti, it had "a mild success."

Gatti kept trying. One summer, in Switzerland, he met Otto Kahn, who suggested that they go to Vevey to hear Reginald de Koven play his new opera, *The Canterbury Pilgrims*. De Koven, onetime music critic of the New York *World* and founder of the Washington Symphony, was a prolific composer of songs and comic operas. His *Robin Hood*, produced in Chicago in 1900, had won immediate and lasting success throughout the English-speaking world; the Boston Light Opera Company was touring with it as late as the Thirties. Now, with Percy Mackaye as his librettist, de Koven had undertaken the more ambitious project of writing an opera based on Chaucer's *Canterbury Tales*.

The story revolved around Chaucer, the Prioress and the much-married Wife of Bath. The Wife, who has her eye on Chaucer, proposes a wager: If she can obtain the brooch bearing the inscription *Amor vincit omnia*, which the Prioress wears on her wrist, Chaucer will be obliged to marry her. Chaucer is incautious enough to agree, the Wife obtains the brooch after much plotting and scheming, and Chaucer faces the prospect of being husband number six to the Wife of Bath. The Poet Laureate appeals to King Richard II, who decrees that if the Wife remarries, it can only be to a miller. This delights the Miller, Chaucer is reunited with his Prioress, and all ends in merriment.

Mackaye's libretto did not help matters, for it contained elements neither authentically Chaucerian nor operatic. In the Drinking Song of Act I occur the lines:

> *Ho, tapmaid, here! Come tipple your man*
> *With a kiss on the curve of his can, can, can!*

And when Chaucer helps the buxom Wife of Bath to dismount from her donkey, she comments:

> *Well swung!*
> *What think you of my jolly heft?*

The Canterbury Pilgrims made its appearance on March 8, 1917, with Edith Mason as the Prioress, Margarete Ober as the Wife of Bath, and Johannes Sembach as Chaucer. Said Gatti: "The public received it well."

The next year, Gatti-Casazza had a near-miss in Charles Wakefield Cadman's *Shanewis*, the first American opera to last longer than one season at the Metropolitan. Cadman, a successful song composer, understood how to write for voices, and the straightforward text by Nellie Richmond Eberhart was free of flamboyant absurdities. Moreover, it seems to be a rule for successful operas that one or more excerpts — the more the better — are capable of standing on their own in the concert hall by sheer musical vitality. And in the "Spring Song of the Robin Woman" Cadman wrote such a piece. It had a great vogue when *Shanewis* was new, and is still heard once in a while today.

The opera begins with a costume party at the home of Mrs. J. Asher Everton, a wealthy and prominent clubwoman of southern California. Mrs. Everton introduces her Indian protégé, Shanewis, whose vocal studies she is financing. Lionel, the fiancé of Mrs. Everton's daughter Amy, is fascinated by the Indian girl. He follows her to the Indian reservation in Oklahoma, where she has gone to enable Cadman to bring in some Indian dances for local color.

Learning that Lionel is engaged to Amy, Shanewis repulses him, denouncing the white man and his dealings with her people. Shanewis's Indian lover then shoots Lionel dead with his bow and arrow, and that is that.

Shanewis was first performed on March 23, 1918, with Sophie Braslau in the title role, Marie Sundelius as Amy, and Paul Althouse as Lionel. The following year it was presented on a triple bill that introduced Charles Breil's *The Legend* and John Adam Hugo's *Temple Dancer*. Both the latter were negligible works by minor composers, reflecting mainly Gatti's determination to present new works by Americans at regular intervals. Thereafter, native opera languished until the arrival of *Cleopatra's Night*, by Henry Hadley, in 1921.

The name of Henry Hadley is one of the most distinguished in American music. Widely performed, in his day, both here and abroad, he also founded the Berkshire Music Festival and conducted its earliest concerts; founded the National Association for American Composers and Conductors; and made guest appearances with the principal orchestras of this country and Europe. Hadley's name is so equated with institutions of conservatism and respectability that *Cleopatra's Night* produces a sensation rather like encountering a bank president in a floating crap game.

The first scene takes place beside Cleopatra's luxurious bath. As Cleopatra is preparing to bathe, an arrow flies over the wall and lands at her feet. Around it is tied a papyrus bearing the hieroglyphics "I love you." In the distance a man is seen swimming.

Cleopatra takes off as much as local circumstances permit, lets down her long hair, puts her toe in the bath, and screams. A dripping man emerges from the bath. He has swum up through the drainpipe. Eunuchs rush forward with lances ready, but Cleopatra halts them. Anyone so enterprising as this swimmer deserves a hearing.

His name is Meiamoun, and Mardion, Cleopatra's favorite maid, is in love with him. He, however, has eyes only for Cleopatra. Now that he has breathed the same air as Cleopatra, he is ready to die.

"Cleopatra refuses to take his life," reads the synopsis in the published score, "and offers to *buy* it — her coin the ensilvered hours of one night of Egypt with her. She warns him, when his hour comes inevitably with the dawn, not to stir the placid surface of her pity. Mardion screams, rushes to him with a dagger, imploring him to let it strike now, unsullied by Cleopatra. The eunuchs seize Mardion. Cleopatra taunts Meiamoun. Will he take his life or sell it to her for a night? He raises the dagger but with a wild cry flings it from him. Mardion breaks from the eunuchs, seizes the dagger and kills herself. Cleopatra bids her be thrown to the crocodiles. She desires to go to the palace. Leaning upon the arm of Meiamoun, she enters the barge. It slowly glides away to the worshipful chanting of the cortège as the curtain descends in the enveloping twilight."

After a pleasant orchestral intermezzo, the curtain rises on an embarrassing situation. The hour is late, the liquor is running low, the guests are hungry but no one can dine because the hostess has not appeared. Everyone is buzzing; Cleopatra has never been known to miss a meal before, not even for Mark Antony. Finally the couple enters. Cleopatra, half-swooning, asks: "Meiamoun, where were you school'd in love?"

Dancing girls perform, giving Hadley a pretext for some pleasant ballet music. The dance grows more hectic. Guests begin to pursue the dancing girls, who, too tired to resist, are carried off into the palace gardens.

This suggests an idea to Cleopatra. Hidden in her garden is a little white temple; the lovers can be alone there.

Meiamoun points out that they cannot reach it in time, since dawn is breaking.

Cleopatra releases him from his pledge. She orders attendants to draw the curtains. She will make it night for six months. But Meiamoun, with Ernani-like fidelity to his promise, drains the cup of poison and falls dead at her feet.

Roman war trumpets sound offstage. After singing a heartbroken farewell to Meiamoun, Cleopatra goes to meet Mark Antony.

The Hadley work had its first performance on January 20, 1921, with Alda as Cleopatra and Morgan Kingston as Meiamoun. Gatti's verdict was temperate: "It was not of great distinction musically and succeeded only moderately."

Six years passed before the Metropolitan ventured to produce another American opera. This time Gatti decided to approach the problem differently, by looking for a composer who had proved himself in the theatre and commissioning him to write an opera for the Metropolitan.

Deems Taylor seemed to be such a composer. He had written vocal as well as instrumental works and had composed effective incidental music for a number of dramas. And in Edna St. Vincent Millay he had a librettist who was an ardent opera-lover, with an exhaustive knowledge of the repertoire.

The King's Henchman had its first performance on February 17, 1927. If a superlative cast, enthusiastic press support and a production that spared neither expense nor effort could make an opera succeed, *The King's Henchman* would have made it. Even so, it was a stout try. It had style and distinction. Its weakness, many listeners felt, was that its story was more literary and poetic than dramatic. After three seasons *The King's Henchman* was withdrawn, but the Metropolitan invited Taylor to try again.

After considering various possibilities, including Elmer Rice's *Street Scene*, Taylor chose Constance Collier's stage version of the George du Maurier story *Peter Ibbetson*. It was performed on February 7, 1931, with Edward Johnson, the Metropolitan's handsomest tenor, in the title role. It was the biggest success of the 1930–1931 season, and with its performance at Ravinia, in the summer of 1931, the Metropolitan could pride itself on launching a work that was felt to be worth staging elsewhere.

Opinions differed sharply about Louis Gruenberg's *The Emperor Jones*, based on the Eugene O'Neill play, which had its first performance on January 7, 1933. There were enthusiasts who declared the work to be an authentic masterpiece. Skeptics contended that what Gruenberg had written was not so much an opera as incidental music and sound effects for the O'Neill play; and that the sung portions of the work, instead of heightening dramatic tension, merely slowed up the action and made the words unclear.

Howard Hanson's *Merry Mount*, with a libretto by Richard L. Stokes, was introduced on February 10, 1934. It showed that one can be a distinguished composer and still not possess the special knack that writing an opera requires. Dr. Hanson's writing for voices was frequently awkward. The role of Wrestling Bradford, about which the virtually one-man opera revolved, made strenuous demands on the vocal powers of even a Lawrence Tibbett. Also, the work presented a somewhat ribald view of Puritan

Massachusetts, and to jest with so hallowed a national institution as the Pilgrim Fathers is always risky.

Seymour's *In the Pasha's Garden* (January 24, 1935) was merely inept. Damrosch's *The Man Without a Country* (May 12, 1937) demonstrated mainly what a considerable amount of opera its composer had heard. *The Island God* (February 20, 1942), an unsuccessful venture into theology, was Gian-Carlo Menotti's first total failure. *The Warrior* (January 11, 1947) was originally a somewhat bombastic radio drama by Norman Corwin that couldn't quite make the transition to opera. Samuel Barber's *Vanessa* (January 15, 1958) struck some listeners as both tasteless and pointless. (Gossip buzzed that Sena Jurinac, originally announced for the title role, had postponed her arrival to get out of doing it.)

The long, unbroken string of failures at the Metropolitan almost made it seem as if the house were under an evil spell as far as new works were concerned — a jinx that affected even so great a genius as Puccini. Of the four Puccini operas that had their world premieres at the Metropolitan, only *Gianni Schicchi* and *La Fanciulla del West* have kept a precarious foothold in the repertoire. Giordano's *Madame Sans-Gêne*, Leoncavallo's *Zaza* and Krenek's *Jonny Spielt Auf* vanished without a trace, and Granados's *Goyescas* is remembered only for a couple of its instrumental numbers.

On the other hand, the record of other leading opera houses during the same period is not much better. The Metropolitan's world premieres coincided with an era during which the orientation of composers was becoming progressively more instrumental and atonal — i.e., nonvocal. To outdo Strauss and Wagner was obviously impossible; to go back to earlier models did not constitute "progress." Atonality, seemingly, was the only way out. It was a dilemma which prompted Verdi's ironic comment: *"Tornare al passato sarebbe un progresso"* ("To return to the past would constitute progress.").

Contemporary operas have failed for a number of reasons, among which trite or ludicrous subject matter, poorly constructed librettos and sheer incompetence on the composer's part could all be named. The basic fault shared by nearly all of them, however, is that they do not sing. So audiences go on listening to operas that do. The libretto concocted for *La Gioconda* by Boito under the anagram-pseudonym Tobia Gorria is one of the silliest works ever produced by a man of genius; but Ponchielli's melodies have stood the test of time. *Faust* was already a trifle *vieux jeu* a hundred-odd years ago, when Walt Whitman was reviewing it for the Brooklyn *Eagle*; but the scene of Valentin's death still has power to move listeners today.

The matter was well stated in the fine lines put by the poet Luigi Illica into the mouth of Carlo Gérard in the first act of *Andrea Chénier*:

> *anchè l'Idea muor;*
> *Tu non muori giammai, tu, l'Eterna Canzon.*

Gian-Carlo Menotti

16

"Farrar Farà"

THEY WERE CALLED "FLAPPERS" because they flapped when they walked. The reason they flapped was that they wore their galoshes unbuckled, in defiance of conventionality and as a form of social protest. The Gerry-flappers were a special breed who attended the Metropolitan and showered Geraldine Farrar with roses when she sang. (The rule against bringing flowers into the house came later.)

When Farrar was seventeen, her parents had cut their ties with Boston and taken her to Germany to study with Lilli Lehmann. A music-loving Bostonian supplied the money, which eventually came to $30,000. Farrar finished repaying it during her first season with the Metropolitan.

After several letters to Lehmann had gone unanswered, Farrar's mother sent a note in copper-plate handwriting. Back came a crushing reply: Lehmann had not answered Farrar's letters because she had not been able to decipher them. She accepted Farrar, and soon was impressed by her American pupil, whose temperament was as hardworking and assiduous as her own.

For years afterward, Lehmann spoke affectionately of Farrar and the diligence she had brought to her lessons. Once, Lehmann recalled, to "test the child's character," she had invented a long series of emergencies, in consequence of which Farrar was to report for a lesson at six o'clock on the morning after an important premiere. Next morning, a carriage arrived. Farrar was pale and tired from only three hours' sleep and the strain of a big performance, but the time was seven minutes to six.

Lehmann was less pleased by Farrar's visits from the Crown Prince, which were anything but a state secret. They were reported by the press in such colorful detail that Farrar's father once invaded a Berlin newspaper office and knocked the editor down.

Lehmann was once staggered by a letter she received from a childless couple she knew. They wanted her help in adopting one of the semi-royal children Farrar was supposed to have borne.

In Berlin, Farrar auditioned for the formidable Cosima Wagner, who was engaging singers for the coming season at Bayreuth. To supply the virginal quality appropriate to Eva in *Die Meistersinger*, Frau Wagner wanted an actual virgin to sing the part. Farrar did not get the role, possibly because she auditioned with an aria from *La Traviata*.

At Monte Carlo, she sang with Caruso. They were unnerved to find the house almost deserted after the first act, until they learned the reason: Everyone had gone out to play *chemin de fer*.

Farrar loved to sing with Caruso but was vexed because his drawings of her always showed her with enormous protruding front teeth. Farrar thought it might have been because she had once slapped his face on the stage, after he had spat over her shoulder during a love scene. It was Caruso who designed the crest Farrar used throughout her career. It showed a robin above the intertwined initials G. F. and the motto *"Farrar farà"* ("Farrar will make it.").

In Paris, she negotiated with Conried for the Metropolitan. Astute Maurice Grau, now in Parisian retirement, coached her on how to handle his successor and how much she could expect to get out of him. When Conried rejected Farrar's terms as exorbitant, Grau said: "Don't worry. He'll come back." And Conried did.

The celebrated quarrel with Toscanini took place at a rehearsal during Toscanini's first season at the Metropolitan. Conductor and soprano took their differences to the manager's office. A candid photograph exists that may have been taken on that or a similar occasion. It shows Toscanini, hand on hip, holding his baton like a duelist's rapier; Farrar glowering and Gatti, seated at his desk with his chin in his hand, looking upward with an expression of the most profound, long-suffering resignation. (Gatti's usual method of dealing with artistic temperament was to hear the performer in stony silence, then walk away without replying.)

A little later, somewhat sheepishly, Gatti telephoned Farrar. Destinn,

Arturo Toscanini (left), Giulio Gatti-Casazza and Geraldine Farrar

who was to have sung her first Butterfly that evening, was ill; would Farrar take over at such short notice? Farrar assented at once. Toscanini was conducting. When Farrar appeared on stage, a faint smile crossed the conductor's face. It was a popular Saturday night performance, but the house was only half full. While it was undoubtedly true that there were stars in the heavens, there were also performers who did and performers who did not fill the opera house.

World War I ended Farrar's annual appearances in Germany but launched her on a new career, in films. Cecil B. De Mille, Samuel Goldwyn and Jesse L. Lasky were just beginning to tap the immense movie market. Farrar worked for all three, appearing in such films as *The Hell-Cat, Flame of the Desert* and *The Woman God Forgot.* In one film with an Egyptian setting, Farrar was obliged to ride a camel. The animal's smell was so offensive that she gave it a daily spraying with Houbigant perfume.

In Hollywood she met and married a film actor named Lou Tellegen. He was the son of a Greek father and Dutch mother, who had gotten his start with Sarah Bernhardt's troupe in Paris. They proved to be an ill-assorted pair. Farrar was a hard worker and an early riser; Tellegen liked to sleep until noon. Farrar was punctual and punctilious; Tellegen was indifferent to appointments and contracts. Anonymous letters, hints from friends and feminine instinct made Farrar suspect he was deceiving her with other women. And when they appeared together in *The World and Its Women*, Tellegen became furious upon discovering that her name was in bigger type than his own. To Farrar this was childish; the value of her name was shown by the huge salary Goldwyn was paying her. The marriage ended, as it was bound to, in divorce.

Between the end of the Metropolitan season and her twelve weeks of summer film-making, Farrar was booked for concert tours. In those pre-jet-aircraft days, a prima donna who had genuinely arrived traveled by private railway car. For fifteen years, Farrar maintained a home on rails. Decorated in chintzes and bright paint, it contained a dining-sitting room with a small piano, comfortable chairs, a wall map for tracing the course of the tour, bedrooms for the Farrar household and closets for the Farrar wardrobe. Dogs and birds completed the homelike aura. The same crew of Pullman porters served Farrar year after year.

Baritone Antonio Scotti, a frustrated impresario, booked several tours that featured Farrar and other Metropolitan artists. When Scotti balked at the fee Farrar asked for the first tour, she suggested, as an alternative, a small fee and a big percentage of the receipts. Scotti accepted with delight, feeling he had driven an excellent bargain. The arrangement was profitable for Farrar but ruinous for Scotti; Farrar walked off with nearly all the profits. Scotti was almost in tears as he thought of the money flowing into all pockets except his own. Farrar left him at the Saint Francis Hotel in San Francisco, chewing a pencil and trying to figure out where the money had gone.

When they sang *Tosca* the following season, as they came out for their second-act curtain call, Scotti muttered reproachfully: "You cost me all my money!"

One tour took the company to a college town in the Midwest. A student critic assigned to review the performance threw himself on Farrar's mercy. The only thing he knew how to write about, he said, was football. Farrar obligingly wrote a review that had kind things to say of every member of the company. Of her own performance, she wrote that Miss Farrar lived up to expectations and her jewels were magnificent.

Next day, every face in the company wore a smile. One performer denounced the metropolitan reviewers; here in the Midwest, he said, was a critic who knew good singing when he heard it. For years he took advertisements in the musical trade journals to reprint the clipping.

A highlight of the 1919–1920 season was the world premiere of Leoncavallo's *Zaza*, with the lovesick music-hall singer portrayed by Farrar.

"Zaza in the role of Geraldine Farrar is a sensation," wrote Huneker. He noted that there were two excellent reasons for her appearance in the part, and she frankly displayed them both.

Although it made her feel squeamish, Farrar's mother admired the dexterity with which her daughter managed the undressing-and-seduction scene of the first act. Farrar's father smoked a cigar outside until the first act was over.

Farrar was idolized by the backstage staff of the Metropolitan. They said of her that she saved her temperament for the conductors. With the staff she was kind, friendly, appreciative of favors, generous at the holiday season and never overbearing. The backstage people detest performers who give themselves haughty airs; they consider it the mark of a second-rate talent.

Each year, on Farrar's birthday, the backstage crew decorated Farrar's dressing room with flowers, brought in an elaborately decorated cake and sang "Happy Birthday." In 1922 they performed the ceremony for the last time. Farrar was forty, and the season would be her last.

There were whispers that Farrar was piqued by the tremendous success of Maria Jeritza in *Tosca* early in the season. In the second-act scene with Scarpia, Jeritza had sunk to the floor and sung *Vissi d'arte* lying on her face, an unprecedented bit of stage business at the Metropolitan. Gatti said the ovation that followed was the loudest he ever heard in any theatre.

Farrar's friends, however, had long known of her intention to leave the opera at forty. Opera, concerts and movies had given her financial independence. And still to come was a decade during which she sang as many recitals as she cared to accept.

The announcement of Farrar's retirement was made just before a *Faust* performance on January 20, 1922, of which Henderson said that "she had never sung Marguerite more beautifully." At its conclusion, Farrar took a solo curtain call. Many of the audience were in tears, alternately dabbing their eyes and waving their handkerchiefs.

"Children," Farrar admonished, "this is no occasion for a funeral."

She made final appearances as Louise, Manon and Carmen. Her farewell role, selected by Gatti, was *Zaza*. It was also a farewell for the opera; the Leoncavallo work was never heard at the Metropolitan again.

The performance took place on Saturday afternoon, April 22. All three lobbies were jammed with floral tributes to be delivered to Farrar. Backstage, there was dismay; the management had issued a last-minute order that no one was to remain backstage at the end of the performance. Chorus and ballet were in tears; stagehands cursed fluently and shoved sets about the stage as if they had Gatti by the throat.

In the audience were nearly five hundred Gerryflappers, each carrying a small white pennant inscribed "Farrar." From one side of the parterre to the other was strung an enormous banner reading: "Farrar Hurrah! Hurrah Farrar!" Balloons floated in the air and flowers rained upon the stage. At the end of Act II, a golden crown and scepter were presented to Farrar before the curtain.

147

After the performance, when the cheering had subsided sufficiently, Farrar made a brief speech. She reviewed her career at the Metropolitan, paying tribute to her parents, who were seated in the front row. She added: "I am leaving this institution because I want to."

Backstage, Gatti's orders were ignored as chorus, ballet, technicians, electricians, stagehands and porters surged onto the stage to say goodbye to Farrar. The crush was so great that stagehands made a seat with their hands, lifting Farrar out through the scenery door on Seventh Avenue. Her flower-banked car stood at the curb. Another huge crowd, consisting of admirers who had been unable to get into the opera house, blocked traffic on Seventh Avenue.

A custom of long standing to honor a particularly admired performer was for admirers to unhitch the horses from the performer's carriage and pull the vehicle themselves. Melba received this accolade in Russia; Rossini, in half the towns of Italy. Something of the sort was attempted by attaching ropes to Farrar's car. But the automobile was a solid 1922 model, and the ropes broke. Another tradition of the opera had ended.

Giovanni Martinelli and Geraldine Farrar in Giordano's MADAME SANS-GÊNE

17

Villa Pace

On an afternoon in the early 1960's, Indian summer lay green and gold along the Maryland hills. It was warm enough for swimming, and conductor Peter Herman Adler said he would, except that his hostess put drowned mice in the pool especially to annoy him. Rosa Ponselle, patting one of the two dozen French poodles within easy reach, smiled and good-humoredly denied the charge.

It had been a busy weekend. The *Aida* at Baltimore's Lyric Theatre for which Ponselle had served as artistic director had been a sold-out, unqualified success. Ponselle, in black velvet, diamonds and emeralds, had taken a curtain call, signed autographs, then joined the "swells," as H. L. Mencken used to call them, for dinner at the Belvedere.

Now there was time to relax in the sun, while members of the Rosa Ponselle Fan Club addressed Christmas cards.

White walls and a red-tiled roof gave the Villa Pace a sun-drenched Mediterranean look. From the terrace one half-expected to see blue water rather than Maryland fox-hunting country. Inside was Florentine elegance, with a touch of Baltimorean polished-brass-and-walnut solidity.

Ponselle designed her house in the shape of a cross for two reasons. One was that the design gave sunlight and air in every room. The other was that the Christian symbol figures prominently in the opera, *La forza del destino*, in which she made her Metropolitan debut. A phrase from the opera, the descending octave with which *Pace, pace, mio Dio* begins, was carved in the limestone frame of the front door. The note-heads, instead

151

of being oval, were in the form of roses. The design, like that of the house and many of the clothes she wore, was Ponselle's.

The Connecticut-born Ponzillo sisters, Rosa and Carmela, were a tremendous vaudeville attraction early in the century. A treasured collector's item is their recording of "Comin' Through the Rye" as it was heard by audiences in the days of World War I. The simple tune is embellished with elaborate trills, runs and roulades, executed as cleanly and effortlessly as a birdcall.

Ponselle had it all from nature. She never objected when Romano Romani billed himself as her only teacher, because the statement was literally true. Romani, however, was a conductor and coach who knew little about the actual mechanics of singing. His function was to show how a phrase should go. Ponselle would say: "You mean — like this?" and do it.

Singers often work for years to develop a trill, and some of them never master it. Ponselle didn't remember a time when she couldn't trill. The coloratura agility, the superb legato, the marvelous shading from full-voice to *mezza voce*, while refined and perfected by diligent work, were in her voice from the beginning.

Ponselle and her sister were appearing at a New York vaudeville theatre in April, 1918. Caruso and Gatti heard them there and Gatti immediately signed Rosa to a contract. By November, she was to be prepared to sing Leonora in *La Forza del destino*. It was a formidable assignment; she had never appeared on an operatic stage.

Also, fantastic and paradoxical as it seems for one of the Ponzillo sisters, she had to learn Italian. "We spoke a dialect at home," Ponselle explained.

The Italian dialects are hard to put into perspective because nothing in this country quite corresponds to them. When we say "dialect," what we really mean is "regional accent." A Philadelphian may smile at the Bostonian's reference to "Hahvahd Yahd"; but the Bostonian is equally amused when the Philadelphian refers to the town across the river as "*Kéy*'m'den." The Brooklynite chuckles at the banjo-twang accent with which the Piedmont Carolinian pronounces "thing" as "thang"; the Carolinian, in return, is entitled to a chuckle over the memory of how, when the Brooklyn Dodgers star Waite Hoyt was injured, the Brooklyn newsboys shouted: "Waite Hert hoit!"

All these, however, are variations on a standard form of speech exemplified, perhaps, by the neutral, basically Midwestern pronunciation of a radio or television announcer. Similarly, Italian has its standard, said to be best attained when it is spoken with the clarity of Tuscan consonants and the purity of Roman vowels — a double standard delightfully summed up in the *double entendre* of "*lingua Toscana in bocca Romana*" — literally, "a Tuscan tongue in a Roman mouth."

Some of the dialects, however, are almost as exotic as the survivals of seventeenth-century French heard in the 'Cajun country of Louisiana, which often constitute a picturesque "jambalaya" that is incomprehensible to someone from a town only ten miles away.

In *Cavalleria rusticana*, the locale of which is Sicily, the hero is called Turiddu because his name is Salvator. The diminutive, "little Salvator," is "Salvatorillo," which in turn is abbreviated to "Torillo." In the Sicilian dialect, the sound of *o* is blunted into *u* ("*Paradiso*," for example, becomes "*Paradisu*"), and the sound of *l* becomes *d*. Hence Santuzza's despairing cry: "*No, no, Turiddu, Turiddu, ah! rimani . . .*"

Having grown up with some dialect such as this, Ponselle had to work at acquiring the beautiful Italian diction which can be admired in her recordings.

The 1918 opening night was memorable. The opera was *Samson et Dalila*. When the curtain rose after the first act, the entire company was massed onstage. The American flag was held by Homer; the Italian, by Caruso; the French, by Leon Rothier; the Belgian, by Robert Couzinou; the Serbian, by Vincenzo Reschiglian, and the British, by Paolo Ananian. One by one, the national anthems of the victorious nations were sung. The date was November 11.

After the performance, a jubilant crowd converged on the Hotel Knickerbocker. They called for Caruso until he appeared at his ninth-floor window to lead the singing of "The Star-Spangled Banner."

Four days later came Ponselle's debut. It was an unnerving moment. *La Forza del destino* had never been performed at the Metropolitan and had not been seen in New York since 1882. Ponselle, a rank unknown, was cast with three of the Metropolitan's greatest artists — Caruso, Giuseppe de Luca and the basso José Mardones.

As they waited backstage, Caruso murmured a heartening "*Coraggio!*"

"Poor devil," said Ponselle, "he was shaking like a leaf himself."

Ponselle was nervous, too; but after the first act she held the audience in her hand. Henderson flatly refused to believe she had never sung in opera before. If that were true, he said, she "must have been born with a ready-made technique." In any case, she had "one of the most voluptuous dramatic soprano voices ever heard."

"A fine figure of a woman, was the opinion of the experts," said Huneker. In her riding boots in the Monastery Scene, however, she seemed awkward and overly conscious of her legs. About her voice, Huneker had no reservations: "It is vocal gold, with its luscious lower and middle tones, dark, rich and ductile."

Ponselle's next role was in another revival, of Weber's *Oberon*, which had not been heard in New York since 1870. After that came *The Legend*, a short-lived work by Joseph Breil, composer of the incidental music for D. W. Griffith's film *The Birth of a Nation*.

Rachel in *La Juive* (with Caruso, in the last of the tenor's 607 appearances at the Metropolitan), Matilda in *William Tell*, Selika in *l'Africana* — Ponselle's repertoire was growing. Her singing in *La Gioconda* helped the work to obtain more than fifty performances in eleven seasons. Her superb *Casta diva* was a highlight when *Norma* was revived on November 16, 1927, after a thirty-six-year absence from the Metropolitan. Ponselle, said Olin Downes of the *Times*, "has probably the most beautiful voice of any soprano of her generation."

Ponselle had a curious quirk. She disliked heat. There could be no heat either in her dressing room or on the stage during a performance; otherwise, she said, she could not and would not sing. No one, of course, minded if the soprano's dressing room was freezing, but a cold stage meant hardship for other performers, in particular the thinly clad ballerinas. Gatti and Ziegler received a stream of complaints from performers who said they had caught cold at a Ponselle performance. But Ponselle's stature by now was such that when she asked for something, she got it. When she sang, the heat was turned off. Many a backstage crewman kept a bottle handy to help get through the ordeal.

Ponselle's first act, on entering the theatre, was to feel the pipes to see whether they were hot. The gesture amused stagehands who had been shivering all afternoon. One bitterly cold night the Metropolitan's engi-

Rosa Ponselle

neer tried to allay the discomfort backstage. Knowing that Ponselle usually came in through the Fortieth Street stage entrance, which was nearest her dressing room, he turned off the heat on that side of the house only. Ponselle foiled him by coming in from Thirty-ninth Street. When she touched a pipe she found it blistering hot. The ensuing outburst taxed Ziegler's diplomacy to its limits.

Ponselle suffered agonies of stage fright. Standing in the wings, awaiting her cue, she was so nervous she made everyone around her nervous, too. She was convinced she would not be able to reach the high notes. But when it was time to sing, she walked on the stage with no visible sign of agitation and filled the Metropolitan with glorious sound.

Ponselle's concern with high notes eventually became almost an obsession. In particular, she dreaded the high C of *O Patria mia* in *Aida*. (Most sopranos do, not only because it is a C but also because of the curiously harmonized passage by which it is approached.) Time after time, Ponselle asked to be released from various roles, insisting she could no longer sing them. When she appeared at Covent Garden, she had the Metropolitan send over a tuning fork. She feared an English orchestra might tune to a higher pitch than she was accustomed to.

Ponselle envied her sister the dramatically juicy music allotted to a mezzo-soprano. Singing Aida, she secretly yearned to sing Amneris. She did not dare risk it, however. Her vocal problem was to keep her big, rich-textured voice light and flexible enough to sustain the soprano *tessitura*. An ever-present danger was that she might venture too deeply into chest-voice and never get out.

Like many other sopranos, Ponselle in particular wanted to sing Carmen. Lilli Lehmann sang it, as did Emmy Destinn. The delightful recordings show that Destinn managed Carmen's lowest notes by transposing them up an octave when necessary. Farrar sang Carmen and thereafter nobody at the Metropolitan had a chance at the part until Farrar retired.

Ponselle got her wish on December 27, 1935. The reviews of her Carmen were undoubtedly the most unfavorable of her entire career. Her singing, said reviewers, was below par; her acting was exaggerated, artificial and unconvincing; her dancing a combination of Charleston and black bottom. Ponselle was probably less devastated by the reviews than she might have been, because she was in love. Her fiancé was Carle A. Jackson, the son of the mayor of Baltimore. They were married in 1936. Ponselle moved to the Villa Pace and has seldom left it since.

Inside the Villa Pace, a record was playing. It was a rarity that had just been reissued, made from the broadcast *Traviata* of January 5, 1935. The music brought the past back vividly as only music can. Well-remembered were Tibbett's dark sonority, Jagel's manly resonance and slightly husky top tones, and the sound that Huneker aptly called "vocal gold." Reliving the performance, Ponselle now and then hummed a phrase or executed a bit of pantomime. She had prepared Violetta with Gemma Belloncioni, who studied the role with Verdi.

"Ah, the right tempi," Ponselle observed with satisfaction. "Mine and Serafin's."

In the finale of Act III, the voice of the reviving Violetta sang faintly:

> *Alfredo, Alfredo,*
> *Di questo core*
> *Non sai comprendere*
> *Tutto l'amore.*

The golden voice lingered tenderly on the name Alfredo. A spoilsport asked why, since there is no *fermata* in the music at that point.

Ponselle looked surprised that the question should be brought up.

"The dramatic situation requires it," she said.

18

Brief Candle

THERE IS NO THRILL quite like that of discovering a great new voice. The Metropolitan's management experienced it in 1922, when a fifteen-year-old coloratura sang an audition. Her name was Marion Talley, and she came from Kansas City. Her voice, like Ponselle's, was pure gold.

She was, of course, not ready for performance. Elated by their discovery, Gatti, Ziegler and Kahn advised her to study for a year, then sing for them again. Chaperoned by her mother and an older sister, Talley settled in New York. Possibly at the suggestion of the Metropolitan, Talley had an interview with Sembrich. The great diva, basking in the afterglow of her career, had become one of the foremost teachers of the day. She was on the faculties of both the Juilliard School and the Curtis Institute of Music, with as many private pupils as she could find time for.

Talley, however, did not become a Sembrich pupil. Gossip was soon buzzing about what had taken place at the interview. One version was that Sembrich had outlined a course of scales, arpeggios, *solfeggi* and other technical studies exactly like that which had produced her own superb musicianship. Talley had replied that she had no intention of undergoing such drudgery; she merely wished to be coached in certain operatic roles. Thereupon Sembrich had signified that the interview was over.

Another version, however, was that Sembrich had already begun to acquire a formidable reputation as a "voice-wrecker." Sembrich, of course, was not the only great vocalist to merit that epithet. It is somewhat curious, in fact, how few great artists have passed on the secret of their vocal mas-

159

tery to pupils. In piano study, an unbroken line can be traced from Van Cliburn, for example, to his teacher Rosina Lhévinne, who studied with a pupil of Rubinstein, who studied with Liszt, who studied with Czerny, who studied with Beethoven. Theodor Leschetizky turned out first-rate pianists as copiously as Leopold Auer mass-produced great violinists.

But no such continuity can be traced in vocal study. Singing is one of the most mysterious of human functions. If one has normal reflexes, begins early enough and is willing to practice eight hours a day for ten years, he can be reasonably certain of acquiring a passable technique, if not greatness, on the piano or violin. But it is a sorrowfully frequent occurrence of the vocal studios that the more one studies, the worse one sings.

The difference, of course, is that whereas the violinist can be taught to hold his left wrist straight and the pianist can be shown how to flex his fingers, the singer is dealing with muscles whose action cannot be seen and whose physiology, even today, is imperfectly understood. What, for example, is to be made of the curious phenomenon called head-voice or *falsetto*? Search the literature of singing technique and you will find half a dozen explanations, all different. Yet the phenomenon can be clearly heard when a bull bellows. Pupils are sometimes told to "breathe from the diaphragm," a physical impossibility, since the diaphragm's movement is a reflex action. Its spasmodic, uncontrollable contraction produces what we call hiccups.

Weird things go on in vocal studios in the quest for the vocal philosopher's stone. One teacher began each lesson by having students inhale some "Caruso air" he had bottled in Caruso's home city of Naples. Another had students sing *crescendo-diminuendo* as he opened and closed an umbrella. Another taught students to "draw out the tone" with a literal gesture like disgorging yards of spaghetti, a mannerism which cost the students much effort to get rid of later on. Teachers sometimes announce they have discovered a "scientific" singing method and write books filled with graphs and diagrams to prove it. Of such methods it can generally be observed that the more scientific the method, the worse the students sing.

One tenor who had acquired a serviceable technique by studying under three different teachers was asked how he had reconciled three such widely divergent theories of vocalism. "I disregarded what was obviously nonsensical," the tenor replied, "and applied the rest."

Singers with this sort of mentality are paid the ironic compliment of being called "teacher-proof."

A hazard when the teacher is himself a performer is that voices are as individual as thumbprints, and what works for one will not necessarily work for another. Or the student may merely copy his teacher's mannerisms; Jean de Reszke in particular lamented that his students copied the externals of his singing style rather than its solid qualities. The performer may sing well through sheer intuition, by a process he is unable to explain; or he may explain it in a way that conveys nothing to students. One soprano said that a well-sung tone produced the sensation of drinking a glass of water; another compared it to smelling a rose. Both had fine operatic careers but limited success as teachers. And Caruso is said to have mystified one of his few pupils by saying, in explanation of the phenomenal Caruso breath control: "Mac, when you go to the bathroom in the morning, you push *down*; when you sing, push *up*."

The final word on the marvelous, mysterious art of singing was undoubtedly that of the tenor Angelo Masini: "*Quando la voce c'è, c'è; e quando non c'è, non c'è;* you can drink, smoke, swim, make love, do anything you like, and still, when the voice is there, it's there, and when it isn't there, it isn't."

It is not necessarily true, therefore, that Talley was foolish and shortsighted to pass up the opportunity to study with Sembrich. The diva, of course, was furious and described the interview with Talley to her longtime friend W. J. Henderson.

Meanwhile, Talley was hard at work with another teacher. Gatti, Ziegler and Kahn kept a close watch on her progress. After three years, even though Talley was still young and immature, they decided to risk a debut, on February 17, 1926.

The opera was *Rigoletto*. During rehearsals, strict orders went out backstage: No one not directly concerned with the performance was to be on or near the stage while Talley was rehearsing. Giuseppe de Luca, who sang Rigoletto, treated the neophyte with fatherly kindness. He told her not to worry about their duets: "Never mind if you cannot hold a phrase; I too will drop it."

Word had gotten around that a remarkable new voice was about to be heard. In addition, the drumbeaters from Kansas City had been busy for a year with publicity to make sure that the local girl made good. At curtain time on February 17, police reserves had been called out to control the 4,200 people crowded into the Metropolitan and the 10,000 milling about outside. A special train had brought 200 opera-lovers from Kansas City. The opera house was swarming with reporters and photographers, and a telegraph line had been installed backstage to enable Talley's father, a telegrapher, to tap out his impressions of his daughter's debut.

Rigoletto was a triumphant success, and Talley's debut was front-page news next day. But Henderson's review in the *Sun* was savage. He ended a lengthy and detailed catalogue of Talley's vocal shortcomings by writing: "Probably the new soprano might achieve a higher artistic success if she would abandon her present vocal method and acquire a sound one. But it is unlikely that this will happen. Singers with methods fundamentally wrong usually patch them up rather than acquire new ones. Miss Talley may perhaps make a career for herself just as she is. It is easier to achieve success in opera than it used to be.

"Mr. Gatti-Casazza gave Miss Talley a good cast to help her, and its members were all trying to give the Kansas City delegation its money's worth. The opera as a whole went with vigor, and doubtless the visitors had a happy evening."

Perhaps it is foolhardy to judge a voice on the basis of a 1925 recording; but Talley's singing of *Je suis Titania* from Thomas's *Mignon* makes it hard to believe her technique was as "fundamentally wrong" as all that. Was it true, as gossip put it, that Sembrich had Henderson "in her pocket" and had prejudiced him against the newcomer? It isn't that easy — despite what people say, and with one or two notoriously venal exceptions — to influence reviews. Did Henderson's opinion and his prestige as dean of music critics influence his colleagues? Brash young reviewers are not noted for reverence toward the opinions of their elders.

At any rate, Talley went on to other roles — Lucia, the Nightingale in Stravinsky's *Le Rossignol*, Olympia in *Tales of Hoffmann*, the Queen of the Night in *The Magic Flute*, Philine in *Mignon*, the Queen in *Le Coq d'Or*. Always it was the same story; the house was sold out but the reviews were hostile. And the Metropolitan now had a brilliant Spanish newcomer in Amelita Galli-Curci, who excelled in the same roles as Talley.

At the end of the 1928–1929 season, the Metropolitan offered Talley a limited contract for the coming season. Talley replied that she was leaving the opera and that the forthcoming spring tour performance in Cleveland would be her last. The management was somewhat taken aback, said Helen Noble; if there was any firing to be done, they preferred to do it themselves.

Talley was twenty-two, and in three seasons of concert tours she had earned, exclusive of her income from opera and record royalties, a total of $334,892. Performers who followed her on the concert circuit said the Talley concerts had wrecked the budget of every concert-giving association in America.

Conductors who worked with Talley said she was intelligent, with a truly beautiful voice; memorized quickly; accepted suggestions readily and ought to have had a long, distinguished career. Perhaps the bad reviews, coming so soon after the exaggerated publicity buildup for her debut, were too sudden a shock. And the glamor no doubt faded quickly; few people, including vocal aspirants, have any idea of how much sheer drudgery the life of an opera singer entails.

Listeners were reminded of Talley years later, when her role of Philine in *Mignon* was sung at the Metropolitan by a seventeen-year-old newcomer with poor posture who moved awkwardly on the stage and was completely beyond her depth in the difficult cadenza of *Je suis Titania*. The debut of Marion Talley can hardly have been more inauspicious than that of Patrice Munsel. But Munsel persevered (among other things, impresario S. Hurok had stuck his neck out to the extent of a $30,000 contract), learning her trade the hard way, on the stage in view of a Metropolitan audience. Eventually she became a polished performer in a variety of roles that included one of the most delightful Despinas of her time.

The usual failing of opera singers is to sing one performance too many. One thinks of the soprano who missed the high B in *Tannhäuser*, while Oscar Thompson of *Musical America* involuntarily covered his ears in pain; the coloratura who missed the E flat of the Mad Scene in *Lucia* in what turned out to be her final Metropolitan performance. In the case of Talley, it is the other way around. One thinks with regret of the career that might have been.

19

Her Grace

THE CRITIC, BIOGRAPHER and accompanist Samuel Chotzinoff, who was fond of her, characterized Grace Moore as a "wench." There were others who used a more specific term.

She startled at least one cocktail party with the statement that she had had 150 lovers. And an apocryphal Metropolitan story concerned the visiting French baritone who showed up in tears. "I am ze only male member of ze company," he explained, "who haff not enjoyed ze favors of Mees Moore zis week."

Her doings brought raised eyebrows, even on the Riviera. The hero of W. Somerset Maugham's famous story "The Human Element" is supposed to have had a real-life counterpart, an admirer who pursued Moore to Antibes but found her to be having an affair with her chauffeur.

Another Moore anecdote is preserved in *The Man Who Came to Dinner*. It is the scene in which Banjo, the Hollywood comedian, tells how he placed a microphone under actress Lorraine Sheldon's mattress and played the recording at lunch next day. "Lorraine left Antibes by the next boat." So did Moore.

Edward Ziegler once greatly tickled his daughter by being skeptical about his star soprano's amorous inclinations. "She never made a pass at me," the white-haired assistant general manager said, "and I'm not that unattractive."

Moore thrived on adulation; it was said in musical circles that the Grace Moore account had changed press agents more often than any other. Next to adulation came love, in which, she wrote, she had always been "perfectly normal, happy and enormously successful."

The aura of semi-divinity that surrounds the attractive daughter of a leading merchant in a small Southern town was lost on Moore. Sent to a fashionable girls' school in Washington, she left it to go on the stage. In the Twenties, she was appearing in *Hitchy-Koo* and *The Music Box Revue,* and aiming for the Metropolitan. She had also, said rumor, become the mistress of one of the wealthiest men in America, a giant of the early days of the automobile industry.

In France, where she had gone for vocal study, Moore fitted congenially into the Elsa Maxwell–Elsie de Wolf group that later came to be called "café society." Meeting Otto Kahn, she bet him a hundred dollars, despite two disastrous Metropolitan auditions, that she would be a member of the company within two years.

Moore won the bet by singing Mimi in *La Bohème* on February 7, 1928. Mimi was not Moore's best role. Her acting was rudimentary; one reviewer described it as consisting of an expression that was smiling and one that was not. She was too obviously full of health and animal spirits to be convincing as the tubercular Mimi. Musically, she disclosed the traits that would make her the despair of conductors. "Moore is a wonderful musician," said one of them. "She always makes the same mistakes."

But the glorious voice made audiences willing to overlook everything else. At her debut, she received twenty-eight curtain calls. It is true that the audience included a Tennessee delegation headed by Senators Tyson and McKellar; but the same thing happened later without a quorum of Tennesseans.

Moore's greatest role was Tosca. It was a part she felt and understood down to her fingertips — Grace Moore as A Famous Opera Singer. She did not have to act; she *was* Tosca, onstage and off. And the music might have been written especially for her voice. A score of later Toscas have not effaced the memory of the way she turned this or that phrase, or of the ferocity with which she spoke the line *"Quest' è il bacio di Tosca!"*

In the early Thirties, Moore left the Metropolitan for a fling in Hollywood. Three years later, somewhat disillusioned, she returned to opera. As a sign of new earnestness about her career, she went to Paris to study the title role of *Louise* with its composer, Gustave Charpentier.

Moore sailed in the company of Chotzinoff, who was going along as coach-accompanist, and her secretary, Constance Hope. On shipboard, Moore's attention was caught by the almost improbable Latin good looks of a fellow passenger.

"Hope," said Moore, "find out who he is."

Miss Hope returned with the information that he was Valentin Parera, Spain's greatest movie idol.

"Hope," said Moore, "invite him to dinner."

Parera's fate was sealed. When the party reached Paris, he and Moore were married.

Moore proved to be a devoted spouse, even though the picture post-cards which she sent to the press at Christmas, an aerial view of a lavish waterfront estate at Greenwich, Connecticut, continued to be captioned: "The Grace Moore Properties."

When Jan Kiepura, "the Polish ham," joined the Metropolitan in 1937, one of his early appearances was in *La Bohème*, singing Rodolfo to Moore's Mimi. During a rehearsal, Philip Crispano, the property master, entered Ziegler's office in great agitation. He reported that Moore and Kiepura had almost come to blows over the placement of Mimi's chair in the opening scene. Ostensibly, Rodolfo's aria *Che gelida manina* is addressed to Mimi; but Kiepura took the position that arias were for singing to audiences, not to fellow performers, and he had placed Mimi's chair far in the background — a sort of upstaging in reverse. Moore, pointing out that she had been in the movies, too, had placed the chair where it belonged. Kiepura had dragged it back. The tug-of-war had been going on for half an hour. Perhaps Ziegler had better come settle it.

Ziegler shrugged his shoulders philosophically. "Let them fight it out," he said, "and may the best man win."

At the performance, the absurd contest was resumed. Kiepura moved the chair upstage, Moore brought it down again. Finally Moore checkmated the tenor by moving the chair and slipping into it in a single motion, before Kiepura could get there.

The volume of applause indicated that the audience either had not been aware of what was going on, or had been and was vastly entertained.

Grace Moore in her dressing room, with a typical floral tribute

The honors of the first contest were so clearly Moore's that opera-fanciers wondered what would happen at the rematch, next time both artists appeared in *La Bohème*. It was widely conjectured that Kiepura would slide the chair away just as Moore was sitting down.

What Kiepura intended, however, can never be known with certainty. Moore had friends backstage and one of them had nailed the chair to the floor.

By the postwar years 1946 and 1947, Moore had begun to put on weight and the golden voice was showing the effects of wear and tear. Listeners who suffered sympathy pains when singers were in trouble were beginning to huff and puff a bit to get their favorite over the hard spots.

Moore was so much the embodiment of youth and vitality that it was impossible to imagine her as a dowager. As it turned out, she was not fated to be one. For her 1947 tour of Sweden, the King sent the Crown Prince to be her escort. A flaming crash at Copenhagen killed everyone aboard the plane.

"Gracie got top billing," said a friend on seeing the eight-column streamer with which the *World-Telegram* headlined the crash. "A Crown Prince beside her, and nothing left in the ashes except a gold ring. I think maybe she would have liked it that way."

20

Bicycle Racer

IN HIS AUTOBIOGRAPHY, Bruno Walter told how Ezio Pinza once came to his apartment to discuss singing the role of Don Giovanni at the Salzburg Festival. A maid answered the door, then returned in a state of blushing confusion. "Ma'am," she told Frau Walter, "there is such a beautiful man outside!"

"I knew then," wrote Walter, "that I had found my Don Giovanni."

Pinza fascinated women, and vice versa. When his wife called the Metropolitan, telephone operators were trained to say either that he was not there or that he was very busy rehearsing. One soprano crossed her arms whenever Pinza appeared, greeting him coolly from a safe distance.

Pinza's first marriage ended when his wife brought a $250,000 alienation-of-affections suit, naming the soprano Elisabeth Rethberg as defendant. Hardly had Pinza extricated himself from this difficulty when he was faced with a $200,000 suit for breach of promise. Eventually the suit was dropped. Pinza's lawyer explained that girls sometimes thought he was being romantic when he was merely being gentlemanly.

Musical gossip buzzed that a young woman, daughter of a world-famous conductor, had killed herself after an affair with Pinza had ended unhappily. The heartbroken father had forgiven Pinza, the story went, and the two men had solemnly shaken hands over her grave.

But there were occasional dissenting opinions, if a favorite Metropolitan story is to be believed. The incident was supposed to have happened during one of the Metropolitan spring tours. Pinza had been telling the story of his latest conquest, using names, dates, places and a generous supply of four-letter words.

At the other end of the car, a famous voice spoke up. "Oh, come off it, Ezio," said Grace Moore. "You're the worst lay in the Met."

Pinza was born in Rome, the puny seventh son of a poor carpenter all six of whose previous children had died in infancy. He was christened Fortunato Pinza, partly in the hope that he would be fortunate enough to survive, partly because the Church objected to his being named for a pagan, the Roman general Aetius, who turned back Attila the Hun at Châlons-sur-Marne. But his family and friends clung stubbornly to "Ezio."

Carpentry, delivering bread, working as a railway brakeman and bicycle racing turned the puny infant into a broad-shouldered, barrel-chested six-footer. His voice was discovered by fellow bicycle racers while he was singing in the shower. Somewhat dubiously, he auditioned at the Bologna Conservatory, and was accepted.

After two years, his studies were interrupted by World War I. Drafted into the Italian army, Pinza came out a captain of artillery. He never returned to the Conservatory; the two years there were all the formal musical training he was to receive. Instead he joined the Rome Opera Company. His singing there made such a hit that Toscanini borrowed him for La Scala to sing in Boïto's *Nerone*. Then it was only a question of time until he received an invitation from the Metropolitan.

Pinza made his debut on November 1, the opening night of the 1926–1927 season, singing Spontini's *La Vestale*, with a cast that included Ponselle, Giacomo Lauri-Volpi, Margarete Matzenauer and de Luca. It was the first of the sixty-odd distinguished characterizations Pinza would offer at the Metropolitan, ranging from relatively minor parts like Don Basilio in *Il Barbiere di Siviglia* to characterizations like Don Giovanni and Boris Godounov, in which he held the center of the stage.

Pinza never objected to performing in minor roles, lavishing on Don Basilio the same meticulous care he devoted to Boris. His makeup for the Rossinian music master, applied by himself, was a masterly stage caricature. Pinza prided himself on his skill at makeup and kept on hand thirty-five false noses, forty-seven beards, fifty-one mustaches, twenty-two pairs of ears, eleven warts, fifteen sets of fingernails and forty-one pairs of eyebrows.

Pinza's voice was powerful but not beautiful, comparing unfavorably as lush vocal sound to that of a Cesare Siepi or Jerome Hines. Pinza's singing was sometimes hard-edged almost to the verge of huskiness. What made his voice remarkable was its range and flexibility. He was equally ready with Sarastro's low E natural in *The Magic Flute* and Figaro's *pianissimo* high F in *Le Nozze di Figaro.* Accordingly, he was heard in an unusually wide variety of roles, ranging from Sarastro, a *basso profundo* part, to Don Giovanni, which can be sung by either a bass or a baritone, to Escamillo, which lies awkwardly for any voice but is most often sung by a baritone.

Pinza was somewhat unusual among Metropolitan performers in that he never vocalized, believing that the vocal organs were strengthened by not being used. Aside from an occasional bellow while shaving, his voice was heard only during working hours.

Three years after his debut, Pinza made his appearance in the role with which he was to be most closely identified, the title role in *Don Giovanni.* A generation of New Yorkers had grown up without seeing *Don Giovanni;* the work had not been previously staged during the Gatti-Casazza regime. Pinza's bicycle-racer legs in tights delighted feminine operagoers, and as one of the handsomest men of his time he made the amorous Don thoroughly believable. (Pinza once confessed, however, that he found making love onstage to be one of the most difficult of the actor's tasks. Stage lovemaking is somewhat stylized, and Pinza as a practical amorist was anything but.)

Pinza added another memorable characterization, as Figaro in *Le Nozze di Figaro* when the Mozart work was revived after a twenty-two-year absence, in 1940. He was rebuked in the press, however, for nonchalantly placing his foot on the prompter's box as he sang his last-act aria.

In 1940, Pinza astonished his colleagues by marrying a pretty member of the Metropolitan corps de ballet. The lovers had been so circumspect that the gossipy world of opera had not even suspected they were seeing each other. Pinza settled down to the life of an exemplary family man and commuter from Rye.

His life was rudely jolted in 1942. A thoroughgoing Italian, he was

Ezio Pinza and Risë Stevens in THE MARRIAGE OF FIGARO

as unreconstructable as Toscanini; and he had been heard making dire predictions of what would happen when Allied troops encountered the Italian army. He had, after all, served in it; what United States Army veteran would say less?

Pinza's disparagements were overheard by, among others, a fellow basso who can be identified as "Corbin." He was an American who had joined the Metropolitan in the Twenties, working his way up through a succession of minor roles to such parts as the King in *Lohengrin* and the Police Commissary in *Der Rosenkavalier*. Corbin reported Pinza to the FBI. His reasoning was that with Pinza detained on Ellis Island as a suspected enemy alien, some of the fat parts that were a Pinza monopoly would be redistributed to other performers such as himself.

Corbin's plan worked perfectly except for two miscalculations. One was that he did not have Pinza's voice; the other was that he did not have Pinza's figure. Like many very tall men, he was spindle-shanked and did not look well in tights. Still, he was a capable performer and for a time sang the Pinza roles with some success.

Then a curious thing happened. Midway through a performance, Corbin began to tire visibly. He finished the part but did so with obvious difficulty. Thereafter his singing was never the same again. His once-sonorous voice developed "holes" and rough edges. After a few more seasons he left the Metropolitan. The more devout members of the company saw the event as an act of divine vengeance.

Pinza, who was soon back singing at the Metropolitan, appeared unruffled by the train of events. He had a somewhat Renaissance turn of mind and one of his hobbies was collecting Florentine poison rings. He displayed no particular animosity toward Corbin, taking the position that it was something almost any brother artist might have done in his place. In Pinza's own dealings with agents and managers, quarter was neither asked nor given. "You have to screw them while you're on top," he once said.

When Pinza went to Broadway to star in *South Pacific*, the superb stage presence and acting skill that Metropolitan audiences had come to take rather for granted struck the drama critics as a revelation. He was hailed as one of a fast-disappearing species, a great romantic actor. Pinza for his part was amused and delighted by celebrity of a kind that had never come to him at the opera.

Movies and television set the capstone on Pinza's career. He had long felt somewhat slighted that singers like Lauritz Melchior, Risë Stevens and Lawrence Tibbett had beaten him in the race to Hollywood. Now Pinza could rest on his laurels; he had done everything.

Soon after *South Pacific* had begun to add a new dimension to Pinza's fame, a fellow panelist on the Saturday broadcast opera quiz told him the story of The Man Who Looked Like Pinza:

"So there's this six-footer with curly hair who's a dead ringer for Ezio Pinza. One day he gets off the train in Pittsburgh. The cab driver says, 'Why, hello, Mr. Pinza — welcome to Pittsburgh!'

" 'Sam' — spreading both hands in an expressive Garment Center gesture — 'Sam Moscowitz is the name.'

" 'OK, Mr. Pinza — Mr. Moscowitz, I mean — hop in and I'll drive you over to the Hilton.'

"At the Pittsburgh Hilton the same pantomime is repeated: 'Sam — Sam Moscowitz is the name.' The desk clerk replies: 'Certainly, Mr. — er, Moscowitz, I understand, and we'll respect your privacy. Now, there's a convention in town, every room in every hotel is taken, but we have one suite we always keep reserved for Conrad Hilton. We're going to put you in there, and if Hilton shows up, he can sleep on the pool table. Front! Show Mr. — er, Moscowitz to the Presidential Suite!'

"After turning down autograph requests from the bellboy and the elevator operator ('Sam — Sam Moscowitz is the name'), our man finds himself in the Presidential Suite. There are flowers all over the place, plus telegrams of welcome from the governor of Pennsylvania, the mayor of Pittsburgh, senators, congressmen, members of the state legislature and the Musical Arts Club of Pittsburgh.

"What especially attracts his attention, however, is a large double bed on which a beautiful young girl is lying. She's nude, d'you see — in other words, she has no clothes on. She looks at him seductively and says: 'Oh, Mr. Pinza, I have something I've been saving for you.'

" 'Sam' — starting to make the Seventh Avenue gesture but instead breaking into song — 'en-chawnt-ed efe-ning . . . ' "

Pinza listened to this ludicrous story in absolute stony silence. Then he asked: "Do I sound like dot?"

21

The Twilight of the Gods

On January 2, 1925, the Metropolitan revived Verdi's *Falstaff*, with Antonio Scotti in the title role and a young California baritone named Lawrence Tibbett singing the part of Ford.

It was not, as is sometimes supposed, Tibbett's debut; he had joined the company the previous season, singing the small role of a Monk in *Boris Godounov*. On that occasion, he confessed later, he was too preoccupied with not stumbling over his beard to be greatly concerned about his singing.

From there Tibbett had worked his way up to Valentin in *Faust*, which he had sung without creating any particular stir, though the New York *Times* had praised the "fine, fresh quality" of his voice and had characterized him as a "tall, spare figure of youth and modest demeanor."

The role of Ford, however, had certain built-in advantages. For one thing, the fresh-voiced California baritone was paired with a stagewise but aging artist whose voice was nearly gone. For another, Ford's monologue ending the first scene of Act II is one of the few genuinely dramatic moments in the *Falstaff* score. Much of the music written by the seventy-nine-year-old composer had a light-fingered Mendelssohnic quality, representing a complete break with his earlier style. There were a few early-Verdian outbursts, however, and one of them was Ford's monologue, with its surprising, magnificent resolution in E flat major:

> *Laudata sempre sia*
> *Nel fondo del mio cor*
> *La gelosia!*

If one has a good high G, as Tibbett certainly did in those days, success is virtually automatic.

What happened next was glossed over in contemporary newspaper reports, and even now the entire story is not clear. For some reason, however, the stage manager, who determines the order in which bows are taken, elected not to send Tibbett out before the gold curtain. Instead, Scotti appeared and reappeared. The audience leaped to the conclusion that Scotti was determined not to share the spotlight with his young American rival and that he had the backing of the Metropolitan's Italian directorate.

Pandemonium broke out. There were shouts of "Tibbett! Tibbett!" The baritone, already in his dressing room, was hastily summoned to keep the house from being torn apart.

Although its causes were not exclusively musical, it was one of the most sensational personal triumphs in Metropolitan history. Olin Downes, covering for the *Times*, hurried back to the office with an account of what had happened. Managing editor Frederick T. Birchall told him: "You have exactly forty minutes to write a story for Page One."

Downes made the edition.

Tibbett's career, once launched, rolled on in an endless blaze of publicity. It has been said, by people in a position to know, that Tibbett never had, or needed, a press agent. That makes it staggering to go through the faded Tibbett press clippings. Tibbett arriving at Grand Central Station, Tibbett boarding a plane for California, Tibbett teeing off at a golf course — everything the baritone did was news.

Tibbett, of course, was doing a good deal that was worth noting. His fine voice, superb English diction and conscientious artistry scored him a personal triumph when he appeared as Eadgar in *The King's Henchman*. Thereafter, he was automatically the chief candidate for the leading baritone role in a new work or an important revival.

His performance of the title role in *The Emperor Jones*, though it could not save that hapless work, was a magnificent display of singing and acting virtuosity. He performed with distinction in *Peter Ibbetson* and managed the taxing role of Wrestling Bradford in *Merry Mount*. The Metropolitan revived *Simon Boccanegra* for Tibbett, and his repertoire gradually included all the standard roles — Iago, Amonasro, Germont, Tonio, Rigoletto. His playing of Scarpia in the second act of *Tosca* was particularly realistic; there were times when the knock at the door came not a moment too soon.

Tibbett was one of the first Metropolitan artists to be discovered by Hollywood, and his film appearances were numerous and profitable. The hardworking management of Evans & Salter booked him for all the concert engagements he had time for. In addition, he earned the highest accolade of a singer in the Thirties: his own weekly radio program. His recording of the Prologue to *Pagliacci* became one of Victor's biggest sellers.

To a generation of Americans, Tibbett symbolized opera. In a Fred Allen skit satirizing opening night at the Metropolitan, announcer Harry von Zell portrayed "Lawrence Tibbett singing a high Q-sharp — highest note ever sung at the Metropolitan."

But Tibbett was also the man who knew of a bar in Harlem that would be open after the legal closing hour of four A.M. His fondness for burning the candle at both ends began to show in his singing. Around 1940, it was clear that Tibbett was in vocal trouble. From time to time, there were flashes of his old grandeur, but the road ran inexorably downhill. On the last night of 1946, listeners suffered with Tibbett through a painful *Rigoletto*, with every note wrenched out by main force, which left no doubt that the great baritone's career was finished.

He was not old, as singers go; one thinks of Giuseppe de Luca, in his seventies, singing *Di Provenza* at Town Hall with never a scrape to mar the sheen of his voice. Tibbett's prominence in the world of music made him the logical choice for president when the American Guild of Musical Artists was founded. There had even been talk of his succeeding Gatti-Casazza as general manager of the Metropolitan.

"People are supposed to drink to escape," said one of Tibbett's long-time friends. "What did he have to escape from? He had money and social position, he was famous, he was doing what he liked to do and women were crazy about him. What more can a man expect out of life?"

Alcoholics are sometimes unwilling to call their affliction by its right name. On one of the periodic occasions when he entered a private hospital for "drying out," Tibbett spoke to an intimate friend of his "compulsion for self-destruction."

It destroyed him.

When he walked in and said "Good morning," it was as if the room had been flooded with sunlight. If ever an artist had genuine sweetness of temper, it was Jussi Bjoerling. He was a modest, hardworking performer who was liked by his colleagues and adored by operagoers. His voice, said Mrs. Enrico Caruso, reminded her of her husband's more than that of any other contemporary tenor.

Although lyric tenors often shy away from the arduous role of Manrico in *Il Trovatore*, Bjoerling reveled in it. For many listeners, the superb lyricism of his *Ah si, ben mio*, followed immediately by the fiery high C's of *Di quella pira*, constituted one of the greatest thrills they ever experienced at the Metropolitan.

Soon after his debut, as Rodolfo in the opening-night *Bohème* of the 1938–1939 season, Bjoerling sang a Town Hall recital that showed he was that rarity, an operatic vocalist of absolutely the first rank whom it was also fascinating to hear in recital. Tenors usually are, like Caruso, operatic singers who give concerts now and then, or, like John McCormack, fundamentally concert artists who take an occasional turn at opera.

Bjoerling's English diction put that of most native vocalists to shame. In a song like Rachmaninoff's "In the Silence of Night," at the words

> *How oft I bade you go,*
> *How oft I call'd you back,*

it was fascinating to observe the skill and accuracy with which he shaded the various modifications of the basic vowel sound of "ah."

When Bjoerling made his debut, he was still in his mid-twenties. It was not long until the musical world was gloomily quoting the ancient maxim: "A young man is a fool if he drinks; an old man is a fool if he doesn't." Bjoerling's custom of gathering with cronies at the Blue Ribbon restaurant on West Forty-fourth Street to polish off a dozen bottles of beer became widely discussed.

Bjoerling spent the war years in Sweden. The official explanation was "travel restrictions." A musical magazine heard from one of its European correspondents, however, that the real reason was different. Bjoerling was said to be in a Stockholm sanitarium that specialized in the treatment of alcoholics. Again the question was asked: Why? Fame, money, a movie-

Lawrence Tibbett as Germont
in LA TRAVIATA

Antonio Scotti as
Don Giovanni

star wife and two handsome children would seem enough to make one content with his lot.

Bjoerling's well-publicized bouts with the bottle may have been a reaction to the drudgery and nervous strain of a profession he found arduous, and out of which he vowed to keep his children at all costs. He was appalled when his son, on reaching adolescence, turned out to have a fine tenor voice and a technique as effortless as his own. He hoped the boy would never take up singing as a career. "It's such a hard life," Bjoerling said. Nevertheless, in 1945 Bjoerling returned to the Metropolitan with his vocal luster undimmed. His fine singing of the title role was a highlight of the restaged *Don Carlo* with which Rudolf Bing opened his first Metropolitan season. He continued to be one of the artists most in demand all over the world. But Bjoerling felt that time was running out.

In the summer of 1956, Irving Kolodin of the *Saturday Review* met Bjoerling in Stockholm. Bjoerling told the American critic that he gave himself only about five more years of singing. The high C that had once been effortless now required a strain. The long, sustained phrases that had once gone on and on were growing shorter.

Ironically, said Bjoerling, this was happening at a time when, from the artistic point of view, he was just beginning to mature. He now perceived the musical logic behind things he had once done dutifully but uncomprehendingly, as a matter of obeying what teacher said. Each passing season gave him deeper insight into his operatic roles and the songs in his recital repertoire. It seemed a pity to be losing his voice just when he was learning how to use it.

Kolodin told him the idea was preposterous. But Bjoerling's words were more prophetic than either of them dreamed. Five years later, he was dead.

22

The Going Concern

As GATTI-CASAZZA gathered power at the Metropolitan more and more firmly into his own hands, the company began to undergo a subtle metamorphosis.

Abbey, Grau and Conried had all been speculative impresarios. An often-quoted Grau sentiment was that nobody ever paid a nickel to see a conductor, and contemporary reviews leave no doubt that this philosophy was sometimes reflected in the quality of performance. Shrewdly reasoning that the public comes to hear stars, Grau engaged the greatest there were. The rest — minor roles, chorus, orchestra, conductor, *mise-en-scène*, lighting — was merely filler. Many early Metropolitan performances must have been rather like opera as it is often staged today at places other than the Metropolitan.

Gatti's thinking, however, had been deeply colored by the quasi-official nature of the posts he had held in Italy. The function of a European *intendant* was not to make money but to see to it that standards of performance remained high. Financial problems would be taken care of through the state or municipal subsidy.

While the Metropolitan received no subsidy, being supported by Society rather than society, it was still, to Gatti's mind, more than just another theatre. It was an institution, with duties and obligations toward its public. When he first arrived, he had found the Metropolitan being run on what he considered rather slapdash lines. Under his guidance, the company assumed the institutional character it retained not only throughout the Gatti regime, but beyond.

What Gatti seems to have brought to the Metropolitan was a thorough-going professionalism. The orchestra, unlike some of those of the early seasons, was no longer a scratch organization casually recruited in Milan, Berlin and London. It was the Metropolitan Orchestra, a permanent and prestigious group. There were Saturdays, with both matinee and evening performances, when the men played steadily for eight hours with scarcely a break; but the season did not last forever, and when it was over one could go up to Woodstock, New York, and spend the summer playing quartets.

Choristers were not spear-carriers who could sing but serious, hardworking professionals able to sing from memory fifty or sixty operas in French, German, Italian and occasionally English and Russian. Conductors, beginning with Mahler and Toscanini, were the best that could be found.

In consequence, the Metropolitan attained a kind of plateau. While some performances were, naturally, better than others, there was a level of excellence below which they were not allowed to sink. When a really great performer appeared, the Metropolitan could be depended upon to provide consistently a musical and scenic background worthy of his talent.

From dozens of *Trovatore* performances, one could recall Leonoras who were great and Leonoras who were terrible, but never an occasion on which the offstage chorus of women's voices, *"Ah, se l'error t'ingombra,"* did not make its pathetic, touching effect.

A scene, among many which could be cited, that never failed to have dramatic impact, no matter who was singing or conducting, was the Storm Scene in *Otello*. The late-afternoon sky darkened, with a lurid band of light along the horizon (possibly un-Mediterranean, but that is exactly how a southwester strikes on Long Island Sound). Scudding storm clouds and vivid flashes of lightning heightened the dramatic tension. As the storm's fury, and Otello's peril, reached their height, brown-robed Franciscans hurried forward, their upheld crosses silhouetted against the livid sky. Then came the joyful outburst *"E salva!"* as Otello entered with the most thrilling press communiqué ever issued by a naval commander.

That the public appreciated the quality of the offerings by Gatti and his Metropolitan Opera Company was shown by the box-office receipts. The figures must have delighted Gatti, who never forgot Verdi's admonition to "regard most attentively" the reports of ticket sales. These soared to, then reached, then passed the million-dollar mark. The season grew longer and longer, reaching twenty-four weeks in 1926. Ticket prices, which were at a seven-dollar top in 1920, rose to $7.70, then to $8.25. And even at the higher prices, the market for Metropolitan tickets was brisk. One subscriber who could not attend an opening night during the Twenties advertised his tickets for sale at fifty dollars.

Throughout most of Gatti's regime, the Metropolitan was in extremely comfortable circumstances. It was a happy exception to George Bernard Shaw's observation that "all the great impresarios, from Handel to Laporte and Lumley, lost money, and lived, as far as one can make out, chiefly on the splendor of the scale on which they got into debt." But not the Metropolitan. From 1910 to 1930, every one of Gatti's seasons was profitable. By 1930, the Metropolitan had accumulated a cash reserve of $1,100,000.

The Metropolitan's very success, in fact, became a boomerang later on, when the deficits began to mount. Many people, remembering Gatti and his million-dollar surplus, could not help ascribing the losses to "mismanagement." Businessmen accustomed to facing the alternatives of staying solvent or going under were made uneasy by any sort of venture that lost money.

The fact is that opera, with rare exceptions, has never paid its way. European opera houses received a subsidy from city, state or both. In Gatti's early Metropolitan years, the subsidy came, in effect, from the boxholders. By paying their yearly assessments, shareholders in the Metropolitan Opera and Real Estate Company provided funds for paying taxes, staffing and operating the building and keeping it in repair. Gatti thus received a rent-free theatre in which to produce opera.

The boxholders for their part received seats for every performance, which they could either occupy themselves or resell to someone else. The classic case was that of Miss Georgine Iselin, whose financial affairs underwent public scrutiny during a tax investigation in 1926. The investigation showed that during the 1920–1921 season, Miss Iselin had subleased her box forty-seven times, for a total of $9,525. At that time, the assessment was $4,500 a year. Miss Iselin thus made a profit of $5,025 and in addition had the use of the box for the season's eighty-odd remaining performances.

In addition to a rent-free house, the Metropolitan had the advantage of a percentage of the fees earned by its artists in concert performances. This was a time-honored custom going back to the days of Grau and Conried, when the Metropolitan's general manager would actually book a Nordica or Caruso on a concert tour. By Gatti's time, the general manager's booking function had fallen into disuse, but the custom of collecting a fee survived.

The Metropolitan also collected a percentage of royalties from recordings made by its artists. In 1925, the company earned over $50,000 from this source. Two years later, its income from a percentage of its artists' radio fees was nearly $100,000.

Payment of these fees, which the Metropolitan had done nothing to earn and which came in addition to the standard twenty percent exacted by concert managers, was bitterly resented by Metropolitan artists. When the American Guild of Musical Artists was established in the Thirties, a key plank in its platform was that payment of concert, radio and recording percentages to the Metropolitan was to be discontinued.

The relatively low wages paid to orchestra musicians, choristers, stagehands and other behind-the-scenes technicians were still another reason why the Metropolitan found itself on a firm financial base. Nevertheless, the Metropolitan's management lost no opportunity to emphasize the difficulties of producing opera and the exertions that were needed to keep the company solvent. When Gatti's contract was renewed in 1926, an editorial in the *Herald Tribune* complimented the Metropolitan on its sound financial condition. It also suggested that the company's solvency should enable it to correct certain artistic shortcomings.

Ziegler at once issued a statement that the company's ledger "shows, and always has shown since Mr. Gatti-Casazza assumed control, a very considerable deficit, the precise amount of the deficit for last season being $226,991. It is only through skillful utilization of sources of revenue other than those which the opera-going public supplies that this deficit has been diminished or covered, or at times somewhat more than covered."

"Somewhat more than covered," for the season Ziegler was referring to, meant a profit of $35,277. In each of the two following seasons, the company earned over $140,000.

Gatti was, if anything, more adept at talking poor mouth than Ziegler.

Farrar maintained that Gatti kept two sets of books: one to show to his board of directors, the other to show to artists who asked for a higher fee in their next contract.

The seven fat years before 1929 brought memorable performances. Caruso was dead and Farrar had retired, but others came to fill the void. Maria Jeritza astounded Metropolitan audiences, and was considered by some a bit of a show-off, when she sang Tosca's aria *Vissi d'arte*, lying flat on the stage. Jeritza's explanation was that she had slipped and fallen during a rehearsal at which Puccini was present, and he had urged her to make that piece of stage business a permanent part of her interpretation.

Amelita Galli-Curci, one of the coloraturas whose appeal to the public Gatti found it so hard to understand, had shown that a great voice and fine musicianship could offset plainness of features. ("When I met her at the boat," her onetime manager said, "I took one look and rushed her to Helena Rubinstein's.")

Lucrezia Bori conquered a public that worshiped her with almost Gerryflapper devotion. Her name was linked onstage, and, by gossip, off-stage as well, with that of Canadian-born Edward Johnson, who as Edoardo di Giovanni had sung Parsifal at La Scala, and who had come from Chicago to join the Metropolitan.

Beniamino Gigli and Giovanni Martinelli engaged in a bitter but inconclusive tug-of-war for the mantle of Caruso. The elegance of Tito Schipa's singing compensated for the shortness of its range; he needed nearly everything transposed down and in consequence was said to travel with trunkfuls of orchestra parts.

Giacomo Lauri-Volpi, "the little man with the big voice," was capable not only of lyric roles but also of the most strenuous dramatic parts in the repertoire. Although "tenor" is sometimes equated with "brainless," Lauri-Volpi was a serious, thoughtful artist who had taken his law degree before going to Rome's Saint Cecilia Academy to study singing. His book of memoirs and reflections, *A viso aperto*,* is a fascinating volume that reveals, among other things, familiarity with the quaint, crabbed poems of Thomas Hardy, little read even in the English-speaking countries. At

---

* Approximately, *Speaking Frankly*. Also an untranslatable pun on the scene in *Il Trovatore* in which Manrico identifies himself by raising his visor.

*Amelita Galli-Curci
in the Mad Scene
from* LUCIA DI LAMMERMOOR

*Maria Jeritza as Octavian
in* DER ROSENKAVALIER

sixty-three, Lauri-Volpi was still singing well enough to make a creditable recording as Manrico in *Il Trovatore*.

Brooklyn-born Frederick Jagel never had quite the career many listeners felt he should have. His voice just missed greatness; its top was marred by a curious veiled, almost husky quality that, in singers' parlance, lacked "focus." But he was a conscientious, dependable artist who almost never missed a performance and was always ready to substitute for someone else at short notice.

Lauritz Melchior, after a few initial uncertainties that accompanied his transition from baritone to tenor, was becoming a pillar of the Metropolitan's Wagnerian wing. Chaliapin, his pantomime more restrained, was back, this time with huge success. His magnificent singing of Boris Godounov and of Mephistopheles in *Faust* were two reasons why Tibbett's earliest appearances were overshadowed.

Elisabeth Rethberg, called at the peak of her artistry "the perfect voice," showed her versatility by singing Aida, Nedda in *I Pagliacci*, Sieglinde in *Die Walküre* and Sophie in *Der Rosenkavalier* during her first season. Soon thereafter, Rethberg's future husband, George Cehanovsky, joined the company to begin the forty-year career that saw him singing more different roles in more different operas than any other artist in Metropolitan history.

A typical performance during the Twenties might have offered *Aida*, with Rethberg in the title role, wearing the striped robe that reminded some operagoers of an advertisement for Aunt Jemima pancakes; Matzenauer as Amneris; Martinelli as Radames; Giuseppe Danise as Amonasro, and Robert Moranzoni conducting.

Around six o'clock, Otto Kahn came uptown from Wall Street to have dinner with Ziegler. Trays were sent into Ziegler's office and visitors were sent out. The two men happily ate chicken with their fingers, relishing the latest opera-house gossip or chuckling over one of the smoking-room stories of which Ziegler had an inexhaustible supply.

Singers, choristers, supers and orchestra players began trooping through the stage door on Fortieth Street, which was guarded by "Captain" John Edgar. Starting as a cabin boy on Great Lakes steamers at ten, he had earned his master's license at twenty-one. Then, having a pleasant tenor voice, he had gone to Europe to study and had sung with opera companies there. Now, his singing days behind him, he was still close to opera. At performance time he wore impeccable evening dress topped by a billowing white mustache and a ten-gallon hat.

On the Broadway side of the house, Thomas J. Bull, white-haired, white-mustached, in evening dress with a shiny silk "topper" and wearing pince-nez, stood at the center door, taking tickets. He was chief of ushers and had stood at the same door on the first Metropolitan opening night in 1883.

The twenty-two ushers began arriving to change into their blue-and-silver uniforms. Nearly all of them worked at other callings during the day; at various times the ushers included bank clerks, lawyers, vocal students with operatic aspirations, Wall Street customers' men, embryo politicians, at least one officer in the Court of General Sessions, and a salesman of cemetery lots.

Backstage, a number of events were beginning to overlap with increasing speed. The stage set was going up under the supervision of Frederick Hosli, head of the stage department, and his master mechanic. Hosli was a veteran who had joined the Metropolitan as an errand boy in the Grau regime. His chief qualification had been owning a bicycle; in those days the Metropolitan paid no carfare for the area bounded by Twenty-third and Fifty-ninth streets, and by Fifth and Eleventh avenues.

Blueprints posted backstage, and chalk patterns on the floor, showed the exact location for each flat. The flats were brought in through the big double doors on Seventh Avenue in exactly the order they would be needed for setting up on the stage. When the sets were struck, they would be repacked in reverse order for returning to the warehouse.

The master mechanic, watch in hand, stood in the center of the stage, supervising the operation and giving the signals for lowering the drops into position. Each step in the sequence was carefully timed and seldom varied more than a few seconds from one performance to another. The timings were important; Sherry's needed to know when to expect an influx of hungry (and thirsty) operagoers; doormen, when to begin posting the numbers on the call-boards that summoned the waiting limousines at the end of the performance; and other people needed the same information for various reasons. Paymaster Aimé Gerber, for example, whose duties included laying in as many bottles of beer as there were acts in the opera on

Feodor Chaliapin as Mephistopheles in FAUST

the nights when Artur Bodanzky conducted, would know it would be time to have the first bottle ready, cold but not chilled, at, say, 8:43 P.M.

The space in the wings was filling up with choristers and supers costumed as Egyptian soldiers and spade-bearded priests. Later, in the Triumphal Scene, they would be joined by the ballet and by other supers dressed as Ethiopian prisoners of war. The supers were drawn from a list of around five hundred names kept on file by rehearsal director Jules Judels. To simplify the fitting of wigs and costumes, and to keep rehearsal requirements to a minimum, the same supers were reengaged, at the standard fee of one dollar a performance, whenever possible. One longtime subscriber and his wife regularly gave away their seven-dollar orchestra seats whenever they had the opportunity to "carry a spear." (The expression was used whether or not a spear was actually carried.)

Backgrounds of the supers were, if anything, even more varied than those of the ushers, except that the Metropolitan was somewhat cool toward college undergraduates. Aimé Gerber said that this was an attitude going back to the days of Grau and Conried. A group of undergraduates, costumed as Brabantian nobles, had once been so carried away by Nordica's singing of *Einsam in trüben Tagen* that they had spontaneously burst into a Yale football yell during the first act of *Lohengrin*.

N. L. Lamzilotti, head of the wardrobe department, and wardrobe mistress Jennie Cervini moved among choristers and supers, checking costumes to make sure that each fitted properly and was in good repair. Costumes for choristers and supers were supplied by the Metropolitan. Principal artists usually had their own. The principals' costumes, too, however, were kept at the opera house. No costume was ever put away after a rehearsal or performance until it had been cleaned and, if necessary, repaired, ready for use again at a moment's notice. In the sewing room, half a dozen expert dressmakers sat at their machines all day, working on the costumes that came in every night.

Makeup artist Senz (he usually dispensed with his given name, which was Adolf) had begun his evening's work by sending backstage a large tray filled with wigs and beards, numbered to correspond with the numbers on the dressing-room tables. Each wig would be collected after the performance, cleaned and recurled next day. An hour before curtain time, Senz, carrying a doctor's black bag equipped with false eyelashes, spirit gum, wax, rubber cement, powder, rouge, cold cream and greasepaint of every conceivable shade, began making the rounds to give final touches to makeup, and approve the adjustment and dressing of wigs.

Property master Philip Crispano and his assistants were making an inventory, with the aid of the *Aida* "prop book," to be sure that all the spears, royal chariots, palm leaves and other needed furnishings were on hand. To an outsider, the distinction between scenery, props and costumes sometimes seemed arbitrary and perplexing. In *Aida*, for example, the platform for the King's throne was scenery and was set up by stage-hands; the throne itself was a prop. The King's sword and crown were props; his robe and mantle were parts of his costume. For the technicians concerned, however, such distinctions were among the few true verities of life.

In the locker room under the stage, adjoining the orchestra pit — known as "Fiddlers' Alley" — the musicians were changing from street clothes to evening dress. A few of the brass players had already gone into the pit to warm up their instruments. Brass instruments, French horns in particular, can be unreliable and out of tune when they are cold. Librarian Lionel Mapleson and two assistants had placed the orchestral full score on the conductor's desk and distributed to the various music stands the proper parts for the night's performance.

On the stage, above it and below it, master electrician Jacob Buchter and members of his twenty-two-man staff were going over lighting cues and special effects that would be needed. Until the Metropolitan, in 1934, installed an automated control panel that was said to be surpassed in complexity only by that at Radio City Music Hall, all lights were manually operated by technicians in various parts of the house, and coordinated by telephoned signals from Buchter. A rough rule of thumb was that on the immense Metropolitan stage an effect which in the ordinary theatre could be achieved with two spotlights would call for twelve.

Backstage, the callboy began making his rounds with increasing frequency, tapping at doors to announce: "Ten minutes before the overture," "Five minutes before the overture" and, finally, "Curtain going up." Performers were effectually isolated from the actual sound of the music by soundproof doors and the building's thick walls. Five minutes before a performer was due to step onstage, the callboy would appear with the announcement: "We are ready for you, Madame."

The space in the wings was becoming crowded with Egyptian courtiers, soldiers and spade-bearded priests. The prompter, carrying a copy of the piano-vocal score, wedged his way from beneath the stage into the prompter's box. Its circular metal hood fitted over his head like the cockpit-canopy of a fighter plane. Ahead and slightly to the left of the canopy he placed an automobile rearview mirror on a tripod, with which to watch the conductor beating time behind him.

Prompters beat time and talk continuously during a performance, delivering lines a moment or two before they are to be sung. Timing is all-important. So is experience and a cool head; when an ensemble goes sour, it is mainly up to the prompter to retrieve it, blocking out this singer and throwing cues to that one until order is restored. While the conductor sets the tempo, it is the prompter's beat that most singers actually follow. When singers first come onstage, one can nearly always see the whites of their eyes flash as they look to make sure the prompter is there. Prompters talk in a conversational tone, making no effort to keep their voices down. The canopy carries the sound of their voices upstage, away from the audience.

The house lights went down. Conductor Moranzoni, in white tie and tails, entered the orchestra pit by the narrow door through which he would return some time later, dripping with sweat and with his starched shirt as limp as a dishcloth. The Prelude began. At its conclusion the stage manager, standing just inside the proscenium, picked up a brass speaking-tube and ordered the curtain raised. The great gold curtains parted, disclosing Martinelli as Radames and José Mardones as the high priest Ramfis.

"*Si, corre voce*," said the prompter. "*Si, corre voce*," sang Mardones. His first note coincided exactly with the conductor's beat and the stab of the prompter's forefinger.

It was a typical Metropolitan *Aida*, well cast, well sung, and well received by a typical Metropolitan audience. One detail, however, might have surprised many in the audience if they had been able to see it. Above the Metropolitan stage was a "paint bridge," eight feet wide and seventy feet long, running clear across the stage at the fourth-floor level.

It had no railings; these would have interfered with painting the canvas scenery that was hung on either side of the bridge. As the Egyptian drama unfolded on the stage, Joseph Novak, chief scenic artist of the Metropolitan, oblivious to the performance taking place four stories below, was touching up the scenery to be used in a forthcoming *Tosca*.

23

Romance

WHEN GATTI FIRST WENT to the Metropolitan, another newcomer was the soprano Frances Alda. After a two-year courtship, carried on in the midst of his struggles to ease Dippel out and to bring order to the Metropolitan's rather slipshod administration, Gatti married her at the close of the 1909–1910 season. One reason given by Alda for marrying was that after an appendectomy followed by a long convalescence, for the first time in her life she felt alone.

They were an odd pair. Gatti's aloofness, his flowing beard and his aura of faint melancholy made the difference in their years seem greater than it was. "I do not talk very much," Gatti said of himself, "and I never discuss my affairs."

Alda, by contrast, was a vivacious New Zealander with red hair and a temper to match. That she could be witty is shown in her memoirs, *Men, Women and Tenors*; but the witticisms often carried a sting. When Giuseppe de Luca sang his fiftieth-anniversary performance at Town Hall, Alda, then, like de Luca, in her seventies, was called on to present the testimonial. Catty to the last, Alda paid de Luca the left-handed compliment of saying that while his artistry had been justly admired, his voice had never been remarkable for power or brilliance.

Soon after she married Gatti, the bride overheard Otto Kahn telling a fellow director that, as the general manager's wife, it would be better if Alda did not appear with the company the following season.

"If I were his mistress instead of his wife, I suppose it would be all right," Alda told the embarrassed Kahn. She informed Gatti she was resigning immediately.

Alda did not appear at the Metropolitan during the 1910–1911 season, although she sang a number of performances in Boston. But prima donnas do not give up that easily. In 1911–1912, Alda returned to the company, and appeared regularly thereafter until her final performance on December 28, 1929.

During the 1914–1915 season, a new ballerina, Rosina Galli, joined the Metropolitan. As a precocious youngster she had begun her career at La Scala while Gatti was still director there. At the age of six, with only three months' study, she had been given a featured role in a ballet called *Meissen Porcelain.*

"After this," said Gatti, "she was always considered a little celebrity, the youngest and tiniest of the company. It is perhaps the only case of a little dancer still in school who never danced in an ensemble with the other children. She was always given special consideration and some kind of little role. The other ballet girls were naturally jealous of this child, since she attracted and held the attention and favor of the public."

At the Metropolitan, too, Galli was given "special consideration." When, on the death of Pauline Verhoeven, Galli was named *première danseuse* and ballet mistress, she became one of two Metropolitan artists with a dressing room of her own. (The other was Farrar.) To complete the picture of a prima donna, Galli owned a poodle. The dog was jealous of her dancing and would bark until she stopped.

A superb artist, Galli was also imperious and exacting. Once she was inspecting the costumes for a new ballet. Each costume had a small rose-colored flower on one shoulder. Although she had previously approved the costumes, Galli decided the color of the flowers was not right. Immediately she began ripping the flowers from the costumes. When the flowers were replaced, Galli was mollified. Metropolitan staff members could detect no difference in the colors.

When "Captain" Edgar, the Fortieth Street doorman, arrived for work in the morning, on his way to the opera house he would stop at a florist's in Pennsylvania Station to buy a rose for a boutonniere. Later, Galli, entering the house, would remove the rose from the Captain's lapel, destroy it petal by petal and trample the petals underfoot.

Frances Alda

Although the Captain was a flower-lover, he pretended to be amused by this byplay. The Metropolitan's people had learned that it did not pay to cross Galli. A backstage technician whose attitude struck Galli as uncooperative received a ferocious scolding from Gatti-Casazza and was told that Madame Galli's wishes were to be carried out exactly and immediately.

The Metropolitan, which like all opera houses swirled with intrigue and gossip, soon had a new rumor in circulation. It was no secret that Gatti and Alda were at odds; they were no longer living as man and wife. Now, it appeared, the void in Gatti-Casazza's life was being filled by Rosina Galli. The relationship developing between the Metropolitan's general manager and its *première danseuse* became the talk of the opera house.

Reversing the usual procedure, Galli began sending flowers to Gatti-Casazza. She either did not know or did not care that Gatti disliked cut flowers. He told Ziegler that he was superstitious about them; they reminded him of funerals. The place for flowers, said Gatti, was in fields and gardens. Nevertheless, he accepted meekly the floral displays that continued to arrive, to the huge delight and amusement of the Metropolitan staff.

The last of Galli's gifts dissolved the opera house in a roar of merriment. Four deliverymen appeared, staggering under the weight of an earth-filled tub. It contained a pink dogwood tree, tall enough to reach the ceiling of Gatti's office, and blooming out of season.

That day everyone in the building found an excuse to walk past Gatti's office to look at the dogwood tree.

"Within a week," said Helen Noble, "the steam heat began to wither it. Perhaps even Gatti's private remarks — in Italian — helped to break its spirit. The tree and the huge tub which held it disappeared one night, to be seen no more."

Abruptly the flowers stopped arriving. Presumably they had served their purpose. Gatti and Alda were divorced in 1929, and at the end of the 1929–1930 season, Gatti married Rosina Galli.

Gatti's divorce and remarriage were to have far-reaching consequences. Although divorce during the Twenties no longer carried the social stigma it had had before World War I, it was still strongly disapproved of by many of the leaders of society who were influential in Metropolitan affairs.

In addition, some directors felt that Gatti had made himself — and therefore the Metropolitan — faintly ridiculous by marrying a woman so many years his junior. Eventually, Gatti's remarriage would prove to be one of the factors that brought about the end of his long regime.

For the time being, however, Gatti's domestic affairs had to take second place. There were more urgent problems at hand.

24

The Crash

On Monday, October 28, 1929, the Metropolitan season opened with *Manon Lescaut*. Singing Manon was Lucrezia Bori, who had made her debut in that role on opening night seventeen years before. Beniamino Gigli was Des Grieux, and de Luca, Lescaut. At an $8.25 top, the receipts set a new record for an opening night.

The event had all the usual pageantry of an opening night — a line of limousines drawing up at the Thirty-ninth Street entrance; subscribers alighting in top hats and ermine, ablaze with jewels, while a curious crowd gaped on the sidewalk; the lobby jammed with reporters and blue with smoke from the magnesium flares used by photographers in the days before flashbulbs.

Despite the traditional opening-night glitter, however, many were undoubtedly too preoccupied to give their full attention to Puccini's music. On the previous Thursday, the stock market, which had been queasy since September, had had a sharp sinking spell. By eleven-thirty, an hour and a half after the start of trading, the ticker was running forty-eight minutes late. Prices were falling five and ten points at a time.

Rumors leaped from coast to coast that the market had collapsed. Telephone lines were clogged as brokers and investors tried to find out what was going on. To allay anxiety and to speed up the tape, the Big Board resorted to "flash printing" — i.e., a stock trading at $72\frac{1}{4}$ — $72\frac{1}{2}$ — $72\frac{3}{4}$ would be quoted as "$2\frac{1}{4}$ — $2\frac{1}{2}$ — $2\frac{3}{4}$." That, as it turned out, only added to the confusion; some stocks had dropped as much as thirty points by the time of their next appearance on the tape.

As news of the disaster spread, crowds began to gather on Wall Street. By noon, so many people had crammed themselves into the spectators' gallery of the Stock Exchange that officials ordered the gallery closed. Among those who pushed their way in was Winston Churchill, the future Prime Minister of England, on a visit to his mother's native city.

When the gong sounded to end the day's trading, Wall Street resembled an armed camp, with four hundred policemen on hand to prevent disorder. Brokers, sweat pouring down their faces, leaned against the trading posts and tried to find out how they stood. By the day's end, 12,900,000 shares had been traded. Four hours after the market's close, the ticker continued to print out prices. The closing quotations made traders wince. The market had suffered a debacle from which the most highly regarded stocks were not exempt. Auburn Motors had fallen from 260 to 190, Johns Manville from 180 to 140, Montgomery Ward from 84 to 50.

News that a group of leading bankers, meeting at the offices of J. P. Morgan & Company, had pledged $250,000,000 to stabilize the market, helped to steady prices on Friday and Saturday. The weekend, however, gave traders an opportunity for hard thinking about the market — some thought about it, perhaps, for the first time in their lives. Speculators operating on ten percent margin had already been wiped out. Now the market was showing that it was no respecter of persons, large or small. On Monday, 9,200,000 shares were traded, and the tape was three hours late. The drop in the averages was even more severe than Thursday's.

For Tuesday, October 29, the Metropolitan had scheduled *Die Meistersinger*, with Grete Stückgold as Eva, Rudolf Laubenthal as Walther, Clarence Whitehill as Hans Sachs, and Joseph Rosenstock making his debut as conductor. A more appropriate choice of an opera might have been *Die Götterdämmerung*. That morning, within thirty minutes of the market's opening, it was evident that the day would be the worst in Wall Street history.

By the time the trading session ended, securities had lost $14,000,000,-000 in values, and 16,400,000 shares had been traded. The market would not match that volume until April 1, 1968, following President Johnson's announcement of his decision not to run for reelection. Stewart Warner and Goodyear had each lost 16 points; Westinghouse, 19; General Electric and American Telephone & Telegraph, 28. The American Exchange had been hit even harder: Gulf Oil was down 20¾, People's Drug, 30¼; Aluminum Company of America, 74¼.

In the midst of the general disaster, a personal calamity was that of Joseph Rosenstock. After reading the reviews of his *Meistersinger*, it is said, he decided not to unpack his steamer trunk. After a few more Metropolitan performances, he departed for Europe and a career that took him around the world and eventually brought him back to the Metropolitan.

Bravely, the Metropolitan attempted to continue business as usual while the market slide went on — not as melodramatically as on October 29, but in a slow, steady, relentless attrition. After eight weeks of panic selling, the averages had fallen 147 points, and two years of bull-market profits had been erased. Surely the market had touched rock bottom? The sad fact was that the decline had hardly begun.

United States Steel and other corporations declared extra dividends; John J. Raskob and other business leaders asserted that stocks were bargains and that now was the time to buy; newspapers printed optimistic headlines. The market paid no attention.

In November, John D. Rockefeller announced that he and his son had placed an order for 1,000,000 shares of Standard Oil of New Jersey, at the market price of 50. Before the crash, "J" had sold for 83. In the next twelve months, it went from 50 to 43. By April, 1932, it stood at 19¾.

It was a time that seared the very souls of those who watched the market going down, down, down and America's mighty industrial empire collapsing in ruins. Jeweled and top-hatted Metropolitan subscribers cringed as they drove past breadlines in the very shadow of the opera house. A whole generation of bright young college graduates bypassed Wall Street in favor of more rational employment. And in the 1950's, when the market began heating up again, a quip going around the boardrooms was: "Nobody over thirty-five is making any money in this market — the psychological obstacle is too great."

America of course was no stranger to financial crises. The Panic of 1837 had been touched off in large measure by President Jackson, out of sheer spite against Nicholas Biddle and his Bank of the United States. It was obvious that the Specie Circular, requiring payment for government lands only in gold or silver, would force the "country" banks to draw on

New York, Boston and Philadelphia, which in turn would draw on London. Gold began leaving the Bank of England, and Bank rate was put up until it sucked gold back across the ocean like a transatlantic vacuum cleaner. Seven lean years followed; but the covered wagons never stopped rolling westward, and at the head of Lake Superior was discovered the fabulous Mesabi ore deposit that gave the nation world leadership in iron and steel.

The failure of overextended Jay Cooke & Company set off a chain reaction that became the Panic of 1873; but Russell Sage, Hetty Green, Commodore Vanderbilt and others who had seen the pinch coming and had taken care to maintain liquidity reaped handsome profits. And the recovery from the panic led to the era of open-handed, confident prosperity that created the Metropolitan Opera.

The disaster that began in 1929 was different. It was a crisis of confidence, in which faith in old values and beliefs was shaken. Many Americans, especially among the nation's intellectual leaders, felt that in the crash Karl Marx's melodramatic prediction of the capitalistic system's downfall was being all too accurately confirmed. Few placed the blame for the market break squarely where it belonged: on the orgy of speculation that had gone on in every part of the country. Some baleful unseen influence must have been at work. "They" were behind it; there was something wrong with "the system."

Herbert Hoover, who was one of the ablest men of his time in everything he undertook except in being President of the United States at the particular time when he had the misfortune to be elected, and who was unlucky enough to occupy the White House from 1928 to 1932, believed the economy had been struck by multiple shock waves such as America had never experienced before. First of all was the excessive speculation against which Hoover, as Secretary of Commerce, had warned as early as 1926. He had battled with Governor Benjamin Strong of the Federal Reserve Bank of New York over the easy-money policies and low margin requirements that stoked the speculative fires.

The 1929 collapse confirmed Hoover's fears; by the spring of 1931, it began to appear that daylight was visible ahead. Then disaster struck from abroad. In 1925, Britain had resumed gold convertibility of sterling at $4.86 to the pound. It was an unrealistic rate; the postwar exchange had dipped as low as $3.60. But it corresponded to the rate fixed by Sir Isaac

The elder J. P. Morgan addressing a photographer

*August Belmont the younger (left) and Otto Kahn at the funeral
of Morgan partner Henry P. Davidson*

Newton when that great scientist brought his intelligence to bear on the problems of the foreign exchanges. Rather than devalue the pound, the British had undergone frightful financial hardships in the Napoleonic wars and World War I; Dr. Hjalmar Schacht, in *Die Stabilisierung der mark*, his book on the postwar monetary chaos in Germany, spoke admiringly of British "tax-heroism" *("Steuerheroismus")*.

The prewar rate of exchange, however, could not be maintained, and in 1931, Great Britain went off the gold standard. That same year, Germany and Austria announced the formation of a customs union. With the Austro-Hungarian Empire dismembered by the Treaty of Versailles, what was left of Austria resembled a head without a torso. Its best hope of survival was in economic union with Germany. But political separation of Germany and Austria had been a keystone of the Versailles Treaty. England and France saw the customs union as a step toward repudiation of the treaty and declared it would not be permitted. To emphasize the point, the French called short-term loans made to various German and Austrian banks. Vienna's great Kredit-Anstalt collapsed, sending shock waves throughout Central Europe and, eventually, around the world.

America was vulnerable to such shocks because of the anarchy of its banking system. There were too many banks — 25,000 of them in 1929. There were fifty-one different regulatory systems; one for Federal Reserve banks, one for national banks and one each for the forty-eight states and the District of Columbia. As a further safeguard, the Federal Reserve System had been created along lines that had worked well in Britain, where bank failures were practically unheard-of, and on the Continent. But a central bank can manage the money supply only if it has centralized authority. There was widespread hostility against the Federal Reserve. Its system of universal free clearings meant loss of income for "country" banks, which cleared checks for their correspondent banks and charged a fee for doing so. In addition, those who, especially in the South and West, clung to the notion that states possessed states' rights resented the Federal Reserve as one more indication of the concentration of power in Eastern seaboard cities. In 1929, only one-third of the nation's banks were included in the Federal Reserve System. A number of states passed laws making it illegal for banks to join. Not until the shakeout of 1933–1934 was the "Fed" able to demonstrate, in a quiet way, who was boss.

It is fascinating to wonder whether Franklin D. Roosevelt, had he been President from 1928 to 1932, would have restored confidence by sheer bluff and nerve. Certainly it was beyond the power of Hoover, who saw all too clearly the extent of the disaster and in his public statements made no attempt to minimize it. He said he never made the inane prophecy often attributed to him, that prosperity was just around the corner.

Hoover was a businessman, closely identified with the business community, and when the depression was laid at his doorstep, business suffered, too. The businessman had been the American glamor figure. His opinions were sought on all kinds of topics and heard with respect. Henry Seidel Canby said that in the small Delaware town of his boyhood, if ratings had been given to citizens, they might have gone like this: a radical thinker — E; a musician, painter or other bohemian type — D; an inventor, scientist or journalist — C; a successful salesman — B; a first-rate businessman, with all that implied —A+.

But the depression was able to do what the muckrakers were not. After 1933, anyone who used the phrase "captains of industry" did so with an ironic smile.

For the Metropolitan, and for the country as a whole, it was the end of an era, called by some historians the Era of Finance Capitalism, during which, whatever else might be said about it, the dollar had been quite literally as good as gold. Now the shadows of the depression began to lengthen across the nation, and they cast a pall on the Metropolitan Opera and Real Estate Company along with everything else.

25

On the Air

IN THE TWENTIES, radio was America's newest toy. Amateurs listened through headphones over home-built crystal sets and joked about sitting up late and getting Chile. A few pioneering stations were on the air, like KDKA in Pittsburgh and WLW in Cincinnati, but radio's potential as an audience-getter and money-maker was not dreamed of. Even so astute a pioneer as David Sarnoff, at thirty-nine the "boy wonder" president of the Radio Corporation of America, thought that radio's greatest value would be for communication between ships at sea, or in similar situations where telephone lines could not be installed. He did, however, circulate a memorandum that became famous, forecasting the use of radio for home entertainment.

In New York, station WEAF, as a means of filling air time cheaply, had hired a young tenor with operatic aspirations, named Milton Cross. On August 28, 1922, a realtor in Jackson Heights placed a commercial on station WEAF. His office was swamped; Milton Cross's singing and story-telling had drawn a listening audience running to many thousands.

At about the same time, William S. Paley of Philadelphia, whose family made La Palina cigars, bought air time on the shaky Columbia Broadcasting System that concert manager Arthur Judson had launched, primarily as a new outlet for his concert artists. In six weeks, La Palina sales doubled. Paley and other businessmen were astute enough to recognize an effective new advertising medium when they saw one, and the gold rush was on. By 1931, CBS had a coast-to-coast network, the National Broadcasting

213

Company had two, Mutual was scrambling for whatever was left and radio was a firmly established national institution.

In its Sunday afternoon Philharmonic broadcasts, CBS had a prestigious series. Merlin H. ("Deacon") Aylesworth, the president of NBC, was determined to get the Metropolitan Opera as a counterattraction.

Gatti was hesitant. While individual Metropolitan artists by now were performing frequently on the radio, giving it the same sort of artistic respectability that Caruso gave recording in its early days, they did not represent the Metropolitan Opera as such. Gatti feared that the dignity of his company would suffer from association with the frivolous new medium that played host to Amos 'n' Andy and the A & P Dance Gypsies, and that the quality of sound reproduction would be poor.

To convince Gatti on the latter point, NBC sent engineer Charles Grey to the opera house to broadcast a forthcoming performance of *Madama Butterfly*. On three days' notice, with no time to study the house and its acoustics, Grey set up his "portable" equipment ("In those days, anything that didn't weigh over a hundred fifty pounds was considered portable," Grey recalled) in Box 44 of the Grand Tier. The first broadcast was private; it went via telephone line to the boardroom of NBC's old headquarters at 711 Fifth Avenue (Radio City was still in the planning stage) and was heard by Gatti, Aylesworth and other NBC officials, and members of the Metropolitan conducting staff.

Soon after the broadcast got under way, a light flashed on Grey's control panel to indicate that his telephone was ringing.

"They say they want a little more orchestra and a little less voices," Aylesworth told him.

Grey turned volume-control knobs up and down. Presently Aylesworth called again.

"Now they want more voices and less orchestra," he said.

Grey complied, feeling a bit like the man in the country-club shower who can't get quite the proper blend of hot and cold water. Another call from Aylesworth, however, brought good news.

"You've done it!" the Deacon said. "We're putting the opera on the air."

It developed that Gatti had not quite believed that by turning black knobs up and down, the balance of orchestra and voices could be controlled at will.

Now Gatti was convinced, and gave the project his blessing. The first broadcast of a Metropolitan Opera performance took place on the afternoon of Christmas Day, 1931. The opera was Humperdinck's *Hänsel und Gretel*, with Editha Fleischer as Hansel, Queena Mario as Gretel and Dorothee Manski as the Witch. Vincenzo Bellezza conducted.

On that occasion, as on all subsequent broadcasts until the interior of the house was rebuilt in 1940, the broadcasters sat in Box 44 of the Grand Tier, in the midst of a jumble of wires, cables and portable broadcasting equipment.

Grey and Deems Taylor, the commentator for the broadcast, were in the box proper. Looking over their shoulders was Milton Cross, seated at a microphone in the cloakroom behind the box. He was to be the announcer not only for the opening broadcast, but for every subsequent performance emanating from the house.

The historic *Hänsel und Gretel* broadcast went out over the largest network that had ever been put together. The performance was carried by the full Red and Blue Networks of NBC, and beamed by shortwave to the British Broadcasting Corporation and the Canadian and Australian networks.

The response to the broadcast was tremendous. Grey was told that in case of a conflict in his schedule, the Metropolitan was to have priority over everything else.

The new medium of broadcasting brought new problems. Singers quickly discovered where the microphones were located and tried to maneuver close to them for their big arias. Those overly successful at this new form of upstaging were called "mike hogs." They might have saved themselves the trouble; Grey simply turned microphones up or down to keep the voices in balance.

That was only one of the problems for which solutions evolved on a trial-and-error basis as the broadcasts continued. Long after the remodeled Metropolitan had been equipped with a properly fitted-out broadcasting booth, NBC old-timers looked back to the days of Box 44 with a sort of awed disbelief. Radio in those days centered in the studio microphone, about which the performers were grouped in the best position for sound reproduction. Outside the studio, a mobile-unit pickup, or "nemo,"* attempted to duplicate studio conditions insofar as possible, and in addition might utilize special gadgets such as the "parabolic" microphones that brought the sound of marching bands closer at football games.

Box 44, however, was used by regular subscribers at five performances a week. The complex tangle of cables, wires, amplifiers and control panels had to be dismantled and stored in an unused freight elevator after every broadcast. The placement of microphones could not interfere with the scenery or performers in any way. Nor could the occupants of Box 44 distract other operagoers, the nearest of whom were seated practically at their elbows.

It was under these difficult circumstances that Grey "rode gain" on an unusually complex monitoring operation. Microphones in those days were highly directional and covered only a limited range; the days when the sound of a big ensemble would be brilliantly reproduced by a single Telefunken microphone suspended above it were still in the future. Of the eight microphones concealed in the footlights and hanging from above, as many as three or four might be in use at once, depending on the vocal-instrumental balance and the location of performers on the stage.

Since control-panel lights had to be inconspicuous, Grey devised notched control knobs that could be operated by touch. Organist-producer Herbert Liversidge, seated next to him, followed the score of the opera under a hooded lamp, warning by means of hand signals when a big crescendo that would require turning down the volume was on its way. Announcer Milton Cross and his guests were soundproofed behind the glass door of the box.

Established broadcasting procedure was violated at every turn. It was found that the sound not only traveled outward but also was reflected upward from the stage; the quality of the broadcasts improved when the overhead microphones were suspended upside-down. The angle at which footlight microphones were placed was adjusted to suit the size and shape of the stage sets and the expected location of the singers. Even with the most careful planning, however, there could be surprises, as when a per-

---

* Nobody seems to know where this odd expression, now also used in television, came from; possibly from Jules Verne's Captain Nemo.

former who had turned stage left at rehearsal turned right in the actual performance.

To avoid possible interference from the Metropolitan's own electrical circuits, the broadcasting equipment was not connected to the opera house in any way. It was grounded to a water main in West Thirty-ninth Street, and the cables that ran through the opera house and up to Box 44 derived power from their own generators under the stage. For every piece of equipment there was a duplicate held in reserve, including a standby amplifier warmed up and ready to go. If a power failure had darkened the opera house, the broadcast could have continued without interruption as long as there was anything to broadcast.

Deems Taylor, anxious to make the broadcasts as enjoyable as possible for the widest possible audience, puzzled over how to surmount the language barrier. He felt that a sketchy summary of the plot would do scant justice to the drama, while a lengthy one would be difficult for listeners to keep in mind during the half hour or more of a typical act of opera. He therefore decided to summarize the plot briefly in advance, then give a running translation of the text as it was being sung.

This plan was shelved when NBC and the Metropolitan began to receive complaints that "some idiot keeps talking" during the broadcast.

From the first, filling the lengthy intermissions during the broadcast was a problem. Intermissions at the Metropolitan customarily ran about half an hour. The usual, if not correct, explanation was that the patrons of Sherry's Restaurant could hardly be served in less time. (Actually, because of the primitive conditions backstage, they needed every minute of an intermission to change a set.)

During the early seasons, Geraldine Farrar came out of retirement to serve as intermission commentator. She described opera plots and played excerpts of the music on a small piano wedged into the cloakroom of Box 44. It was the special midget piano Steinway had made for her private railroad car.

Since *Information Please* was one of the most popular radio programs, the Metropolitan set out to develop a quiz program of its own. It was not easy, however, to find a quizmaster as urbane as Clifton Fadiman, or panelists as lively as John Kieran, Oscar Levant and Franklin P. Adams.

Eventually the right choice turned out to be Edward Downes, whose wonderful broadcasting voice radiated geniality, erudition and a Harvard accent.

A dramatic moment was shared by radio listeners during the broadcast of *Aida* on February 26, 1938. On the previous day, Giovanni Martinelli, who sang Radames, had dined with a friend in the Bronx on shrimps and beer. (Milton Cross later mentioned that fact on the air, to the great dismay of the seafood industry.) Martinelli arrived at the opera house feeling unwell, but not wishing to cancel at the last moment, tried to sing the performance. After a few phrases, *Celeste Aida* died out in incoherent gurglings.

At the Metropolitan switchboard, Irene Barry heard the debacle over the house intercommunication system that was always turned on during a performance. Her mind began making calculations as rapidly as any digital computer. No matter what was wrong on the stage, another tenor was needed in a hurry. Who was in town and not singing somewhere else? She dialed the always dependable Frederick Jagel. He was at home, but about to take his two sons to the zoo. Barry told him to come down to the opera house instead; there would be plenty of baby-sitters for the boys.

Jagel leaped into a taxi, hurried into his costume and, within thirty minutes of Martinelli's collapse, the performance was under way again. In Box 44, Milton Cross mopped his forehead. Cross, who hated ad-libbing, had just spent one of the most uncomfortable half hours of his broadcasting career.

Another broadcasting highlight occurred when Jeritza, taking a curtain call with Gigli, felt the tenor had taken more than his share of the limelight. When they went offstage, Jeritza kicked his shins. Gigli slapped her. Jeritza, in tears, went before the gold curtain again to confide to audience and radio listeners: "Mr. Gigli has not been kind to me."

A clause in the contract for the Metropolitan broadcasts stipulated that if a matinee should conflict with a Rose Bowl game, the opera would not be presented "live" but would be recorded for later broadcast. Once this happened when Lily Pons was singing the title role in *Lucia*. Noel Straus, covering for the *Times*, reported that Pons had sung the first E flat of the Mad Scene badly but had redeemed herself with the second.

The Straus review appeared in the Sunday *Times*, which is circulated nationally, and Straus soon began to receive letters from all over the country, upbraiding him for his "unfair" review. Astonished — he had heard the performance with his own ears — Straus investigated. He found that the engineers had re-recorded the good E flat and spliced it into the tape to replace the bad one. That was what the indignant radio listeners had heard. Straus said it was the sneakiest thing he had ever heard of.

The Metropolitan Opera *Auditions of the Air* gave the Metropolitan still another radio link to the nation at large. And Leonard Warren, Eleanor Steber, Frank Guarrera and other gifted Americans joined the company as a result.

Gossip buzzed during the 1938 auditions, won by Warren and tenor John Carter. A picture on the society page of the *Journal-American* showed Carter sitting in a box at the opera. The caption identified him as "this year's winner of the Metropolitan Opera Auditions of the Air." At that time, not only had the winners not been officially announced; the auditions were still going on. Carter did win, eventually, and sang at the Metropolitan for several seasons, though his success did not match that of his baritone co-winner.

One of the first questions that naturally arose in connection with the opera broadcasts was: Is anybody listening? It was taken for granted that the audience was, by radio standards, relatively small. Opera in the United States could hardly be said to exist outside New York City. It was exotic entertainment presented in a foreign language, staggeringly expensive to produce, and having the deadly connotations of being "intellectual" and "highbrow." Where people went was to the movies, which were cheap and universally accessible.

In the early stages, any opinion about the opera-broadcast audience was largely guesswork. Audience measurement, hardly an exact science even today, was then in a very rudimentary state. NBC did, however, maintain a correspondence department which replied to listeners' queries and requests for autographed photos. The volume of mail, with certain qualifications, served as a rough index of popularity. One qualification was the discovery that, all else being equal, a program that was generally disapproved would draw about fifteen times the mail of a popular success. Presumably, then, people were fifteen times as quick to complain if they didn't like something as to praise if they did.

When the Saturday matinee broadcasts began bringing opera into people's living rooms, making it even cheaper and more accessible than the movies, NBC's correspondence department began receiving queries of a sort it had never seen before. Where could one purchase opera librettos, and how much did they cost? Could not the Metropolitan announce its schedule longer than a week in advance? Where could one get information about Metropolitan singers? What was the best book of opera plots?

Another type of letter might be signed by the president or secretary of, for example, the Saturday Matinee Opera Club of Council Bluffs. If all thirty-five of the club's members purchased librettos, would that entitle them to a special rate? Where could one obtain a bibliography of good solid material — music history, biography, descriptive analyses — for the benefit of members whose turn it was to lead the discussion that preceded (or followed) the opera broadcast?

Before long, the very special opera-broadcast audience was to give an even more striking proof of its existence.

In 1940, when the hard-pressed Metropolitan was obliged to make a public appeal for funds, it was primarily the radio audience to whom it turned for help. The response was immediate and heartwarming. In donations of one dollar, five dollars and ten dollars, more than a third of a million dollars was contributed by radio listeners. Many of them had little reasonable expectation of ever attending a Metropolitan performance in person; but radio had made the Metropolitan a part of their lives.

To aid the fund drive, NBC launched an essay contest. Listeners were invited to send in their thoughts on "What the Metropolitan Opera Broadcasts Mean to Me" — accompanied, of course, by a contribution. The contest winners were brought to New York at NBC's expense, installed at the Waldorf-Astoria and taken on a round of entertainment climaxed by the opening night of the 1940–1941 season. The winners were a cross section of America: a welder from Oregon, two telephone operators from the Midwest, a schoolteacher from Georgia, a small-town New England merchant — all with the common denominator of loving opera, and the Metropolitan in particular.

Another development took place in 1940, when the broadcasts for the first time acquired a long-term sponsor. Until then, NBC had had little success in selling the opera. Saturday afternoon was not prime time, and the Blue Network in those days was the "dog" which carried shows for which space could not be found on the Red. The opera had been sponsored briefly by Lucky Strike, Listerine and RCA. The latter, since NBC was a subsidiary of RCA, was merely transferring the money from one pocket to another.

At about that time, the Texas Company had come under heavy fire in the press for doing business with the Axis nations. It was perfectly legal, since the United States was not then at war; but in view of the political climate of the time, the discovery was unfortunate for Texaco. Shrewd, mustached Benjamin Sonnenberg was Texaco's public relations counsel. He felt the situation required the company to perform a lavish, large-scale public service of some kind. By a happy coincidence, Sonnenberg also represented NBC. Texaco's sponsorship of the opera broadcasts was practially a foregone conclusion.

Texaco proved to be an admirable sponsor. Its commercials were kept to a minimum and were models of brevity and dignity. To give the intermission features a professional touch, Texaco engaged producer Henry Souvaine and, later, Souvaine's widow, Geraldine.

When word reached NBC that the Texaco contract was in the house, there was a universal sigh of relief. It was known that "Uncle Dave" (he was not yet General Sarnoff) had passed the word that if the Blue Network carried the opera one more season "on sustaining," the network would get a whole new sales department.

To impress the new advertiser, NBC's Press Department exerted itself to the limit. The news releases and other mailings that announce a newly launched program were followed up by personal calls to editors, reporters and radio columnists; a news release doesn't mean a thing until it gets in the paper. Wires were pulled, pressures exerted, friendships strained. NBC men strove in particular to get the press to violate its taboo on naming advertisers by referring to the "Texaco–NBC Metropolitan Opera broadcasts."

The hard-fought battle raged all summer, and at its close the NBC men could look on their handiwork with satisfaction. The newspaper and magazine clippings were mounted in scrapbooks bound in blue leather, on

221

which was stamped in gold letters "Texaco–NBC Metropolitan Opera Broadcasts." A deputation from the press gang took the scrapbooks to a cloud-high suite of offices in the Chrysler Building.

The executive concerned admired the handsome volumes. Then he opened one. His face darkened. "What's this?" he asked.

Apprehension filled the NBC group. Perhaps, if they had tried just a little harder . . .

"These are newspaper clippings," the executive said. "I wanted to see the publicity."

For a moment the NBC men were stunned. When they had recovered, they went back to Radio City, collected several trunkfuls of the mimeographed press handouts that had been mailed, and sent them to the Chrysler Building. The executive was happy.

26

The Press

OF ALL THE CRITICS who reviewed the first Metropolitan opening night in 1883, W. J. Henderson lived longest. He committed suicide on June 5, 1937, at the age of eighty-two. One of his last reviews was of Gian-Carlo Menotti's first opera, *Amelia Goes to the Ball*. His review concluded: "It is very probable that Mr. Menotti will be heard from again."

A famous Henderson witticism resulted from the frequency with which the Metropolitan performed *Faust* in its early seasons. Henderson pictured a New Zealander, far in the future, wandering through the excavations of Manhattan Island. "They will pause at the ruins of a vast arena on upper Broadway, and the New Zealander will say, 'I suppose this was the arena.' The guide will reply, 'No, it was the sacred Faustspielhaus.' The New Zealander, knowing German, will say, 'You mean Festspielhaus, don't you?' And the guide will answer, 'No, honored sir, the Festspielhaus was in Germany, where they played dramas by one Vogner. Here, they played *Faust*, and it is, therefore, the Faustspielhaus.' And the New Zealander will marvel greatly."

Henderson in his later years was a lean old Yankee who appeared more like a prosperous New England farmer than a musician. He was utterly without affectation and liked to describe himself as "just a reporter with a specialty." In the summer, as a change of pace, he reported on yacht racing.

Henderson lived in a hotel in the Times Square district. He was driven from his hotel to the concert halls by a chauffeur in a big black limousine. Back in his hotel room, he would dash off his review in twenty or thirty minutes and a messenger would deliver it to the *Sun* office on lower Broadway.

Henderson's colleagues deferred to him because of his vast knowledge and experience. When he heard new singers, he compared them to Patti, Melba, Calvé and the de Reszke brothers. At intermission, Henderson's opinion would sometimes be sought by his colleagues, especially the younger men whose self-assurance was shaky. (Noel Straus once said that if people waited to learn everything they needed to know in order to be a capable music critic, no one would become a critic until he was seventy years old. Straus was then seventy-five.)

On such occasions, Henderson often tricked his fellow critics by delivering a set of preposterous opinions which were the reverse of what he actually thought, and which were promptly contradicted by his review next day.

The witty, urbane reviews of composer-critic Deems Taylor were a feature of the famous "page opposite editorial" in the *World*. Colleagues loved to recall a story about Taylor's early days as a newspaperman. He had been sent to review a performance by the brilliant but unpredictable pianist, Ethel Leginska. A few hours before concert time, Leginska experienced a sudden, uncontrollable desire to be alone. Without saying a word to her manager or anyone else, she boarded a bus and left town.

Next day every paper but the *World* had a story on the mysterious disappearance of Ethel Leginska. Herbert Bayard Swope, the *World's* irascible editor, called Taylor to find out what had happened.

"I don't know," Taylor replied. "I went to Carnegie Hall, but nobody showed up, so I came home again."

Samuel Chotzinoff, Taylor's successor on the *World*, had been accompanist for Efrem Zimbalist, Jascha Heifetz and other artists before turning to journalism, and had married Heifetz's sister.

Chotzinoff once became so engrossed in a gin-rummy game with his crony Ira Hirschmann that he forgot he was to review a concert by Leopold Stokowski and the Philadelphia Orchestra. At two A.M., he remembered the concert. After walking the floor in perplexity, he commenced his review.

"A mid-October cold kept me from attending the concert by Leopold

Stokowski and the Philadelphia Orchestra at Carnegie Hall last night,"
it began. "That, however, need not prevent me from writing about it."

The review went on to describe the audience arriving with "that ex-
pectant look the Philadelphia subscribers always have." Chotzinoff continued with the works chosen by the "king of program-makers," and how
he imagined Stokowski had played them — which, as it turned out, coincided quite closely with what had actually happened. His superiors at the
paper were too amused to scold him.

Lawrence Gilman of the *Herald Tribune* was a tall, ascetic-looking man
with a slightly husky speaking voice that was familiar to audiences of the
Sunday Philharmonic broadcasts, for which he was the commentator.
Gilman attended Metropolitan performances wearing a fur-collared overcoat, with plugs of cotton in his ears. On reaching his seat, he would remove his overcoat, bow ceremoniously to his colleagues, take out his ear-
plugs and listen with polite concentration. When he left the opera house,
the cotton plugs were again in place to shut out the sounds of the nonmusical world.

Robert A. Simon of the *New Yorker* was a large, amiable, soft-spoken
man who delivered pungent witticisms in a barely audible voice. Having
less space at his disposal than his newspaper colleagues, he was free to
pick and choose among the week's musical events. His usual rule of thumb
was that a performance did not qualify for his presence unless at least
fifty people were taking part. Consequently, he was likelier to be found at
the Metropolitan than anywhere else.

A gifted versifier and a believer in opera in English, Simon translated
numerous operas. One of his diversions was to set a phrase like "to finish
it" in such a way that the performer would be compelled to sing a four-
letter word on high B flat.

Simon was also a minor composer. He published a volume of *Bronx
Ballads*, with words and music by himself, together with a scholarly intro-
duction assessing the influence of Schubert on the Bronx and vice versa.
One of the ballads began:

> *Old Man Stein*
> *Had a daughter who was very fine*

> *In her own particular line,*
> *Which happened to be —*
> *Brain-*woik*!*

Simon was often accompanied to the Metropolitan by his young son, John, who pleased everyone with his gracious manners and his ability to remember people's names. Long afterward, when John Simon was editing the Harvard *Crimson*, his father was asked how the boy had acquired his Chesterfieldian polish at such an early age.

"It was easy," Simon replied. "When I took him to the opera, I promised him a dime for every person he spoke to."

Olin Downes of the *Times* loved to tell the story of how he got into the newspaper business. As a young man in Boston, he supported his musical studies by odd jobs that included playing the piano in a gymnasium for calisthenics, followed by "selections" for dancing. The piano, with a net to protect it from flying basketballs, was on a balcony, access to which was gained by means of a ladder. From time to time, a couple would dance to the foot of the ladder and call up: "Say, Professor, how about a turkey trot?"

In some way or other, Downes had gotten to know the editor of the Boston *Post*, whose drama critic also reviewed the opera. A big story was coming up in Geraldine Farrar's first Boston appearance after her sensational triumphs in Germany. When the editor quarreled with his drama critic, the editor — perhaps to show the critic how easily he could be replaced — offered young Downes the post of music critic.

In those days they did *Faust* in five acts, and Downes stayed to the end. It was past midnight when he left the theatre. He returned to his office in a horse-drawn trolley. It did not occur to him to take a cab and put it on his expense account; he did not know expense accounts existed.

At the office he found a state of pandemonium. The paper was late. On a stone in the composing room was the chase for Page One, with a gaping hole that contained only Downes's by-line and the headline FARRAR TRIUMPHS AS MARGUERITE IN 'FAUST'. The editor seized Downes by his lapels. "Where's the story?" he demanded.

"I — I haven't written it yet," said Downes. The editor wasted not a second in recrimination. He yelled across the city room to a rewrite man: "Hey, Joe, write a column of slush quick for the first edition!"

Slowly and painfully, Downes turned out his first review. "Writing, always difficult for me," said Downes, who always talked as if he were quoting from one of his own reviews, "was at that time well-nigh impossible."

Downes never did acquire facility; but in time he became a very able reporter and a highly esteemed critic. His discovery that Fritz Kreisler's "arrangements" of eighteenth-century masters were really his own compositions constituted a major "exclusive" for the *Times*. When the pianist Simon Barere died on the stage at Carnegie Hall, Downes rushed backstage to get a statement from the attending physician, obtained vital statistics and names of survivors, assessed Barere's artistic career and, best of all, put the whole package together in time to make the Late City Edition.

As a reviewer, Downes was almost painfully conscientious. He had been known to express one opinion in a review, change his mind after sleeping on it and take just the opposite position in his Sunday column.

Downes was tall and rather heavily built; when it was found necessary to repair the *Times* seat at the Metropolitan, the management facetiously threatened to bill the newspaper, on the grounds that Downes had sat the bottom out of it. For a big man, however, he was surprisingly agile, still playing a vigorous game of tennis in his fifties.

Downes played tennis as he did everything else, with fervor and conviction. His reactions were always vehement. What he liked, he liked enormously; what he disliked, he detested. Sitting across the chessboard from Downes was like being on the receiving end of a cavalry charge, with pawns surging forward, bishops slashing, knights galloping in all directions. If not unnerved by the fury of the opening attack, one could usually hold his own; Downes was an erratic player and sooner or later would make a mistake that nullified his gains. "If only I could learn to play carefully!" he would say at such times.

Because of his enormous zest, Downes escaped the *ennui* that sometimes oppressed his more jaded colleagues. George Bernard Shaw, speaking from firsthand experience, observed that critics would not go to concerts "when they are no longer paid for their soul-destroying sufferings." But after

227

forty years of reviewing, Downes retained his zeal and enthusiasm. Once the *Times* publisher, noting that his critics reviewed more or less the same operas and orchestral works over and over, expressed wonder that they could find anything new to say about them.

"Give me thirty great performances of the same work on thirty consecutive days," was Downes's rejoinder, "and I'll show you something new to say — that *demands* to be said — about every one of them."

Downes wrote slowly and laboriously, and his copy showed it. His style was ponderous, humorless but explicit. His infrequent attempts at humor or whimsy were generally unsuccessful, but readers always knew where he stood. His prose recalled what someone said of Theodore Dreiser's, that it was like some huge beast crashing through the jungle, trampling down the underbrush but leaving a well-marked trail for lesser animals to follow.

After writing, Downes would rewrite, until it was not clear whether the copy had been written in pencil and corrected with a typewriter or the other way around. On Thursdays, when his Sunday article was set up in type, he would rewrite it on the page. Downes's Sunday column could be spotted halfway across the composing room by the shiny type-metal of freshly inserted corrections.

By union rules, printers are not obliged to set anything they can't read; and the *Times* printers considered Downes a borderline case. Once the printers celebrated Downes's birthday by printing a poem for private circulation. After paying tribute to Downes's zeal, scholarship, integrity and so on, the poem concluded:

> *But when it comes to setting type,*
> *That Olin really Downes us!*

A trip to New Orleans brought back vivid memories of Noel Straus, who had written for the *Times-Picayune* before coming to the *Times*, and had interviewed Caruso during the tenor's last tour to Mexico and Havana in 1919.

There were the streets of the Nine Muses — Euterpe, Melpomene and so on — familiarity with which had made Straus so formidable an opponent in crossword-puzzle contests.

There was Saint Louis Cathedral, where the organist Marcel Dupré had improvised brilliantly on a fugue subject submitted by Straus. It was a subject on which Straus had been working for some time and whose possibilities he felt he had about exhausted. Dupré looked at the theme for several moments, then began to play. In that brief glance, he had seen that, by changing one note of the fugue subject, it would be possible to work up a tremendous concluding *stretto*, with the fugue subject appearing simultaneously in its original form, in diminution in the treble and in augmentation in the bass. (Later Dupré brushed aside Straus's compliments, observing with a smile: "It's all just a bag of tricks.")

Gaping like a missing tooth was the space in the Vieux Carré once occupied by the French Opera House, an exquisite smaller-scale replica of the Paris Opéra. Straus had stood all one night, watching it burn. Earlier, he had seen a performance there at which a soprano, coming out for a curtain call, had been struck on the shoulders and bent double by the descending curtain. Understandably, the stage crew became rattled. The curtain fell again, hitting the soprano's rump and straightening her up; then it struck her shoulders and bent her double again. Then the soprano had enough presence of mind to step two paces forward. There, safe from the wayward curtain, she acknowledged the applause, which by now had become thunderous, and walked offstage with dignity unimpaired.

Straus had visited the dives along Bourbon Street, not as a customer — his tastes were rather too fastidious for that — but to investigate the odd new sound called jazz, which was being produced by Negro musicians. On one such occasion he found the madam, an amateur magician, giving an exhibition of bawdy sleight of hand with the aid of two of her girls. In another corner, the Negro "professor" was playing the piano and singing:

> *I know a fine way*
> *To bang a Steinway.*

All these events were taking place in front of a flag-draped photograph of President Woodrow Wilson. The year was 1918, and patriotic sentiment was high.

Straus once visited an island in Lake Pontchartrain that had some connection with the pirate-patriot Jean Lafitte. On the way, the wind freshened and some of the passengers in the open boat became nervous. The captain told them that this was nothing; in a real blow, he said, waves sometimes broke completely over the island. To reassure his passengers, he took a worn photograph from his wallet and passed it around. It showed his mother, drowned, hanging by her long hair from a limb of a live-oak tree.

Straus was born into a well-to-do and cultivated family in Chicago. He recalled, as a boy, reading Aristophanes with his father, inwardly cringing at his parent's "barbarous Greek accent." At twelve he became the organist of the reform synagogue ("so reformed they were practically Episcopalians") attended by his family. In his teens he accompanied his mother on the first of a number of trips to Europe.

Straus was not, except for his youthful organ-playing days, a performer. He was not, in his own judgment, a very good writer, because writing as such did not interest him. He had developed a musico-journalistic style that made his meaning clear, and for reviewing purposes that was sufficient. He was by taste and temperament a scholar. He had heard Amalia Materna in 1893, and every important artist, without exception, since. At Metropolitan intermissions he could be seen smoking a cigarette in a long black holder, regaling colleagues with opera-house gossip or recalling minute details of performances that had taken place forty years before.

Conversation with Straus was often a sort of unconscious one-upmanship on his part that left everyone else rather deflated. Once Ernest Bloch sent the *Times* a pebble from his home at Agate Beach. That started a geological conversation during which one speaker quoted the authors of his college geology textbook, Chamberlain and Moulton. It turned out that Straus had studied with Chamberlain and Moulton at the University of Chicago. Wild flowers? Straus had spent a summer in the Jersey pine barrens, where more different varieties grow than anywhere else in the country. Italian primitives? He had once gone up and down the Italian peninsula to study them. Once someone mentioned a "busybody," the curious device for looking down the street without being seen, which is found only in certain Philadelphia neighborhoods. Straus had once lived in Philadelphia in a house that had a "busybody."

Straus had studied German lieder with Riccardo von zur-Mühlen, who had studied with Julius Stockhausen, who had studied with Clara Schumann, the composer's widow. In consequence, Straus would often surprise people with fresh insights into familiar works. He maintained that if Schumann had foreseen what singers would do with his well-known "Ich grolle nicht," he would have made the tempo indication *nicht zu langsam* rather than *nicht zu schnell*. Brahms's "Immer leiser wird mein Schlummer" is almost invariably sung in very slow tempo. Straus pointed to the tempo marking and *alla breve* time signature as evidence that the song should have hectic, feverish urgency; the *"Kummer"* lying like a veil over the girl is delirium.

Another misconception, Straus maintained, concerned Pergolesi's "Tre giorni son che Nina." In modern editions, only the first verse is published: "For three days Nina has lain on her bed. Sound pipes, drums, cymbals! Awaken my Ninetta, that she sleep no more."

Somewhere or other, Straus came across the remaining verses, which make clear that the pathos is mock-heroic. The trouble is simply that Nina doesn't want to get out of bed. The doctor got into bed with her, but that didn't help; the musicians did the same thing, but that didn't help either. Straus derived much quiet amusement from hearing vocalists perform the song as if to portray the anguish of a lover who will not admit that his sweetheart is dead.

Those who were saddened to think how much knowledge would pass out of the world at Straus's death urged him to write a book on music. Straus laughed at the idea. He carried his learning as jauntily as a feather in his hat. Beneath the erudition was a puckish, ironic humor that peered out at every opportunity. A gifted young pianist was "Kitain on the keys"; Tanglewood, scene of the Berkshire Music Festival, was "Tanglefoot"; and lines from Brahms's setting of "The Bonny Earl o' Moray" that went

> *Und ach, der edle Moray*
> *Die Königin gefiel*

were translated as

> *And ah, the noble Moray*
> *He gave the Queen a feel.*

To a favored few, Straus would show his poem *Truthann und Insult.* Written in German but unprintable in any language, it was a hilarious parody of the love duet from Act II of *Tristan und Isolde.* Straus detested Wagner and vowed to reduce the four operas of the *Ring* to a single *Rigoletto*-length work by cutting out the repetitions and redundancies. He hated modern music even more, and would groan audibly when compelled to listen to it.

Straus's ironic humor did not desert him even on his deathbed. One evening around seven o'clock, he said to a visiting friend: "The smartest thing for me to do would be to roll over and croak." Two hours later, he did just that.

27

Hard Times

WHEN THE GREAT DEPRESSION set in, Gatti and the Metropolitan were as well prepared as it was possible to be. The astute Italian did not share the unbounded optimism felt by nearly all Americans, high and low.

"Even during the [First World] War," said Gatti, "I made it my business and my unswerving policy to keep our administration solvent, efficient and effective. I felt that after the war the time would come when its consequences would make themselves felt. The prosperity that seemed to be heaped up and overflowing I believed in only up to a certain point. I always believed that it was more superficial than real. I always maintained that there must not be the slightest looseness of administration, that there must be no blindness on our part, no succumbing to the false prophets. I believed that we must prepare for the reaction that was inevitable. I believe in building up a fund for the rainy days.

"And I say now that if I had not seen to it that we continued to guard our reserve fund with constant vigilance, and that we built it up to the best of our ability, the Metropolitan could not have continued to live and have its being . . ."

Even so, with hard times, Gatti's $1,100,000 reserve fund began shrinking like snow shoveled into a furnace. In 1929–1930, for the first time since Gatti had assumed sole direction of the company, the Metropolitan failed to show a profit. True, the deficit was not large — a little over $14,000 — but it was an ominous foretaste of things to come. The next season's deficit of $322,000 swallowed nearly a third of the carefully hoarded reserve fund. In three years the reserve was entirely gone. During

233

the same period, the Metropolitan lost more than thirty percent of its subscribers. Box-office receipts fell by nearly a million dollars a season. The season's length was cut back from twenty-four weeks to sixteen, and Gatti was obliged to drop twenty-eight singers from the roster.

Another blow fell a few days before the opening of the 1931–1932 season, when Otto Kahn resigned his dual post as the Metropolitan's president and chairman of the board. The official explanation was that Mortimer Schiff of Kuhn, Loeb & Company had just died, and Kahn's increased responsibilities with the firm precluded daily concern with the affairs of the opera house.

Also a factor, however, was the failure of Kahn's plan to build a new Metropolitan Opera House on West Fifty-seventh Street. Kahn felt that the Metropolitan's directors had failed to honor "the solemn obligation of a semi-public institution such as the Metropolitan to provide amply and generously for music lovers of small or modest means."

Kahn's place was taken by his lawyer and longtime associate, Paul D. Cravath, who made the best of things by saying: "I should not feel very disappointed if we had to stay on in the old house. It has associations and traditions which attach audiences to it."

Kahn's retirement, said Gatti, brought "public apprehension" about the Metropolitan's stability. It also deprived Gatti of a loyal, time-tested ally. Not all the Metropolitan directors were equally sympathetic. Most of them were so business-oriented as to feel that any operation which lost money was being mismanaged. The European concept of an opera house as a cultural asset to be maintained for public benefit — along with art galleries, museums and libraries — had not developed in New York. David Sarnoff, on becoming a member of the board, sent down an efficiency expert to look over the Metropolitan's operations, and proposed an audit of the company's books. The auditors would probably have been somewhat staggered by what they found; Gatti was said to run the company by means of slips of paper stuffed in his pockets and the phenomenal memory of his secretary, Luigi Villa.

The shadows of the depression grew darker. The breadlines grew longer. The toll of unemployment mounted — eight, nine, ten million Americans were out of work. Brokers sold apples on Wall Street. (This, said Herbert Hoover, was a publicity stunt arranged by an apple-growers' association on the West Coast. But it made a profound impression.) In colleges and universities all over the country, undergraduates were acquiring the viewpoints that would give journalism, the academic world and intellectual circles generally a prevailing leftward slant for years to come.

When the grim financial returns for the 1931–1932 season were in, Gatti addressed an appeal to all members of the Metropolitan. After pointing out that the very survival of the company was at stake, Gatti urged its members to accept whatever pay cuts might be necessary.

"Since the personnel of the Metropolitan is composed of Americans and foreigners," Gatti added, "I affirm that the former are obliged, out of patriotism and duty, to sacrifice themselves for the good of a great American institution where all or almost all of them began and continued their artistic careers; and the foreign-born artists are obliged to do the same, out of gratitude toward the Institution where they found, and find, a long and faithful hospitality and generous rewards for their services.

"For myself, I state that I do not believe that I can do enough to liquidate my debt of gratitude to the Metropolitan. I offer to serve it in the coming season with any necessary reduction of salary which circumstances require, and even without salary if this be necessary."

Members of the company acceded to Gatti's request with one conspicuous exception — Gigli. On the advice of his lawyer, the late Fiorello H. La Guardia, the tenor returned his contract unsigned. Gigli said later that he had offered to take a cut in salary if Gatti did. He added that he would have been prepared to take a cut of up to thirty percent in salary, except that Gatti had told him the contract was "not worth the paper it was written on."

As a matter of fact, Gatti *had* taken a sizable cut. In 1932, his salary was $57,736; for 1933, the general manager received $43,108. Even so, the 1933 figure was a handsome one; had the board of directors taken Gatti up on his offer to serve without salary, it would have covered nearly a third of the season's deficit.

Gigli was unwise enough to announce publicly that he was not returning to the company because of "conditions and impositions that would have diminished my dignity as a man and an artist." Gatti retaliated by releasing to the press a round-robin letter signed by every reengaged member of the company. The letter described Gigli's conduct as "inexcusable," and he was accused of "lack of co-operation and *esprit de corps*." It was commonly believed that the protest was anything but spontaneous; Gatti was said to have received his artists with a contract in one hand and the round-robin letter in the other.

Gigli departed for lucrative engagements in Europe and South America, and his glorious voice was absent from the Metropolitan for seven years.

"Gigli is an artist with good qualities who has rendered important services to our company," said Gatti blandly, "but as we have carried on without artists even greater than he, we can continue to do so."

The financial plight of the Metropolitan became graver and graver. In 1933, Gatti had to pocket his pride to the extent of making a public appeal for funds. The campaign was launched during the *Manon* matinee on February 25, 1933, at which Richard Crooks made his debut as Des Grieux. Farrar came out of her Connecticut retirement to plead with audience and radio listeners to put up the $300,000 needed to keep the opera going. The response was overwhelming. Soprano Marion Telva sent a thousand-dollar check to the stage via an usher. Rosa Ponselle telephoned her pledge. "Had the intermissions been as long as the performance," said Farrar, "I feel sure we should have attained in cash and pledges the entire sum, then and there, for the opera's guarantee."

Similar appeals were made during intermissions of every broadcast for the rest of the season. The money was raised, and the crisis was averted for the time being.

There was no public appeal during the next season; the New York Philharmonic-Symphony, also deep in financial trouble, was conducting a million-dollar fund campaign of its own, and no one wanted to kill the ailing goose that still laid a few golden eggs. The Metropolitan undertook private fund-raising, however, by selling tickets to a costume ball held in a Louis Fourteenth setting at the opera house, and a "Surprise Party." The latter event was an all-star vaudeville show during which, among other things, diminutive coloratura Lily Pons, dressed as an Apache, "hoisted" the giant *Heldentenor* Lauritz Melchior, in a little girl's dress and curly wig, by means of a wire attached to his costume.

There was a short-lived proposal to solve the financial problems of both the Metropolitan and the Philharmonic by merging them into a single institution — an arrangement like the one that existed between the Vienna State Opera and the Vienna Philharmonic. A prompt outcry went up that jobs for live musicians, thanks to radio and recordings, were disappearing fast enough as it was. The WPA was launching a series of projects for musicians, to keep the species from becoming extinct altogether. Toscanini, by now the Philharmonic's musical director, administered the *coup de grace* to the merger plan by pointing out that the Metropolitan's acoustics were unsuited to orchestral performances, the Philharmonic would have to curtail its season and Philharmonic standards would be lowered.

More bad news came in the spring of 1934. The supervision of electrical wiring in public buildings had just passed from New York's Fire Department to the Superintendent of Buildings. The wiring of the Metropolitan's stage area, which had been approved by the Fire Department ever since the interior was rebuilt in 1903, was judged a fire hazard by the new inspectors. Before the building could be occupied for the 1934–1935 season, it would need repairs costing more than $500,000. In view of the New Deal shock waves that were emanating from Washington with such awesome regularity, the stockholders of the Metropolitan Opera and Real Estate Company were not remotely likely to appropriate such a sum. Instead, the building, after sixteen unencumbered years, was mortgaged for $600,000.

Another crisis had been surmounted; but the stockholders' nerves were becoming frayed. At about this time, Allen Wardwell, counsel for the Metropolitan Opera and Real Estate Company, had cocktails with author-pianist John Erskine at the Century Club. Erskine headed the Juilliard School of Music and was president of the foundation set up by the will of Augustus D. Juilliard, textile manufacturer and longtime holder of Box 2 at the Metropolitan.

A first proviso of Juilliard's will was that income from the foundation was to be used "at such times and to such extent and in such amounts as the trustees may in their discretion deem proper" to aid the Metropolitan Opera. If the Metropolitan did not need the money, it was to go to the Juilliard School.

Under the terms of the will, the Juilliard trustees had offered the Metropolitan financial assistance in 1924. At that time, however, prosperity was in the air, Gatti's surplus had already topped $50,000 a season, and it is very likely that Gatti feared that Juilliard money would be followed by a Juilliard voice in management. Kahn had politely but firmly refused the Juilliard offer. Thereafter, nearly all the income from Juilliard's $13,000,000 estate went to the Juilliard School.

Now, Wardwell told Erskine, Juilliard support was urgently needed. The Metropolitan board of directors were about ready to close the house. "They want to leave their baby on the Juilliard doorstep," Wardwell said.

It was no secret that Erskine felt the time had come for Gatti to retire. He had intimated to Wardwell, however, that with a different management, Juilliard money might come to the Metropolitan's rescue. Now, in a letter to Wardwell, Erskine spelled out his conditions in detail. Juilliard would offer $250,000 provided its conditions were met. The subscription must be increased by at least ten percent. Expenses must be slashed until the budget balanced. More young American singers must be engaged. A supplementary season of opera in English was to be presented, under the direction of Edward Johnson. Erskine, Ernest Hutcheson (pianist and dean of the Juilliard School) and two Juilliard directors, John M. Perry and Felix Warburg, were to be named to the Metropolitan board. Productions were to be supervised by an Opera Management Committee composed of Erskine as chairman, Lucrezia Bori, Johnson, Wardwell and Cornelius Bliss, of the Metropolitan board. And Gatti must be replaced by the basso Herbert Witherspoon, who had managed a season of opera in Chicago in 1931–1932. When Blanche Witherspoon heard the news of her husband's appointment, she was stunned; she had married Witherspoon earlier that year only on his solemn pledge that he would never take the job.

Gatti arrived in November to a *fait accompli* quite different from the one he had encountered in his first season at the Metropolitan. The strong right arm of Otto Kahn could no longer be relied on for support; the opera-loving financier was dead. Some of the directors were cool or openly hostile; in addition to the financial plight for which Gatti had been unable to find a solution, they were put off by Gatti's divorce and remarriage to Rosina Galli. Alda, though no longer a performer, had influential friends, a fact she emphasized in *Men, Women and Tenors*.

While Witherspoon, not yet officially named as Gatti's successor, set about familiarizing himself with the Metropolitan's operations, Gatti launched what would obviously be his last season as general manager. It opened on December 22, 1934, with *Aida*. Rethberg sang the title role,

The farewell party for Giulio Gatti-Casazza aboard the REX

with Maria Olszewska as Amneris and with Martinelli, Tibbett and Pinza in other principal parts.

An unexpected highlight of the season was the debut, on February 2, 1935, virtually without advance fanfare, of a new Norwegian soprano named Kirsten Flagstad. She scored a triumph as Sieglinde in *Die Walküre*, and four days later had even greater success in her first Metropolitan Isolde.

At the season's final broadcast, a *Lakmé* on March 30, Farrar persuaded Gatti to say a brief farewell during an intermission. Gatti crowded himself into the anteroom of Box 44, along with Farrar and the miniature Steinway originally made for Farrar's private railroad car. Dutifully he read the speech Farrar had written for him and which he had been rehearsing backstage all week. He finished with extemporized Italian and a kiss for the astonished commentator.

Next night there was an "Operatic Surprise Party" as part of the regular Sunday evening concert. Pons and Melchior, dressed as acrobats, performed a tumbling act with the aid of a wire attached to Melchior's tights. Comedienne Beatrice Lillie sang a scene from *Carmen* in various known and unknown languages, while her colleagues sang in French. At the conclusion of the drollery, basso Emanuel List, made up to look like Gatti, came forward to acknowledge the applause. The real Gatti watched from the director's box. Next to him sat Toscanini, who in honor of the occasion had broken his vow never to enter the Metropolitan again.

Still another farewell was the party given by Rosa Ponselle aboard the *Rex*, as the Gatti-Casazzas were about to sail. Tears and champagne flowed freely. By now Gatti's hair was thin and his beard was completely white. He looked tired. Rumor said he had spent most of the previous night in a violent quarrel with his wife, who did not want to leave New York. But Gatti's mind was made up.

Singers and stagehands crowded around for a last farewell. Then the gangplank was run ashore, tugs slowly nosed the *Rex* into the North River current, and New York had seen Giulio Gatti-Casazza for the last time.

28

Flagstad

GATTI'S MOST VALUABLE LEGACY to his successors at the Metropolitan was a consequence of the fact that Frida Leider, the company's leading Wagnerian soprano in the early Thirties, wanted to be released from her contract. Gatti was willing; he disliked keeping artists who were unhappy in the company. Before releasing Leider, however, he needed to find someone else to sing her roles.

It has been said that the Metropolitan thought so little of Flagstad's talent that she was engaged for secondary roles, which would be a wonderful story if it were true. The roles for which she was specifically engaged — the three Brünnhildes of the *Ring*, Isolde, and Leonora in *Fidelio* — could hardly be called secondary. On the other hand, the extent to which Gatti was impressed can be gauged from the fact that he signed Flagstad only to a one-year contract without a renewal option. It seems clear that Gatti had no idea he was bringing to America one of the greatest Wagernian sopranos in Metropolitan history.

For that matter, neither did Flagstad herself. At that time, she was not, strictly speaking, a Wagnerian soprano.

The soprano then was practically unknown outside her native Norway, although Oscar Thompson, editor of *Musical America* and one of the most knowledgeable critics of singing, had heard her in Oslo in 1932 and had sent a glowing report to his magazine. Three years earlier, during a Scandinavian business trip, Otto Kahn had heard her sing Tosca and had suggested that she might be worthy of consideration by the Metropolitan. But nothing came of the suggestion.

When Gatti heard Flagstad, she was nearly forty and had been singing in public more than twenty years. Since her marriage to a wealthy Norwegian businessman, she had enjoyed living in a big house in Oslo with plenty of servants, and was less and less inclined to leave it for the grind of touring, rehearsals and performances. She considered herself, in fact, to be practically retired.

But her career kept intruding. Urgent calls would come for her to replace an indisposed soprano or to learn a new role on short notice. (She was famous as a good musician and a quick learner.) One such part was Isolde, which she learned for an Oslo *Tristan und Isolde* in 1933. It was her first big Wagnerian role. The King Marke of that performance was the Metropolitan basso Alexander Kipnis. When Kipnis learned from Eric Simon, Gatti's European talent scout, that the Metropolitan needed a Wagnerian soprano, he recommended his Oslo Isolde. And in Bayreuth, where she was singing small roles in the summer of 1934, Flagstad received an invitation to audition for Gatti in St. Moritz.

Years afterward, Flagstad remembered the ordeal of her audition. The weather was hot, and the thirteen-hour train ride had been tiresome. The salon in Gatti's hotel had thick carpets, overstuffed furniture and heavy drapes — a decor which, however comfortable, swallows the resonance of a voice. She had had only six days in which to prepare for the audition. She had begun to study the *Siegfried* Brünnhilde but knew practically nothing of the other two. She knew Isolde and Leonora in Norwegian and would have to relearn them in German; but in Bayreuth, the Wagnerian capital of the world, she had been unable to find a score of *Tristan und Isolde*.

Gatti, conductor Artur Bodanzky and Eric Simon could not help smiling at the long string of excuses. But in spite of everything, Flagstad's voice made an impression.

Bodanzky sent her to Prague to coach with George Szell, the stern drillmaster who would later make the Cleveland Orchestra a virtuoso ensemble of the first rank. Szell terrified Flagstad; he did not say a kind word until the final lesson. Then he said: "I'm going to write Mr. Bodanzky that he needn't worry about your learning the music in time."

While studying Isolde for Oslo, Flagstad had discovered that her voice had deepened to a darker, more resonant timbre. Another discovery was somewhat disconcerting at first: All her dresses were splitting down the back. She had not gained weight, however. Singing Isolde's long, sustained phrases had merely developed her back and shoulder muscles.

Flagstad and her husband arrived in New York early in January, 1935. Her voice was first heard at the Metropolitan in a *Götterdämmerung* rehearsal on January 15. By now Brünnhilde's music was securely memorized. Flagstad sang, as she always did at rehearsal, in full voice. When she had sung half a dozen phrases, Bodanzky sent a messenger for Gatti. Then he turned over the baton to Karl Riedel and went to the back of the house to listen.

Word raced through the building like a forest fire: "My God! Drop everything and come hear this voice!" The auditorium began filling as if for an actual performance. When they heard Flagstad's high C, Bodanzky shouted, "*Brava*, Flagstad!" and the orchestral players stood and cheered.

Flagstad's debut in *Die Walküre*, on February 2, was a matinee performance, heard by a nationwide radio audience as well as by Metropolitan patrons. It was a performance that, as Henderson put it, "began in calm and ended in pandemonium." The enthusiasm that greeted Flagstad's singing was matched in the reviews next day. Olin Downes wrote that "for once the Metropolitan has engaged a singer who is in her prime." (A standing joke, not always unfounded, was that singers were engaged for the Metropolitan only when they were too old to appear anywhere else.) Lawrence Gilman compared the new singer to Olive Fremstad, which was the highest praise he could think of.

Flagstad had made such an impression as Sieglinde that the first of many sold-out, standing-room-only audiences was on hand four days later to see what she would do with Isolde. The performance left no doubt; the Metropolitan had found a voice such as is heard only once in a lifetime.

The five seasons that followed brought a magnificent Wagnerian renaissance at the Metropolitan. *Tristan und Isolde*, with Melchior and Flagstad in the title roles, became, in terms of actual money taken in at the box office, the hottest attraction on Broadway. His association with Flagstad brought new lustre to Melchior's career. The tenor's voice was not a pretty sound and his musicianship often left much to be desired. But he had the requisite power, and he made a commanding figure on the stage. Flagstad was a big woman, but Melchior was even bigger. Together they were the most convincing Wagnerian lovers the Metropolitan had seen in many years.

Flagstad's voice was huge, but that was not its most striking quality. Her voice, even in her first Metropolitan seasons, never had the trumpetlike brilliance of Helen Traubel's during the American soprano's great days. What was remarkable about Flagstad's voice was its freshness and the effortless ease with which it was produced. To the end of her career, she sounded like a young girl. Traubel's voice seemed to penetrate the orchestra; Flagstad's, to soar above it.

At a typical end-of-season *Tristan* in the late Thirties, most of the cast showed the effects of a hard season's wear and tear. Melchior was dryvoiced and husky; others in the cast were hardly better off. Only Flagstad sounded as if she had just come back from a month's vacation.

Flagstad once told an interviewer she believed her voice had lasted because she had taken extreme care never to force it. She had begun her career by singing in operetta and musical comedy. As the added bigness came of its own accord, she had cautiously gone on to more dramatic and taxing roles.

At the opening of the 1939–1940 season, an event occurred that was to have far-reaching consequences. On November 23, 1939, four days before the *Simon Boccanegra* performance that opened the season, Arthur Bodanzky died unexpectedly. A lean, efficient orchestral technician with a fantastic sense of tempo (he used to win bets by doing the second act of *Die Walküre* in one hour, no more and no less), Bodanzky for twenty-four years had been the mainstay of the Metropolitan's German repertoire. In 1937, as an understudy for Bodanzky, the Metropolitan had engaged a gifted twenty-five-year-old Viennese, Erich Leinsdorf. He was to assist Bodanzky in preparing the operas of the Metropolitan's German repertoire, and eventually conduct them himself. Bodanzky's death, however, knocked all plans awry. On Leinsdorf's untried shoulders was placed the responsibility for the Metropolitan's entire German repertoire. During the season he led fifty-five performances, five of them of operas he had never conducted before.

It is to the credit of Leinsdorf's nerve and musicianship that he survived the ordeal. But he did so at the cost of immense nervous strain. There is, moreover, a tendency to overassert oneself when unsure of one's position. (That is true of other fields as well as music.) A newly-promoted business executive, for example, may drive with an unnecessarily taut rein until he gains confidence as he sees his instructions being carried out. There seems to be no doubt that Leinsdorf stepped on people's toes. Among other things, he apparently attempted to get Melchior to sing the notes correctly, an undertaking given up by most other conductors as hopeless.

On January 25, 1940, an attack on Leinsdorf appeared in the *Herald Tribune.* In an interview, Melchior questioned the conductor's fitness for his Metropolitan post, because of his youth and inexperience. Other singers, including Flagstad, supported Melchior. Edward Johnson, the onetime tenor who by now had become the Metropolitan's general manager, replied with an angry statement that there were certain "old boats" who believed the Metropolitan would sink without them, and the smoldering feud was out in the open.

Flagstad now did a very unwise thing by attempting to have her accompanist, Edwin McArthur, engaged at the Metropolitan as a conductor. At that point, another inexperienced conductor was the last thing Edward Johnson wanted. Although Flagstad's leverage at the box office was powerful enough to get McArthur several performances, in the long run it did McArthur's conducting aspirations little good. In the spring of 1941, Flagstad returned to Norway, and McArthur's career as a Metropolitan conductor was over.

Flagstad's official position was that she had wished to help the career of a gifted young American who wanted to conduct. Some people, however, were cynical enough to look for a more personal explanation of Flagstad's interest in McArthur.

Because of the war, Flagstad did not return to America until the spring of 1947. Her return was preceded by a series of hostile items in Walter Winchell's column, charging her with "collaboration" during the German occupation of Norway. Her recitals in both New York and Philadelphia were picketed by a veterans' group, the American Veterans Committee. In Philadelphia, a stench bomb was thrown into the hall.

The charges against Flagstad were vague. A magazine sent John Bartlow Martin to Europe to run down the Flagstad story. Martin spent a year abroad, talked to dozens of people who had known Flagstad during the war, and wound up more mystified than ever. Flagstad had returned to

246

Lauritz Melchior and Kirsten Flagstad, as Lohengrin and Elsa, carefully noting the location of a footlight microphone during rehearsal for a Saturday matinee broadcast

Norway in the first place because of her husband's failing health. She had traveled part of the way in a German plane. But we were not then at war, and United States government officials were doing the same thing.

Reports that Flagstad had been a regular wartime member of the Berlin State Opera were shown to be without foundation. Flagstad had spent the war years living quietly in Norway. She told friends, in fact, that her great regret was that she had spent the best years of her life, vocally speaking, sitting at home with no place to sing.

Flagstad's husband had been accused of wartime collaboration, but he had died before the charges could be proved or disproved in court. With his death, the Norwegian government saw no point in pressing the investigation further. In any case, Flagstad had been specifically exempted from the charges, and a certificate to that effect had been issued to her by the Norwegian Supreme Court.

What was most puzzling about the anti-Flagstad demonstrations was their inconsistency. Within weeks of Flagstad's performance, Tito Schipa, who had ended his prewar recitals with the fascist salute, sang at Carnegie Hall with never a protest from the American Veterans Committee. There was no public outcry when the Metropolitan engaged Ljuba Welitch, who had sung throughout the war at the Vienna State Opera, and Max Lorenz, "Hitler's favorite tenor."

The explanation, as it turned out, was that "collaboration" was merely a pretext. The real reason went back to the heated days of the Leinsdorf-Melchior-Flagstad controversy. At the height of the dispute, Flagstad was said to have referred to Leinsdorf disparagingly as "that Jew."

Flagstad vowed she never made such a remark. But someone said she did, someone told someone else and eventually the story got to Winchell.

Jews came to Flagstad's defense. Marks Levine, her longtime manager, wrote to concert managers all over the country that, as a Jew, he could not in good conscience book Flagstad's engagements if he believed the collaboration charges were true. Arthur Bronson wrote in *Variety* that the bombed and picketed Philadelphia concert involved two separate rights: the right of the demonstrators to demonstrate, and the right of the audience to hear the concert for which it had purchased tickets. (The Philadelphia group tried to have Bronson fired for making this reasonable remark. All it got them, however, was the rough side of editor Abel Green's tongue.)

Flagstad herself behaved with impeccable dignity. She made no public statements and did nothing to add fuel to the controversy. Vindication came when Rudolf Bing, as the newly arrived manager of the Metropolitan, invited her to return. Bing ignored the criticism aroused in some quarters. Flagstad was a great artist, he said; she belonged at the Metropolitan.

Flagstad took her leave of the Metropolitan with six memorable performances of *Alceste* in the spring of 1952. If her voice was not quite the matchless instrument of a decade earlier, nevertheless Flagstad's admirers could observe with satisfaction that their idol had ended her Metropolitan career as she had begun — one of the greatest artists ever to be heard there.

Licia Albanese (wearing apron) with well-behaved fans backstage

29

In Arrears

On May 10, 1935, Herbert Witherspoon, the new general manager of the Metropolitan, paused at the door of his office for a word with his secretary, Luigi Villa. In preparation for a meeting with the board of directors, Witherspoon had just been conferring with his associates, Ziegler and Earle R. Lewis (newly promoted from the box office). Without warning, the new manager collapsed and died on the spot. The strenuous hours of planning for the new season had taken their toll.

John Erskine hastily convened the Opera Management Committee. Edward Johnson, who was to have managed the spring season, was advanced to the general manager's post. It was said that Gatti had favored Johnson as his successor all along.

Johnson, now no longer a performer, let his auburn-dyed hair go white, becoming in the process somewhat handsomer, if anything, than before. He was a highly eligible widower; his wife had died on the eve of his first Metropolitan success and he had never remarried, although many women would have liked him to.

Johnson's light, high-pitched speaking voice, conventional good looks and ingratiating manner gave an impression of weakness. It was obvious that he liked to be liked. He found it difficult to discipline colleagues with whom he had been on a first-name basis for years. Moreover, as a performer himself he had known the immense loneliness of the artist onstage, with only his own gifts and resourcefulness to see him through. Metropolitan vocalists found Johnson a sympathetic general manager. On the other hand, they often found it hard to get a straightforward Yes or No out of him about anything. "He's charming," one artist said. "Too *damned* charming."

Yet, in the changed environment in which the Metropolitan was forced to operate, a certain pliability was perhaps a desirable trait in the general manager. Johnson bent to the wind when a stiffer plant might have broken. *"Il turbine rovescia la quercia"* ("the hurricane blows down the oak tree"), as Cio-Cio-San says.

There was, in the first place, the sheer difficulty of doing anything in the uncertain climate of the Thirties. The hard times that began in 1929 were not to end, really, until the nation entered World War II. New ideas were stirring; old certainties had become uncertain. The New Deal labor-management philosophy brought the Metropolitan under increasingly heavy pressure from the unions, augmenting both the difficulty of negotiating contracts and the cost of presenting opera.

Mounting costs of production made it even more difficult to carry out the Juilliard directive for a budget with some hope of remaining in balance. Increased revenues seemed out of the question in view of prevailing economic conditions; opera was among the first of the luxuries people found they were able to do without. Instead, Johnson, Ziegler and Lewis looked for ways to save money.

One step they took was to place a maximum limit on artists' fees; a thousand dollars a performance. This accomplished the desired result of saving money; nor is it likely that it deprived the company of very many artists it wished to engage. The prestige of the Metropolitan was still a magnet for singers all over the world.

But a singer worth a thousand dollars to the Metropolitan could earn double or treble that amount in recital, to say nothing of earnings from radio and the movies. Consequently the Metropolitan could not command the first claim on its artists' services. A tendency developed for top artists to sandwich their Metropolitan performances between appearances at Hollywood, Radio City and the concert circuit. In the days before the American Guild of Musical Artists eliminated the Metropolitan's commission arrangement, Lawrence Tibbett curtailed his Metropolitan season on the ground that he lost money by singing there; the Metropolitan collected more in fees from his radio, film and concert earnings than it paid him to sing.

Johnson temporized and conciliated as necessary in order to patch his seasons together. He never had the free hand enjoyed by Gatti-Casazza, with Otto Kahn's powerful backing, after Gatti had succeeded in nailing Dippel's hide to the door. Johnson was responsible to the Juilliard trustees as well as to the board of directors, and soon a third potent force made itself felt in Metropolitan affairs.

Eleanor Robson, third-generation member of an English theatrical family, had been brought to this country at seven, had made her stage debut at seventeen and had become a star of the legitimate theatre in her twenties. In 1910, she had given up her career to marry the younger August Belmont, son of the onetime president of the Academy of Music's board of directors.

The radiant new Mrs. Belmont, who would still be a strikingly beautiful woman half a century later, fitted quickly and gracefully into the Newport–Long Island–Saratoga–Palm Beach world of yachting, polo and thoroughbred racing.

"A private railroad car isn't an acquired taste," she once said. "You take to it immediately."

During World War I and after, Mrs. Belmont proved remarkably effective as a fund-raiser and organizer of benefits for the Red Cross. Her skill at raising money impressed Cornelius N. Bliss, a co-worker on various Red Cross projects, who was also a director of the Metropolitan. His admiration led to an invitation to Mrs. Belmont to join the Metropolitan's board of directors.

In 1935, to help ease the Metropolitan's financial plight, Mrs. Belmont proposed to form a new organization called the Metropolitan Opera Guild. Its purpose would be to raise money for the Metropolitan. Members, in return for their financial contributions, would be permitted to attend rehearsals and in various other ways would be brought into "closer association with glamorous artists."

Although somewhat skeptical, the board told Mrs. Belmont to go ahead. As director of the Guild, Mrs. Belmont engaged Blanche Witherspoon, the widow of the recently deceased general manager.

Third of the trio of Guild founders was Lucrezia Bori, who retired at the end of the 1935–1936 season. No longer a performer, Bori revealed that her real name was Borja. She was a member of the great Spanish family that in Italy had called itself "Borgia" and had produced both worldly Popes and saintly princes. Bori brought to the Guild not only glamor, but also firsthand knowledge of the realities of opera production.

Mrs. Belmont began by lining up a nationwide group of honorary sponsors for the Guild. Eventually the list of two hundred names included President Franklin D. Roosevelt, the governors of nine states and New York's mayor, Fiorello H. La Guardia, an ardent operagoer who never missed a Metropolitan *Ring* cycle unless there were riots somewhere.

At the end of its first season, the Guild had recruited two thousand members and raised enough money to buy a cyclorama. Astonishing as it seems, the Metropolitan had never had one before. The Guild's publication, *Opera News*, was flourishing under the editorship of Mary Ellis Peltz, who was frank enough to state that she had become a music critic because she realized she could never become a performer.

Ziegler hardly knew what to make of the Opera Guild ladies. He was particularly unnerved by the hats that some of them wore. But the Metropolitan needed their help. And the help grew more generous year by year. At the end of its first decade, the Guild's membership had grown to 24,000; its contribution toward the Metropolitan deficit, to $30,000, and its spending for new productions, to $175,000. About 100,000 students from public, private and parochial schools in New York, New Jersey and Connecticut had had their first taste of Metropolitan opera by means of low-priced tickets for which the Guild made up the difference. The Guild had provided scholarships for young singers, redecorated dressing rooms, replaced the proscenium border of the stage and added a crystal chandelier to the buffet lounge.

Mrs. Belmont's purpose in founding the Opera Guild had been "to broaden the base of participation in support of grand opera." The broadening came none too soon. As the Thirties drew to a close, the Metropolitan, which had staggered from crisis to crisis throughout its history, faced a threat more ominous than any it had ever confronted before. The Metropolitan Opera and Real Estate Company, the very basis of the Metropolitan's existence, was breaking up.

The Real Estate Company's troubles could be summed up briefly: Too many of the stockholders were dead. By 1939, half the boxes were held by the estates of former investors. So many of these had refused to pay their assessments that the Real Estate Company did not have sufficient money to pay its taxes. On July 19, 1939, the musical world was staggered by an announcement that the Metropolitan Opera and Real Estate Company had decided at a special meeting to propose "the sale of the famous old structure to the Metropolitan Opera Association."

A great deal of criticism has been leveled at the boxholders for giving the hard-pressed Association the alternatives of buying the house or suspending. It has been argued that the snobbish rules for eligibility made it more difficult for estate executors who would not pay their assessments to sell to new owners who would. That may be, although an executor normally liquidates an estate without unnecessary delay, and it is hard to believe that an executor would deliberately place obstacles in the way of turning assets into cash. A more direct cause was that given by Robert Brewster, president of the Real Estate Company: There was simply no market for the shares. Frazier Jelke had paid $200,000 for Harold S. Vanderbilt's box in 1926; in the nervous climate of 1939, there were no takers at any price. In somewhat the same way, the price of a seat on the New York Stock Exchange, which had been as high as $625,000 in February, 1929, by 1942 was selling for $17,000, or less than the amount paid by the Stock Exchange to the heirs of a member who died.

Moreover, by 1939, snobbery was no longer the potent force in Metropolitan affairs it once had been. The social season no longer revolved around a box at the opera. Cabarets had begun to make their appearance in New York around 1912, and with repeal of the Prohibition Amendment the former speakeasies that were being renamed "night clubs" became the places to go. A generation was growing up that preferred Billy Rose's Diamond Horseshoe to Edward Johnson's. Society had changed so radically that there was really little point in attending the Metropolitan unless one enjoyed going there.

Some opera-lovers felt that if the executors did not wish to pay their assessments and could not sell their boxes, the public-spirited thing to do would have been to donate the house to the Association or sell it for a nominal sum. That might have been done rather easily had the Metropolitan been, say, a simple partnership made up exclusively of opera-lovers. But the Opera and Real Estate Company was a corporation, and its operations accordingly were somewhat more tricky to bring to a close. Moreover, an executor, no matter how great an opera-lover, might not have cared to justify giving away a share of a property appraised at $5,000,000 (an offer of $7,000,000 had been refused in 1924), occupying a choice site in the heart of the Garment Center.

The terms finally proposed, and accepted by the Association, were neither as generous nor as onerous as they might have been. The purchase price was to be $1,970,000, slightly more than the original cost but less than half the current appraised value. Of that sum, $500,000 was to be paid in cash by the following summer. The Association would also take over the 1934 mortgage, on which $470,000 was still due, and would pay the rest in four-percent bonds.

Although a majority of stockholders approved the terms of the sale, a smaller group protested, arguing that a sale on the open market would bring a much higher return. In that case, of course, the house would almost certainly have been torn down to make way for an office building. The dissidents were Jelke, who had paid a considerably higher price for his box than some of the other shareholders; Robert Goelet; Mary W. Harriman; Forsyth Wickes and the executors of the Clews brothers, James and Henry; Georgine Iselin; Elbridge T. Gerry and Mrs. Arthur Little. The dispute continued until 1942, when appraisers appointed by the New York State Supreme Court ruled that the price was fair.

Even $500,000, however, was more cash than could be found in Johnson's all but empty coffers. Obviously, an appeal would have to be made to the public. George A. Sloan, the Rockefeller son-in-law who headed the drive, and his associates decided, while they were about it, to try for a million dollars. That sum would cover the purchase price, with something left over for repairs and for the emergencies that were certain to occur.

A vast nationwide fund-raising campaign got under way. Mayor La Guardia headed the drive, aided by the Opera Guild, the American Guild of Musical Artists, the governors of ten states and a committee of 175 civic and educational leaders. All during the 1939–1940 season, appeals for contributions were broadcast during intermissions of every Saturday matinee.

When the results were tabulated in May, 1940, it was found that the drive had exceeded its million-dollar goal by $42,000. Several boxholders had donated their receipts from the sale of the house to the opera company, for a total of $144,000. Another $149,000 came from fifteen foundations, the largest contribution being the Juilliard's, of $70,000. Business and financial concerns contributed $143,000. Smaller sums were donated by opera subscribers, directors of the Association, out-of-town opera groups, artists, employees, members of the Metropolitan Opera Club and labor unions. But the greatest single source of funds was the Saturday afternoon radio audience, which sent in $327,000 — nearly a third of the total.

On June 28, 1940, the Metropolitan Opera Association formally took title to the building in which it had presented opera for fifty-seven years. The company still had a roof over its head, even though in future it would have to keep that roof mended for itself.

30

Wartime Opera

RENOVATING WORKMEN HAD REMOVED two truckloads of dirt from the auditorium floor. Despite the many years during which women had been wearing jewels to the Metropolitan, no gems were found, though one ten-cent ring caused a brief flurry of excitement.

When the season opened on December 2, 1940, with *Un Ballo in maschera* (with Zinka Milanov, Stella Andreva, Kerstin Thorborg, Jussi Bjoerling and the Hungarian newcomer Alexander Sved), the exterior of the "yellow-brick brewery" was as dingy as ever. Inside, however, it was gleaming with fresh opera-house red, white and gold. When the asbestos fire curtain was raised to reveal the new gold curtain, there was an outburst of applause. The old curtain had been cut by the Opera Guild into six-inch squares and sent to those who had contributed a dollar or more to the fund campaign.

The unsalable boxes of the Grand Tier had been converted into rows of seats, adding thirty additional chairs and $150 of potential revenue, while still leaving room for a properly glass-enclosed broadcasting booth for Milton Cross and his co-broadcasters. Also on the Grand Tier was a new meeting room for the Opera Guild, created by combining the former ladies' lounge and the onetime press room. (The Metropolitan's press department led an almost furtive existence in one backstage cubbyhole after another, finally ending as an annex of the box office.) The new decor of Sherry's Restaurant suggested nothing so much as a 1903 Baltimore bordello as nostalgically recollected by H. L. Mencken.

The 1940 opening marked the dividing line at which the process of "democratization," as Mrs. Belmont called it, was to begin. It took a practiced eye, however, to detect the difference. Mrs. Cornelius Vanderbilt III was, as usual, in Box 3. Mrs. George Washington Kavanaugh, with her six-inch diamond tiara, was there. Cuttings, Goelets, Wetmores and Whitneys were on hand.

The John Jacob Astors were missing; they were at Madison Square Garden, attending an Ice Follies benefit for the Musicians Emergency Fund. So was Mrs. Lytle Hull, who confessed she had never cared much for singing, and soon transferred her loyalties to the Philharmonic. James Whittaker, who according to newspaper scuttlebutt had quarreled with the managing editor of the *Mirror* and had been made its music critic as punishment, had an explanation for other missing faces: "A socially significant minority stood in bed, letting almost anybody with a few hundred loose dollars supplant them on the Big Night."

A significant change was seen in Box 35, at the center of the Diamond Horseshoe. It was occupied not by J. P. Morgan but by one of the new millionaires, Thomas J. Watson of IBM. Another newcomer was Mrs. Harrison Williams, longtime occupant of the "best-dressed" lists.

The occasion had a hectic, feverish air unusual even for a Metropolitan opening night. What some journalists had called "the phony war" was turning into grim earnest. France had fallen; the British army had been driven into the sea at Dunkirk; the London blitz was at its height and the Japanese were driving into French Indo-China.

Army and navy uniforms were plentiful in the opening-night audience. During the Presidential campaign just ended, candidate Roosevelt had vowed "again and again and again" that American troops would not be sent to fight in a foreign war. Many young men of draftable age were skeptical enough, however, to enlist in order to get their military service over with. For many, the ironic sequel would be that their tour of duty lasted five years instead of four.

The outbreak of war in Europe had brought fresh perplexities for the hard-pressed Johnson regime. Gatti-Casazza had faced similar problems in 1914; but Gatti had had a far abler company to draw upon in 1914 than did Johnson in 1939. In both instances, the supply of fresh talent from Europe was cut off; but Gatti had managed to get out with more. The all-American Johnson administration (Canadian-born Johnson had become a

United States citizen) had announced it would favor Americans as a matter of policy; it found itself obliged to make good on its promise because it had no alternative.

True, some of its voices would have done credit to any opera house in the world. Helen Traubel, who had sung in the ill-fated 1937 spring season without creating a great stir, was engaged after a 1940 Town Hall recital that was so magnificent it earned column-long reviews in the *Times* and the *Herald Tribune*. Robert Weede never fully came into his own until he went from the Metropolitan to the Broadway theatre. He was hemmed in to some extent by the vocally ailing Tibbett and the rapidly rising Leonard Warren. Among his performances, however, there were some memorable ones. Nobody of his time sang better in the difficult declamation of Scarpia's monologue in the second act of *Tosca*.

John Charles Thomas, at the height of his splendid powers and already famous from musical comedy, radio and concerts, was a valued addition when he could be induced to take opera seriously. He had gained his first experience at the French-language Théâtre de la Monnaie in Brussels and had been known, in the second-act duet of *Rigoletto*, to address Gilda absent-mindedly as *"Ma fille."* In the Shaving Scene of *Il Barbiere di Siviglia*, his standard quip was to address Dr. Bartolo as "Dr. Barbasol." The story was told of him that at a Chicago performance of *Aida*, he came out in Amonasro's leopard-skin costume to take a bow, and encored with "Home on the Range."

Dusolina Giannini, whose infrequent appearances mystified many operagoers, had returned to this country after Farrar-like success in Germany. She was the daughter of Ferruccio Giannini, a Chicago-born tenor who had sung in Colonel Mapleson's companies as a young man and who had worked in Philadelphia with Emile Berliner while that luckless inventor was perfecting flat disc records to replace Edison's more cumbersome cylinders. Some of the early Giannini-Berliner recordings, made by singing through a primitive speaking tube, are still treasured by collectors.

Church authorities were scandalized when Giannini proposed to name his daughter for Dusolina, a pagan character in *I Reale di Francia*. Giannini retorted that he only went to church to please his wife, and he would as soon not have his daughter baptized at all. Here the archbishop,

Mrs. George Washington Kavanaugh admiring Mrs. Frank Henderson's orchid during an opening-night intermission

at whose home Giannini often sang after Sunday dinner, intervened, and Dusolina was duly baptized.

Years later a niece, who happened to be going through the baptismal records in the old family parish in South Philadelphia, found that the Church and not Giannini had had the last word. His daughter's name was entered in the register as Ursulina.

Jacob Pincus Perlmutter reached the Metropolitan after graduating from violinist-vocalist in a jazz band to tenor of the Radio City Music Hall quartet. Old hands at the Music Hall still called him "Pinky" even when he had changed his stage name to Jan Peerce.

After he had been singing at the Metropolitan for some time, Peerce happened to meet his old violin teacher from the Lower East Side, now far along in years. A friend asked the teacher if he recognized his former pupil.

The teacher did. "They tell me you have had a great success," he told Peerce. "They say you are playing first violin in the Metropolitan Opera orchestra."

Eleanor Steber and Risë Stevens were other native singers who developed into versatile, distinguished performers. A dozen others could be named. But there were some for whom an opportunity to sing at the Metropolitan was a dubious kindness.

Why this was so was once made clear by the Viennese soprano Leonie Rysanek in recalling the early stages of her own career. It had begun at the small opera house in Innsbruck, where she had a year-round contract with civil service status. She had learned everything about how an opera house operates; when not actually singing, she did everything from helping with makeup to shifting scenery. Most important, she had an opportunity to appear frequently in a wide variety of roles, and being in the lineup often is as important for an operatic beginner as for a rookie in big-league baseball. No part of an opera singer's craft, any more than an actor's, can really be learned off the stage.

At Innsbruck, Rysanek was a local celebrity. Everyone spoke to her on the street, and if the high C didn't go quite right at a performance, there was always next time.

From Innsbruck the trail led to Breslau, eventually to the Vienna State Opera and finally to the Metropolitan. It had been a gradual transition, by easy stages, from small opera houses to large. Even so, Rysanek confessed, she found her first appearances at the "yellow-brick brewery" a terrifying ordeal.

Jan Peerce, with all his Music Hall seasoning, suffered stage fright at his debut, in the broadcast *Traviata* of November 29, 1941, that was clearly apparent from the audience. (Adding to Peerce's mental stress was the fact that Gennaro Papi, the scheduled conductor, had collapsed and died just before the performance.)

If such experienced performers were intimidated by a Metropolitan debut, it could be traumatic for young Americans with little experience who were put on the big stage to sink or swim. What we most urgently need, and seem least likely to get, is a nationwide string of smaller opera houses like those in which Rysanek and others learned their trade. Workshops are fine as far as they go; but there is something about the professionalism of the most routine third-rate company that is unaccountably missing from a student performance, however polished.

Several disastrous Metropolitan debuts resulted from the Metropolitan's efforts to find a replacement for Lily Pons. During most of the Johnson regime, Pons had no understudy. Without her, the Metropolitan's coloratura repertoire would have been eliminated. Fortunately for the Metropolitan, Pons was as plucky as she was gifted. Watching her from the wings one night, a veteran stagehand shook his head in admiration and said: "I've seen that little woman go out on that stage when she wasn't fit to be out of bed."

But even Pons had to give up sometimes. One such occasion was a scheduled *Lakmé* on December 2, 1942. Someone recalled that a young soprano named Marie Wilkins had sung the Bell Song during the previous year's *Auditions of the Air*. She was hastily summoned to the opera house.

Had Wilkins been prepared, the occasion could have had a storybook ending in the launching of a brilliant new career. Unfortunately, she wasn't. It was a most uncomfortable evening, during which listeners admired the soprano's courage, enjoyed her pretty face and figure, sympathized with her obvious lack of experience, but wished they were somewhere else.

If such events at times gave the Johnson administration an air of desperate hand-to-mouth improvisation, there were others that seemed based

Lily Pons as Lakmé

Lily Pons and Lauritz Melchior

on sheer opportunism. One such event was the appearance of the Icelandic soprano Maria Markan, who made her debut as the Countess in *Figaro* on January 7, 1942. She proved to be a routine, rather hard-voiced singer whom there seemed little reason for bringing in except publicity; Iceland just then was in the news as an important stop in the wartime shipping routes.

The Johnson regime had emphasized not only the desirability of native singers but also of performance in the native tongue. The English-speaking opera houses are unique in always presenting operas in their original language. In Paris, *Die Götterdämmerung* is *Le crépuscule des dieux*; in Italy, *Die Meistersinger* is *I maestri cantori*, and a German Radames addresses his love song to *Holde Aida*.

At first sight it seems absurd not to present opera in the language spoken and understood by the audience. There are, however, a number of practical obstacles. One is that many listeners prefer the original language. One subscriber leaving a Metropolitan English-language performance was overheard to comment: "When they do it in English, it doesn't sound like opera."

Another objection is that the performers would be compelled to relearn all their roles in English. And the greatest hurdle of all is the sheer difficulty of obtaining good English translations. English is a heavily stressed, relatively inflexible language, whereas Italian, for example, can be stretched out and squeezed like a concertina. In Mimi's last-act aria in *La Bohème*, elision of the vowel sounds makes it possible to sing the seven syllables *"Sei il mio amor"* on only three notes.

No doubt one would become accustomed to the sound of opera in English; the Germans do not appear to be put off when Carmen's Habañera is sung as *"Ja, die Liebe hat bunte Flügel."* Many listeners feel, however, that a bad English translation is worse than none. Besides, the native language does not add all that much to comprehension; even in Italy, natives take libretti to the opera. One's most complete enjoyment of a work comes when the text is practically committed to memory.

A Johnsonian experiment with opera in English was a revival of *The Bartered Bride* on February 28, 1941. An observer who wandered into a rehearsal found Bruno Walter in the pit, with Felix Wolfes of the Metropolitan's musical staff seated behind him with the score. Principals on the stage included Ezio Pinza, Italian, and not yet as fluent in English as he became on Broadway; Jarmila Novotna, Czech; Karl Laufkoetter and Ludwig Burgstaller, Germans. From time to time Walter would turn to inquire over his shoulder: *"Kann man das verstehen?"*

"Ja," Wolfes would reply. And the rehearsal proceeded.

To Johnson's wartime problems of singer shortages, rationing, blackouts and persistent deficits were soon added others in the form of competition. The new Opera Company made its appearance on October 15, 1941, with a performance of *Così fan tutte*. Its repertoire included such infrequently performed works as Verdi's *Macbeth*, Tchaikovsky's *Pique Dame* and Moussorgsky's *The Fair at Sorochintzy*. Its social backing was at an impeccably high level. Nevertheless, this time the Metropolitan did not have to buy off its competition. Despite an interesting repertoire, promising new talent, and a revival of *Die Fledermaus* that became a long-running Broadway success, the New Opera Company was essentially a dilettantish venture and soon went under.

More substantial was the New York City Opera Company, founded by Laszlo Halasz and launched with a performance of *Tosca* on February 21, 1944. But the new company proved a complement, rather than competition, for the Metropolitan. It quickly attracted a knowledgeable and loyal audience with novelties and new works which the Metropolitan thought unsuitable for its own more conservative subscribers. Also, after a few disastrous experiences, it left to the Metropolitan large-scale works like *Aida*, for which its own stage facilities were inadequate. The seasons of the two companies were staggered, the New York City Opera preceding the Metropolitan in the fall and following it in the spring.

The hard wartime years finally came to an end, and white ties and ermine were back on November 26, 1945, when the Metropolitan season opened with *Lohengrin*. Prominent in the audience were President Truman's wife and his daughter Margaret, whose vocal aspirations were beginning to be known. Miss Truman, with her Secret Service escort and, later, without it, would become a familiar figure to Metropolitan subscribers.

A striking feature of the immediate postwar seasons was the new snap and precision at close-order drill shown by the choristers and supers in

Standing in line for the 1942 opening night

such scenes as the Changing of the Guard in *Carmen*. The army had left its mark.

The war years, too, had left their mark on the scenery. The *Ring* sets were so tattered it was felt they would not survive another performance. Johnson and his colleagues* could take satisfaction, however, in the fact that the previous season's receipts had been the highest in fifteen years and had resulted in a profit of nearly $6,000.

There was still another trial in store for the much-tried Johnson administration. The labor unions with which the Metropolitan did business not unnaturally wished to adjust their members' wages to the new, higher postwar price levels. The Metropolitan said it couldn't pay more. In the summer of 1946, during a protracted wrangle with the American Guild of Musical Artists over choristers' salaries, the Johnson regime threatened not to reopen. Two years later, in the course of negotiations with the musicians', the stagehands' and three other backstage unions, the Metropolitan announced for the first time in its history that the coming season had been suspended.

"To those versed in operatic affairs," observed Irving Kolodin, "a season's lapse for any reason but lack of a place to perform was merely a threatening gesture, no matter how seriously it impressed the public."

Kolodin was writing with the knowledge, even cynicism, of a longtime opera-lover. Others, however saw the threat to the Metropolitan as immediate and real. Among them was Billy Rose, whose long string of successes ranged from winning a shorthand competition (with an injured fist clamped around a potato because it was too swollen and painful to operate in normal position) to songwriting; a night club on West Forty-second Street; *Jumbo*, the Aquacade at the 1939 World's Fair, and *Carmen Jones*, an updated version of the Bizet opera with a vaguely Southern United States locale, "Negro dialect" lyrics by Oscar Hammerstein II that infuriated the Harlem newspapers, and an all-Negro cast.

During the *Carmen Jones* rehearsals, Rose decided it would be a nice time to give up smoking. When the craving overpowered him, however, he would borrow a cigarette from whoever was handiest. Chain smokers were afraid to go near him.

* Still Ziegler and Lewis. Ziegler, however, had already been attacked by the illness that would cause his death in 1947.

When the labor disputes threatened the 1948–1949 season, Rose offered to operate the Metropolitan for one year "without loss" if "given a free hand and allowed to clean house." The offer was not accepted; it would have been interesting to see what came of it.

The season duly opened, three weeks late, on November 29. But the strain of the protracted negotiations, which are carried out not by artists but by the tough-minded professionals who represent them, undoubtedly was a factor in Johnson's decision to retire. The board persuaded him to stay until May 31, 1950, to round out fifteen seasons as general manager.

At the end of Johnson's regime, television arrived at the Metropolitan. The first telecast was of the opening-night *Otello* in 1948. The 1949 opening-night *Rosenkavalier* also was telecast, offering an unexpected comic touch during an intermission interview backstage with Johnson. A member of the cast who had obviously had several himself kept wandering before the camera with a glass of champagne in his hand, urging the general manager to have a drink.

While a network might televise opening night as a public service, it was inconceivable that any sponsor would pay for an entire performance, running three hours or more regularly during the season. Filling the long intermissions also was a problem, with cameras sometimes reduced to panning rows of empty seats. By and large, radio remained the means by which the Metropolitan communicated with its audience across the country.

One of the most absorbing performances of the Johnson era, and possibly of all Metropolitan history, took place on February 4, 1949, with the experienced hand of Fritz Reiner leading the orchestra and with Ljuba Welitch making her debut as Salome. Operagoers accustomed to sopranos who blasted their way through the role by main force listened as if to a revelation as Welitch's silvery voice floated effortlessly above the rampaging Strauss orchestra. One felt this must have been exactly the effect Strauss had had in mind — a performer with the voice of a young girl and the sensuous body of a voluptuary. Strauss had wanted fragile-voiced Elisabeth Schumann for the role, and had prepared a special reduced orchestration in the hope that she would accept. Schumann had sense enough to refuse.

Welitch's first-season Salome was an experience as brief as it was memorable. Thereafter her singing never quite reached the same high standard. Various explanations were put forward, ranging from a throat operation

*Composer-critic-commentator Deems Taylor and Mrs. Taylor at an opening
night in the Forties*

to an unfortunate love affair. (Welitch once told an interviewer she loved men and money, in the order.)

Welitch was perhaps most thoroughly miscast as Musetta in *La Bohème*. The improbable carrot-red hair and surplus pounds that added to Salome's aura of decadent luxury merely made Musetta dowdy.

During one memorable *Bohème*, at the close of the Cafe Momus Scene, Welitch prepared to ride offstage on the shoulders of the Bohemians Schaunard and Marcello. The soprano misjudged the distance, and Schaunard received her full weight on his right forearm, bent at an awkward angle. He barely made it to the wings.

At intermission Virgil Thomson, then of the *Herald Tribune*, asked a group of colleagues in the lobby: "Do you like female impersonators?"

31

Who Hired Bing?

JOHN ERSKINE said Mrs. Belmont did.

Mrs. Belmont denied it; she said she had merely gone to England to investigate Bing's eligibility from a social point of view.

At any rate, the general chronology of events seems clearly established. Early in 1949, a group called the National Arts Foundation began negotiating to bring England's famed Glyndebourne Opera to this country. Rudolf Bing, the general manager at Glyndebourne, came over to have a look at the National Arts group.

Nothing came of the negotiations; but meanwhile Bing had arranged through Fritz Stiedry, an old friend from Berlin who was now conducting at the Metropolitan, to pay a courtesy call on Edward Johnson. During the course of their conversation Johnson startled Bing by asking: "How would you like to have this job?"

Bing thought Johnson surely must be joking. To prove he wasn't, Johnson arranged a meeting with board chairman George Sloan for the next day. Thoroughly bemused, Bing returned to England.

In May, he was summoned back by a peremptory telegram from Sloan. After a series of interviews with board members — and a favorable report from Mrs. Belmont — Bing was offered a three-year contract starting June 1, 1950. During the intervening year, he would be paid as an "observer" in order to acquaint himself with the Metropolitan and its workings.

Bing hesitated. Glyndebourne, the small, intimate theatre created by the wealthy Englishman John Chrystie on his country estate, was unique among the world's opera houses. The Edinburgh Festival which Bing had created almost single-handedly was an immense success that drew thousands of summer visitors to the Scottish capital. By any standard, Bing was well fixed where he was. On the other hand, the magic of the Metropolitan name lured him as it did the world's great singers. He ended by accepting.

On his arrival in New York, the new general manager proved to be a slightly built, middle-aged man whose slenderness and erect carriage made him seem taller than he actually was. He spoke English in an odd and rather fascinating Oxford accent with Viennese overtones. His lean, high-cheek-boned face, bald spot like a clerical tonsure, nervous energy and general air of having the situation under control made one think of an ascetic-looking monk who once had been a riverboat gambler.

Bing's tenure of office got off to a bad start. The Metropolitan's press department sent out a release stating that he had been director of the Darmstadt and Charlottenburg operas in Germany, that he had organized the first Glyndebourne Festival in 1934 and had been general manager ever since. The mistake was so embarrassing that Bing felt obliged to correct it in an open letter to the press. Conductor Fritz Busch and stage director Carl Ebert were the founders of Glyndebourne. In 1934 Bing had been a concert agent in Vienna; his contribution to the first festival had been to round up a group of singers at Chrystie's request.

The concert agency was one of a series of jobs that began with an apprenticeship in a secondhand bookstore. Born into a solid Viennese mercantile family (his father was head of the Austrian iron cartel), Bing by the age of fifteen had been expelled from several schools and had convinced his family that he would never amount to anything. He studied singing and once auditioned for Lilli Lehmann, then living in retirement in Salzburg. After hearing him, Lehmann called: "Let's go, Fifi!" to her little dog and left the room. Looking back on his brief singing career, Bing said he was glad it came to nothing; he would not have hired himself even for the Metropolitan chorus.

A series of theatrical and managerial odd jobs led him to the Darmstadt Opera as Ebert's administrative assistant, then to Charlottenburg and finally Glyndebourne. When Glyndebourne was suspended during World War II, Bing, who by then had become a British subject, got a job as assistant to the manager of a London department store. He soon was in charge of all departments except ladies' fashions. After the war, he was one of the group that got Glyndebourne started again, eventually becoming its general manager.

Fritz Busch good-naturedly forgave the overstatement of the Metropolitan's press release. Ebert, however, held Bing responsible; it was the end of a twenty-year friendship.

Although Bing's role as "observer" seemed workable enough in theory, tension mounted as the season went on and it became necessary to complete plans for 1950–1951. The main responsibility, naturally, was Bing's. That Bing intended to run things in his own way, with his own team, was shown by his not retaining Frank St. Leger as musical secretary. An Irishman born in India, St. Leger had toured as Melba's accompanist from 1912 to 1917, had been Johnson's vocal coach in Italy and had conducted not only at the Metropolitan but also at Covent Garden, the Chicago Opera and the restored opera house in Central City, Colorado. Being practical as well as musical, he had taken over more and more of the day-by-day administrative tasks that Ziegler was unable to perform during the illness that preceded his death in 1947.

St. Leger was succeeded as artistic administrator by Max Rudolf, and as general assistant by John Gutman, two old friends of Bing's from the Darmstadt days. To Rudolf, Bing confessed frankly that he could not afford to keep St. Leger; he was too much older and knew too much more about the local scene.

Bing's first confrontation with an artist was handled in a manner that soon became typical. Leonard Warren and Melchior both had the same concert manager. In this way, Melchior learned that Warren's contract had been renewed while his had not. Melchior issued an ultimatum. It was a Saturday evening; if Bing did not offer him a contract by Monday morning, he could find himself another *Heldentenor*.

Max Rudolf, knowing his man, replied that ultimatums were not a good idea with Bing. But Melchior was adamant. Bing was, too.

"I will not be dictated to," Bing said in a public statement. "No doubt I shall make mistakes, but I can assure you that I will attempt to run this house — unmoved by promises or threats — on the principle of quality alone."

It was the end of Melchior's Metropolitan career — which would have ended soon in any case, since the tenor was in his sixties.

Melchior was the first of three dozen artists to be dismissed. Another was Robert Merrill, who had notified the management rather casually that he would not be available when the company wanted him. He was going to Hollywood to appear in a film called *Aaron Slick from Punkin Crick.* Bing informed the baritone he had breached his contract and was no longer a member of the company. Shocked and sobered, Merrill promised to mend his ways. Being the valued artist that he was, he had no trouble being reinstated.

Bing's position was that an artist's first loyalty belonged to the Metropolitan. "To appear at the Metropolitan," he once said, "is a spectacular honor and should even be worth a financial sacrifice." And it must be admitted that to run the company on any other basis was to court disaster. The frequent crises of the Johnson administration often were the fault of the easygoing management itself. Many times, when a singer became indisposed, it had been necessary to look frantically for a last-minute replacement because the alternative artist supposed to be covering that performance had taken an out-of-town engagement.

A revealing contrast between Johnson's manner and Bing's was shown when Antoniette Stella demanded a solo bow, in violation of the Metropolitan's no-solo rule, after her Nile Scene aria in *Aida.* Otherwise, she said, she would not finish the performance.

Johnson once faced an exactly similar situation, when Grace Moore arrived at the opera house out of sorts and refused to go on. Johnson put his arm around her shoulders, propelled her out the stage door — meanwhile keeping up a soothing stream of badinage and flattery — walked her around the block, back through the stage door and into her dressing room. Moore sang.

But when Bing was summoned to the stage, he looked at his watch and told Stella he was giving her exactly three minutes to make up her mind to sing. If not, he would suspend the performance, refund admissions and inform the audience why he was doing so. He would then sue Stella for the evening's box-office receipts. He would also file a protest with the American Guild of Musical Artists.

"Incidentally," he said in conclusion, "you now have only two minutes and a half."

It would have been interesting to see the public's reaction if Bing had carried out his threat. But Stella lost her nerve, as Bing had shrewdly anticipated that she would. The performance went on.

A tenor once called two hours before an important rehearsal to announce that he was too ill to sing. Within minutes an ambulance arrived at the tenor's hotel, manned by two husky attendants who informed the tenor they had come to take him to a hospital for treatment at the expense of the Metropolitan's general manager. The tenor decided that he was feeling better.

Bing soon showed that displays of artistic temperament left him unmoved. While Gatti-Casazza's attitude toward artists had been a sort of resigned paternalism, and Johnson had treated them as valued fellow artists, Bing's manner was often one of icy disdain. "I find that artists are more often uneducated than genuinely temperamental," he once observed. He could be unbelievably cutting at times, and the withering nature of his comments was reinforced by the somewhat supercilious manner in which he delivered them.

Once a baritone who had appeared with the company in numerous roles found that for the coming season he had been offered only six performances of Lescaut in *Manon*. The singer told Bing that while he would be happy to perform the relatively minor and quasi-comic role, he was not a beginner and would like to display his talents in a more diversified range of parts. Bing looked at him coldly and replied: "My dear sir, there isn't a role in your repertoire that another member of the company can't do better."

Episodes of this kind aroused such resentment among performers that word of it began getting back to the board of directors. One director asked Bing whether, if some truths had to be faced, they couldn't be delivered in a way less upsetting to the singers. Bing replied that it would be a waste of effort, since singers were bound to be upset about something most of the time, in any case.

Not only artists felt the whiplash of Bing's tongue. Once, during a protracted labor negotiation, a union official raised his voice to emphasize a point. In his most lordly Anglo-Viennese manner, Bing said: "Would you mind screaming that again? I didn't quite get it."

Both Gatti-Casazza and Johnson had been at considerable pains to cultivate the goodwill of the press. Bing, of course, understood the value of publicity, but his manner toward newspapermen could hardly be described as servile. Once a group of reviewers, backstage during an intermission, were discussing Franco Corelli. The tenor had just made international head-lines during a performance in Italy by drawing his prop dagger and leaping into a box to attack an operagoer who had hissed his singing.

"Bravo!" Bing exclaimed. "Corelli is coming to the Metropolitan next season, and when he gets here I shall train him to bite critics."

Bing was incensed by what he considered incompetence on the part of a reviewer. "Criticism should be made a licensed profession," he once said. "Why should an experienced artist be subject to public ridicule by a young man who has just started in his job? There are schools for mu-sicians and singers. There ought to be a school for critics."

Once when the Metropolitan was in Chicago on tour, its performances had been blasted daily for a week by Claudia Cassidy, the deceptively fragile-looking critic of the *Tribune*. Then Bing happened to meet her during an intermission. Bing beamed, and said in his suavest tone: "Why, hello, Miss Cassidy. I didn't know you were in town."

Bing's comment about his fellow impresario Herbert von Karajan had widespread repercussions. "Karajan says he had thirty-seven lighting re-hearsals for his *Götterdämmerung* in Vienna," Bing observed. "I could get the stage that dark with two."

Summing up the impact of Bing, the late C. D. Jackson of Time-Life-Fortune, then a member of the Metropolitan board, once said regretfully: "Our problem is that we have a witty general manager." Other board members, particularly George Sloan, took a less lenient view. The board had questioned the wisdom of dropping St. Leger and felt that some of the dis-missed singers, Melchior in particular, had been treated rather shabbily after long years of service. And Bing had trodden on too many toes for his own good. At board meetings, the sentiment "Bing must go" began to be heard with increasing frequency. When it became known that George Sloan was determined to have a new general manager, some members of the staff began to operate openly on the assumption that Bing's current con-tract would be his last.

Those were dark days for Bing; he had few friends inside the house ex-cept Max Rudolf and Gutman. Then George Sloan died. Insiders believed it was only Sloan's death that saved Bing's neck. With Sloan gone, the anti-Bing drive collapsed. As is usual in such cases, the board was split into a pro-Bing minority, an anti-Bing minority and a remainder that did not feel strongly one way or the other. Besides, it was coming to be appreciated that while Bing was an easy man to dislike, he had charted a course for the Metropolitan and was steering it with a firm hand on the tiller. As one observer put it: "You always know where you stand with Bing, even if the knowledge doesn't make you particularly happy."

Bing fired the backstage mutineers and life at the opera house settled back, more or less, to normal.

32

The New Broom

ON A TYPICAL MORNING, Bing arrived in his office at ten o'clock. On his desk was a typed list, which he studied at odd moments during the day, of the guests who would be sitting in the director's box that evening. (Even so, he sometimes got the names wrong.) After a day of conferring with department heads, artists, managers, newspaper reporters and board members, he would go home to early dinner at his thirty-sixth-floor apartment in the Essex House. After dinner, in white tie and tails, he would head back to the Metropolitan for the evening performance. His wife Nina, a Moscow-born former dancer, seldom went along. She preferred the Russian Tea Room on West Fifty-seventh Street.

Bing first went backstage to wish the singers well for the performance. He felt that such amenities not only helped company morale, but also served to let people know that "the boss is in the house." And an observant boss at that.

In the Johnson days, when whole rows of seats were being given away merely to fill the house, a ticket-taker at one entrance had fallen into the easygoing habit of admitting his friends and friends of friends without tickets. No graft was involved; he was a good-natured fellow who did it out of sheer hospitality. Once inside, a dollar handed to an usher would get an orchestra seat that wasn't being used that evening.

The ticket-taker, however, made the mistake of carrying over his hospitality to the Bing regime. It was not long before Bing caught him red-handed. Approaching a couple who had just been admitted, Bing asked to see their ticket stubs. When they couldn't produce them, Bing fired the unfortunate ticket-taker on the spot.

Bing also barred the motley horde of artists' relatives, fan clubs, press agents and assorted hangers-on who had formerly had the run of back-stage. It was no longer possible to use the stage entrance on the strength of being a correspondent for an obscure publication in Brooklyn. The buzzer that released the stage-door latch sounded only if one had good reason for being there.

The sharp break with Johnsonian custom had been apparent as early as the first production of Bing's first season. In one of his last interviews as general manager, Johnson had said: "At the Metropolitan, we try to hold to the pattern of the past while designing new policies for the future. But all this is done on a trial and error basis—it doesn't change overnight."

It did under Bing, however. The new general manager was a man who knew his own mind. He had strong likes and dislikes, which inevitably began to be reflected in the Metropolitan's performances. The list of his ten favorite operas which he gave to the *Times* included *Wozzeck* but not one work by Wagner.* The Metropolitan did not go Wagnerless on that account, however; Bing was astute enough to know that Wagner com-manded a loyal public. Besides, the Lee Simonson sets had been used for only one *Ring* cycle, and some wear had to be gotten out of them.

Bing was frankly bored by *Pelléas et Mélisande.* "This is as long as *Götterdämmerung,*" he said, "only not as funny."

After the opening night of November 22, 1949, Irving Kolodin had com-mented in the *Sun* that opening night was no longer viable either as a social event or as an opera performance. Why not, he suggested, treat it frankly as a clambake, perhaps at higher prices, get it out of the way and then turn to the really serious business of the season?

Bing "made the professional's improvement on the amateur's suggestion," as Kolodin put it, by combining opening night and two other galas into a three-performance package selling at sixty dollars per seat. Both patrons and box office were delighted. The three events brought in $53,671.46 more than would have been realized from sold-out houses at normal rates.

Bing's choice of an opera for his first opening night was a bold one.

* The others on the list were *Der Rosenkavalier, Fidelio, Otello, Don Carlo, Aida, La Bohème, Le Nozze di Figaro, Carmen, Boris Godounov.*

Instead of selecting a surefire success — Metropolitan history afforded abundant precedent for *Faust* — he chose Verdi's *Don Carlo*, which had not been heard at the Metropolitan in nearly thirty years. It was to be staged by the Shakespearean actress and director Margaret Webster, the first of the many talents Bing was to import from the Broadway theatre.

By dismissing the most routine-minded of the Metropolitan's stage directors, Bing had made it clear that tradition would no longer be as highly esteemed a quality as in the past. Many felt the reform was long overdue. Gian-Carlo Menotti in particular had been a voice crying in the wilderness to urge the Metropolitan to bring in people from the commercial theatre who, unfettered by reverence for the past, could look at opera from a fresh point of view. Menotti's comments about "the poor old Met," delivered during a Saturday intermission broadcast, had not endeared him to the management.

Bing's *Don Carlo* was a solid ten-strike. Margaret Webster's staging had dignity and grandeur; Rolf Gerard's sets and costumes gave the production distinction. Two fine new voices in Fedora Barbieri and Cesare Siepi; good performances from veterans Jussi Bjoerling, Robert Merrill and Jerome Hines; deft work by Fritz Stiedry in the pit — except for the somewhat pallid singing of Delia Rigal, it was everything a manager could have hoped for.

The *auto-da-fé* scene, showing the burning at the stake of the Flemish patriots, which is omitted in some productions of *Don Carlo*, was retained in Bing's. Roman Catholic clergy and laity picketed the Metropolitan in protest. Bing was unruffled.

More legitimate-theatre talent arrived. Garson Kanin staged a *Fledermaus* that was so successful and had so many performances — more in a season than any work in Metropolitan history — that Edward Johnson said it should be called "*Fledermice.*" Alfred Lunt staged a graceful *Così fan tutte*, Cyril Ritchard offered a bubbling, high-spirited *Barbiere di Siviglia*. *Madama Butterfly* came to life with authentically detailed sets by Motohiro Nagasaka and staging by Yoshio Aoyama, who had been a Kabuki expert before turning to the opera house. Aoyama threw out Goro's shuffling gait and hands-in-kimono-sleeves posture (Chinese mannerisms, he explained, not Japanese), as well as the fireflies of the love scene, traditionally represented by miniature light bulbs on fishing rods.

"In my country," Aoyama pointed out, "the fireflies do not appear while the cherry trees are in bloom."

Listeners realized, come to think of it, that they don't in this country either.

Best of all was the fact that Herbert Graf, who for years had had a monopoly of the Wagnerian repertoire and as a consequence sometimes tended to be rather perfunctory, was put sufficiently on his mettle by the outside competition to stage a really striking *Rigoletto*, one of the best of the dozen productions he staged during the Bing era at the "yellow-brick brewery."

But the Broadway-Metropolitan interaction was not always fruitful. Charles Elson's single-unit set for *Don Giovanni* reminded Virgil Thomson of a turnpike cloverleaf. Oliver Smith's *Traviata* sets included two mammoth staircases, the one in the third act occupying so much space that the farandole had to be danced on a supper table. Rolf Gerard's staircase in the first act of *Carmen* offered a temptation to move the players up, down and across it, which director Tyrone Guthrie was unable to resist. Noel Straus found the result was unconvincing and marred the effect of massed choral tone. Straus maintained that the most effective way to manage a chorus was also the simplest: to have it function frankly as a chorus, moving on and off the stage with nearly the precision of close-order drill.

Howard Dietz, the fine librettist of *Die Fledermaus*, proved unable to supply an English text for *La Bohème* that was singable, understandable and dignified — qualities it needed to be successful. Horace Armistead designed *Cavalleria rusticana* in a contemporary setting, with such then-contemporary touches as Sicilian peasants wearing castoff GI battle jackets.

In brief, from the new productions of Bing's early years it could be pointed out that designers and directors from the legitimate theatre brought much-needed originality and fresh points of view to the Metropolitan. It could also be pointed out that a little learning is a dangerous thing, and that it helps if directors know what they are doing and understand what the operas are about.

One production that made some listeners have second thoughts was the brownstone *Faust* staged by the English director Peter Brook. On hearing the music, Brook was struck by the fact that it was the quintessence of mid-

Rudolf Bing

nineteenth-century French romanticism. Accordingly, he proposed that the locale be changed from medieval Germany to France of the Second Empire. On the same line of reasoning, one could justify an *Aida* set in Genoa of the Seventies.

The updated *Faust* made nonsensical such lines as Mephistopheles's *"L'epée à cote, le chapeau d'autrefois."* The "hat of other times" was not an antique but a shiny modern silk topper, as of the 1850's. In the Chorale of the Swords, Valentin and his fellow soldiers are supposed to hold up their sword hilts to ward off the power of Mephistopheles. Cross-hilted swords, however, went out with plate armor, and in the Second Empire setting would have been an anachronism.

Even more ludicrous, was the superficial basic premise of the performance. *Faust* is a medieval opera; its Gothic mysticism is an essential element. Imagine a rationalist-skeptic Frenchman of the Age of Pasteur, the spiritual and intellectual heir of Descartes, Bayle and Lavoisier, brought up in the *ambiance* from which the Age of Enlightenment had spread all over Europe and America — imagine such a one even believing in the Devil, let alone performing the incantations needed to summon up the Prince of Darkness. Or a Siebel relying on holy water to break the evil spell that caused flowers to wither at his touch. A French Siebel of the 1850's would have been more likely to try Bordeaux mixture. *

One thing about *Faust*, however, was certain: It lingered in the memory. It was the Bing touch. Even his failures had style.

Bit by bit, Metropolitan productions came to reflect the tastes and personality of the new impresario. Bing made no secret of his coolness toward Wagner, and though the Metropolitan dutifully performed his works from time to time, the great Wagnerian renaissance of the Thirties and Forties was ended. It was suspected that Bing favored European performers over Americans. Certainly his regime was not marked by the forthright pro-Americanism of the Johnson era. Bing's stars came from everywhere.

Bing created something of a furor by engaging the Negro dancer Janet Collins as prima ballerina, supposedly a "first of her race." Everyone had forgotten that Negro dancers had performed, without fuss or fanfare, in

---

* The slurry of lime and copper sulphate that proved effective against *Phylloxera*, the scourge of French vineyards in the mid-nineteenth century.

The Emperor Jones twenty years before. As John Martin of the *Times* observed, "How can you be more colored than colored?"

When Alexander Sanine, the Russian director who staged *The Emperor Jones*, first met with his dark-skinned cast, he asked whether anyone in the group spoke French; his English was poor.

One of the dancers stepped forward.

"Speak Russian," she said in Russian. "I will interpret for you."

Sanine found that she was part gypsy and had performed all over Europe. She had in fact appeared at the theatre in Moscow where he made his debut as stage director.

Bing took another step toward integrating the Metropolitan by engaging Marian Anderson as Ulrica in *Un Ballo in maschera*. It was an intentional miscasting that would have made sense a dozen or more years earlier, when the singer's voice was at its peak. At the later stage of her career, however, to have criticized the Metropolitan for engaging so distinguished an artist as Marian Anderson would almost have been equivalent to opposing motherhood. Bing reasoned, shrewdly and correctly, that the precedent established would make possible the later engagements of such artists as Leontyne Price, George Shirley and Gloria Davy.

Whatever else might have been said about Bing, and a good deal was, he was never known to back away from a controversy. He characterized opera as "basically a brutal profession," and to its exigencies, as the occasion required, he could apply Viennese charm, British superciliousness or hardheaded American-businessman practicality. He was not offended when his regime was characterized as "dictatorial." He felt that, by the very nature of opera, it had to be. Ultimate responsibility for everything rested with the general manager. "What goes right is the result of teamwork," he once said. "What goes wrong is my fault."

Bing's autocratic temperament would again be in evidence in the spring of 1961, when negotiations for a new contract with the musicians' union became deadlocked. Bing again asserted that he would not be dictated to, and at the end of the season departed for Europe and his annual combined vacation and talent search. ("The way Rudy drives," John Gutman commented, "it might also be considered a kind of suicide pact.")

Anthony A. Bliss and other members of the board of directors sighed, took up their picks and shovels again and resumed negotiations. On

Franco Corelli and Leontyne Price with Rudolf Bing after their
Metropolitan debut

August 9, it was announced that the 1961–1962 season had been canceled.

Here newly inaugurated President Kennedy, in the interest of preserving one of the nation's great cultural assets, intervened, sending Secretary of Labor Arthur J. Goldberg to act as mediator.

The season opened.

Unlike some of his predecessors, Bing was not in the least embarrassed by the Metropolitan's deficits. He had been brought up in the tradition of Vienna, where the Vienna State Opera receives an annual subsidy from the government that is bigger than the budget for the Austrian Foreign Service. Metropolitan directors who hoped for a resumption of the good old Gatti-Casazza days, with prosperity and a million dollars in the bank, were doomed to disappointment from the start. Bing's position was that opera had always lost money and, with infrequent exceptions such as the Metropolitan's early days, always would. He planned his seasons on the assumption not that the budget could be balanced, but that the Metropolitan would in some way or other find the money it needed.

Deficits accordingly began mounting to Abbey-like levels and beyond. During Bing's years at the old house, the deficit increased from $300,000 to $2,000,000 a year. During the same time, the annual budget rose from $3,000,000 to $10,000,000. Although the deficits made the Metropolitan's directors unhappy, they became resigned to them as inevitable. For one thing, in the generally inflationary postwar period when nearly everything else cost two or three times what it used to, it was not unreasonable that the cost of the Metropolitan should go up also. For another, it is easier to meet a deficit if it is anticipated ahead of time, and Bing projected his a year in advance. He was meticulous with figures, and his London department-store days had given him valuable experience in money management. His projections of Metropolitan income and expenditures, on target within relatively minor amounts, earned the professional admiration of George S. Moore, president of the First National City Bank and treasurer of the Metropolitan Opera Association. And probably all the directors, when the bad news finally came out, were relieved to find that it was not much worse than Bing had said it would be.

"They may not like the deficits," Bing once said, "but they know they can trust my figures."

33

The Penguins

ONE FEATURE OF THE HOUSE that did not change greatly during the Bing regime was the Metropolitan Opera Club.

On the evening of many Metropolitan performances, there could be seen dining on the Grand Tier, served by waiters in maroon livery, a group that was predominantly male, white-haired and in full evening dress.

Around curtain time, the "penguins," having finished their brandy and cigars, would stroll across the hall and take seats in the omnibus box at the extreme left of the Grand Tier.

The Metropolitan Opera Club had such an aura of wealth, social position and respectability that it was the last place one would have expected to have been the object of a police raid. It was once raided, however, and apparently with good reason.

Tradition says the idea of the Metropolitan Opera Club was born in the spring of 1892 when Preble Tucker, a prominent young lawyer, homeward bound from a theatre on West Twenty-third Street, met his friend Oliver Sumner Teall in Madison Square.

Tucker complained that it was not yet midnight and there was nowhere to go. New York at that time had not one supper club of the type that was fashionable abroad. Tucker was thinking in particular of London's Corridor Club, which had its own box at Covent Garden, and of the older, more famous Jockey Club of Paris with its loge at the Opéra.

Teall had an idea. Why not form a similar club in New York? If such a club had its own box at the Metropolitan, the box could serve as a base of operations for eligible, unattached club members. The boxes which figured so importantly in the Metropolitan's early history at intermission became drawing rooms where hostesses could receive visitors. Young men took less expensive seats elsewhere or simply bought general-admission tickets and cruised the boxes until they found a vacant chair. They were welcomed as escorts for the unattached ladies who were usually present.

Carrying the idea a step farther, why not have the club itself within the opera house?

Reginald de Koven, music critic of the *World*, whose *Robin Hood* at that time was enjoying immense success, was taken with the idea. So were architect Stanford White, James Otis, Elisha Dyer, Jr., and others. At a founders' dinner in the Knickerbocker Club, the Vaudeville Club was organized, with de Koven as president.

Not long thereafter occurred the disastrous 1892 fire which wrecked the stage and part of the auditorium of the Metropolitan. The Vaudeville Club persuaded Abbey, Schoeffel and Grau to lease to the club their undamaged foyer and "assembly rooms" on the Grand Tier. The latter were redesigned by club member Stanford White into a small, charming theatre-supper club for dining with vaudeville.

The Vaudeville Club opened on January 10, 1893. Because repairs to the opera house were not completed, there were no Metropolitan performances that season. Consequently the first attraction at the Vaudeville Club was almost like opening night at the opera. "Bohemia," noted a society page with satisfaction, "was conspicuous by its absence." In the fashionable audience was Louis Keller, founder of the Social Register.

The opening bill featured an artist named Papinta and her "chromatic and serpentine dances." The programs, changed weekly, presented the best talent of the day. The new club soon became immensely popular. At the end of its first season, with a healthy surplus in its treasury, the club renewed its lease. It also rented the large, newly renovated omnibus box on the Grand Tier, opposite the clubroom.

Next season the Metropolitan was again presenting opera. Obviously its performances and those of the Vaudeville Club could not take place simultaneously. The timetable eventually worked out was that variety shows in the clubroom would begin immediately after the opera — at midnight or thereabouts — on Mondays, Wednesdays and Fridays. They would start at nine-thirty on Tuesdays, Thursdays and Saturdays, when, according to the schedule of those days, the opera house was dark.

During the second season, performances at the Vaudeville Club declined in quality and the members' high jinks grew more boisterous. Exact details of what the police raid discovered have been lost; but the revels were clearly bacchanalian enough to call for stern reforms. In its third season, the club abandoned vaudeville and reopened as the Metropolitan Opera Club. It was incorporated on October 10, 1899, with the rising dramatist Clyde Fitch as a member of its board of directors.

The club's first financial crisis occurred in 1901, when it found its treasury bare and its membership down to thirty. Wealthy members dug deep to supply fresh funds and a membership drive was launched. By 1906, the club had 97 regular members and 145 associate members, and had enlarged its omnibus box by acquiring the stall-box on its right. By 1910, the club was in a position to limit memberships and to ration guest invitations. Overcrowding in the clubroom on occasion had inconvenienced active members, "whose comfort," Huneker said, "should be the first consideration."

On November 26, 1906, a letter on the club's official stationery, signed by various members, was addressed to "Signor Enrico Caruso." It read:

We the undersigned wish to express our sincere sympathy for you and to say that we feel you have been most unjustly adjudged, and that you are entirely innocent of the charges that have been made against you.

We hope to greet you on Wednesday evening, and with best wishes for your great success during the coming season, we beg you to believe us, etc., etc.

The occasion was Caruso's famous misadventure in the monkey house at the Central Park Zoo. Treasured in the club's archives was Caruso's handwritten reply: "As long as I live, I shall remember your exquisite kindness. . . . Your letter will be kept by me as one of the most cherished 'mementos' of my artistic career."

Since the Metropolitan Opera Club had been founded for men only, women from the first were determined to be admitted. Club members were equally determined to keep them out. The fight to bar women, however, was a rearguard action. By 1910, they were being grudgingly admitted. They were relegated to a corner, however, and hidden behind a large screen.

An exception was made for the Saturday matinee. At that performance, ladies occupied the first two rows of the box, and tea was served during the final intermission.

During the 1916–1917 season, a crisis of the first magnitude developed. It arose because an elderly Metropolitan Opera clubman had established squatter's rights to the front row, left-hand corner seat in the club box, next to the directors' loge. The best place in the box to see and hear, it was also farthest from the exit, which was at the right-hand rear corner of the box.

The squatter usually left before the end of the last act. To avoid stepping on a dozen pairs of patent-leather toes, he would swing himself over the low partition and go out through the directors' loge.

Soon other members began to use the same shortcut. The Metropolitan's directors quailed at the sight of such acrobatics by elderly clubmen two stories above the orchestra level.

Shortly thereafter, clubmen strolling into the box found that the low partition had been replaced by a brass grill as large and ornate as the head of a Victorian bedstead. Not only was there no question of vaulting over; from that side of the box it was now almost impossible to see the stage.

The club was in an uproar. Younger, hotheaded members were all for drafting a stiff letter of protest to the Metropolitan's management. Older men advocated a cautious policy of wait-and-see.

Meanwhile the grill disappeared as suddenly as it had arrived. One of the Metropolitan's directors, brushing past it in the dark, had snagged his trousers.

In the 1929 market crash, some members of the Metropolitan Opera Club were badly hurt, but there were relatively few resignations. The Metropolitan Opera Club held its own despite the far-reaching changes wrought by the depression. By then, business suits, even sweaters, were being seen at the Metropolitan, even at the traditionally formal Monday performances. White tie and tails, however, held their own in the Metropolitan Opera Club box. It took World War II and gas rationing to change that.

Rationing cut down on the use of limousines, cabs were hard to get and nobody wanted to wear a top hat in the subway. Reluctantly, the club switched to black tie for the duration.

At the annual meeting of the club for the 1940–1941 season, there were only 51 members. The treasury was so depleted that it seemed impossible to guarantee its $10,000 annual rental to the opera house. In addition, the club had authorized extensive alterations in its clubroom and new uniforms for its employees.

Henry Hope Reed, the club's new president, made a rental offer to the Metropolitan — $5,150, plus $100 a head for each new member over and above the 51 on hand. The Metropolitan accepted. Reed and David Shaw-Kennedy, the treasurer, arranged a loan at the New York Trust Company and relaxed. One more season was assured.

By 1946–1947, the club had 104 active members, with 67 associates, and was solvent enough to contribute $42,000 to the Metropolitan Opera Association. In return, the Metropolitan gave the club headquarters a thorough face-lifting, throwing out the Spanish-mission-style furniture with which the club had made do since early in the century.

During the Bing regime, the club began raising money for the opera company by holding an annual gala ball. Bing was delighted, although he was said nevertheless to chafe at having no control over the block of seats set aside for the club on Mondays, Wednesdays, Fridays and Saturday afternoons.

The club had now reached its arbitrarily fixed maximum membership of 125 active members, plus 90 junior and associate members. Even with the limit in size, some observers wondered what would happen if all the members should happen to wish to attend a performance at the same time.

Club officials said they would worry about that when it happened. It never did.

34

The Claque

FOR SO SHREWD AND THEATRE-WISE a professional, Bing occasionally had moments of surprising naïveté. One of them produced a confidential memorandum which, dated December 5, 1952, was circulated to all hands:

This is addressed to every member of the company, although the management is, of course, aware that only a few are really affected by it.

It concerns the claque and the intolerable and undignified level to which this business has now degenerated. Naturally, the management is aware that certain artists employ a claque and, of course, the leaders of the claque and indeed a good number of those employed by those leaders are known to the management. Although the management disapproves of the claque in any shape or form, as long as the claque worked reasonably well and within certain acceptable limits, the management has refrained from taking any active steps to stamp it out.

However, as indicated above, the management is not prepared to tolerate the scandalous behavior which the claque has recently adopted and must ask all artists concerned to cooperate with the management in stamping out this nuisance. Complaints from subscribers and others are mounting. Singers are vastly mistaken if they think that the public cannot perfectly well distinguish between what is a genuine success and what are ridiculous attempts of the claque to force success that never comes.

The management will take every step to prevent the claque, as far as possible, from obtaining tickets and this is a request to all singers concerned to pledge that for the rest of this season they will not employ a claque. Let us see how it works. I feel sure that the vast majority of our outstanding singers have no need for a claque; they could save money and at the same time save the dignity of the House.

I would be grateful if any member of the company who disagrees with the views expressed in this memorandum would see me and discuss it. Anybody who does not, I take it approves of the plan to eliminate the claque and I shall be very grateful for your cooperation in this matter.

Rudolf Bing
General Manager

In the opera house, it is virtually impossible to keep a secret very long, and the substance of Bing's memo soon appeared in the *Times.* Next day the Metropolitan's veteran claque chief was shaking his head sorrowfully and repeating a well-known saying: "Amateurs are ruining the profession."

What had happened was that the presidency of the Zinka Milanov Fan Club had been taken over by a very able and energetic professor from the University of Pennsylvania. At a performance in which the leading roles were sung by Milanov and Kurt Baum, the Milanov Fan Club greeted its idol with such vociferous applause, cheers and whistles that the Baum Fan Club, put on its mettle, tried to outdo them. Curtain calls became virtual hog-calling contests. Eventually the Metropolitan was driven to the extraordinary step of having uniformed Pinkerton detectives in the house when Milanov and Baum appeared together.

At this point, a quiet hint was dropped to Bing that it might be well to scrutinize the door list for the names of those to be admitted backstage after the performance.

The affair was watched with huge amusement by a man with the odd name Voice of Experience. Friends called him "Vox" for short.

"I have to laugh when you newspaper fellows write about the claque," said Vox. "A lot of young punk kids start screaming and you fellows say the claque is doing it. Let me tell you that in the professional claque a ham who did that wouldn't get re-engaged.

"The noise-makers weren't the claque — they were a couple of rival fan clubs. La Scala had the same trouble with Callas fans who hissed when Tebaldi sang, and vice-versa.

"Fan clubs create excitement and are good for business as long as they don't get out of hand. Farrar had a fan club, the famous Gerry-Flappers. Caruso had a clause in his contract to buy fifty standing-room tickets at regular prices for any performance he sang in. That was for the Caruso Fan Club.

"But don't confuse fan clubs with the regular claque. The claque doesn't do anything to make itself conspicuous. It is almost as mysterious as the Mafia. Even today I don't know who runs it. I got in through a friend of mine who knew I was an opera buff.

"Some people are surprised to learn the claque aren't paid. In fact, they pay to get in. They are dedicated men who live for opera. Some of them are dishwashers in midtown restaurants. They don't care how or where they live. They really start living only when the curtain goes up at the opera house. The satisfaction of being there, plus not having to stand in line for standing-room tickets, is all they get out of it.

"I'd get a call from my friend maybe two or three nights a week. We'd meet at the gold Caruso statue in the Broadway lobby. Each of us would give a dollar to a stocky man with iron-grey hair — I never found out his name — and he'd give the money to a doorman. If there were ten dollars, the next ten guys got in. If you lost your place in line, you were out of luck and out a buck."

The Metropolitan was always curiously shamefaced about its claque. Edward Johnson had two stock answers to reporters' queries: There had never been a claque at the Metropolitan; or it had been abolished the previous season.

In most European opera houses, by contrast, the claque is openly sold as a concession. The claquer buys it, as he would the right to check coats or rent opera glasses, and gets out of it what the traffic will bear.

The Metropolitan's claque chief would not discuss business arrangements, pleading that his clients were entitled to the same privacy as those of a lawyer, or a doctor's patients. In a general way, however, it was known that arrangements were flexible. The higher the fee, the larger the claque. An artist scheduled to sing in the Saturday matinee, and wishing to impress a nationwide radio audience, might feel justified in spending more than for an ordinary performance.

"This is interesting," said Vox, "because it tallies with my own empirical observations. The size of the claque varied. Sometimes there would be six or seven of us, sometimes a dozen, sometimes twenty or more."

Metropolitan claquers took standing room on both sides of the house, as near the stage as they could get. One man was stationed in the Dress Circle to watch for the conductor. When the conductor entered the orchestra pit, he was invisible to most of the audience, so the man upstairs started the applause. Conductors did not pay; the claque did it as a professional courtesy.

Then the conductor took up his baton, and the claque was ready for work.

"Next time you are at the opera," said Vox, "listen to the way the professionals start the applause. It's like — if I may be poetic — the first patter of rain on dry leaves. If the audience doesn't take the hint, they stop instantly. If it 'takes,' as we say, that is the time to pour it on. Enthusiasm feeds on itself. The trick is to make the second curtain-call a little bigger than the first, and so on. We call that 'stoking the fire.' After the third or fourth bow it is time enough to yell 'Bravo!'

"And, by the way, don't say 'Bravo' for a lady artist; the feminine form is 'Brava.' Use both with great caution. Too much repetition dulls the edge.

"Sometimes, after a really brilliant vocal feat, you'll hear a quietly murmured 'Brava.' If timed just right, and uttered in just the right tone of hushed reverence, like a churchwarden saying 'Amen,' this will bring the house down. Then you can be sure an old pro is at work."

What happens if one artist pays the claque and another doesn't?

"I can't tell you," said Vox. "In all my years in the claque I never got any instructions. Nobody told me to applaud, nobody told me not to applaud. Maybe they had their orders in the higher echelons."

In this respect, the Metropolitan was somewhat unusual. In most theatres, nothing is left to chance. Berlioz told how conscientiously Auguste, chief of the Paris Opéra claque in his day, worked at "preparing" a new work:

Hidden in his parquet box, he was present at every rehearsal. Then, when the maestro said to him, "Here you will give three rounds, there you will call out encore," he would answer imperturbably: "It shall be done"; or, "Sir, it is dangerous"; or, "I will think about it; my mind is not yet made up on that point. Have some amateurs to attack with, and I will follow them if it takes."

Auguste would resist a composer who tried to get dangerous applause from him: "Sir, I cannot do it. You would compromise me in the eyes of the public. Your work is very difficult to direct."

Not only composers but also performers can be unnerved when expected applause is not forthcoming. Tradition says that was why the Metropolitan's claque began. Caruso was singing in a 1910 production of Gluck's *Armide*. The work, then as now, was unfamiliar to most operagoers. Caruso's finest efforts received scant applause, and the tenor was in despair.

"We must organize a claque," said Alessandro Bonci, the fellow tenor whose handlebar mustache rivaled Caruso's own, "and I know just the man to do it."

"Who?"

"My valet. He knows every note of every opera."

And the Metropolitan claque was born. It continued to operate, the Bing memo notwithstanding, as long as the house itself.*

"That only proves my point," said Vox, "that the claque performs a useful and necessary function. With the best of intentions, the public doesn't always know when to applaud. An opera house without a claque is a vacuum of the sort abhorred by Nature. Let me tell you about a war-time example that came under my notice."

When Manila was retaken [said Vox], the local opera company soon was presenting quite respectable performances of standard Italian opera fare.

The operas were popular with United States troops, among whom were two Midwesterners named Edwards and Zimmerman. Edwards, who haunted the Metropolitan during his trips to New York, explained the plots of the operas and added other backstage lore, such as the workings of the claque. A group of opera buffs soon was in the making.

Once, after *Rigoletto*, Zimmerman asked whether the tenor had not

---

* And it has continued to operate at Lincoln Center, although the more open interior design of the new house, and the absence of a brass rail, make it somewhat more difficult to remain unobtrusive. And from time to time, the fan clubs still get out of hand.

done pretty well with *Questa o quella*. Edwards allowed that he had. Then why, asked Zimmerman, had he not received any applause?

Edwards explained that *Questa o quella* is very difficult to direct. It is in two stanzas, like a hymn tune; an inexperienced audience might expect still a third stanza. Unlike some Verdi arias, which end with a high note that triggers applause practically by reflex action, the conclusion of *Questa o quella* is a simple descending phrase. The tenor's final line, "*Una qualche beltà*," and the first spatter of applause must coincide exactly; otherwise the minuet starts up again and all is lost.

Zimmerman's sense of fair play was outraged. He proposed the formation of a claque to see that the tenor received his just due next time.

Nothing easier. At the next *Rigoletto*, the buffs were on hand with cues carefully memorized, as well prepared as any dishwasher leaning over the Metropolitan's brass rail.

At the proper moment, Zimmerman cupped his hands and shouted through them a tremendous, ear-splitting "*Bra-VO!*" The conductor dropped his stick, the concertmaster dropped his bow, the tenor dropped a cue and the house vibrated with quiet merriment.

Zimmerman was astonished and asked whether that was not the approved way of showing enthusiasm at the opera.

"Yes," said Edwards, "except that for a minute there, I thought Illinois had just made a touchdown."

35

Callas

CONSIDERING THE IMPACT of Maria Callas on the Metropolitan, it is somewhat surprising to be reminded that she appeared there in only four roles — Norma, Lucia, Tosca, and Violetta in *La Traviata*. All told, in three seasons she sang twenty-one Metropolitan performances. John Brownlee used to sing three times that many in a single season.

The revival of Bellini's *Norma* that opened the 1956–1957 season confirmed what some listeners had already guessed from the recordings — the voice was uneven, with a curious hollow timbre in the middle register. Although she sang coloratura roles, Callas was not really a coloratura, and proved it by cracking repeatedly on the high E flat in *Lucia*. As an actress, she was more than somewhat of a ham.

But Callas was a personality. She made an immediate, vivid impression on people, either for good or bad. She was one of those performers about whom it is impossible to feel lukewarm. Listeners either loved or hated her performance. Gian-Carlo Menotti was probably right in his comment that of the audience that packed the theatre for a Callas performance, half were hoping to see her fall on her face.

She could not by any stretch of the term be called beautiful. But she fascinated men. She married the wealthy Italian Gianbattista Meneghini, whose position as a large shareholder of Electric and Musical Industries, Ltd, facilitated her early appearances on Angel records. Later she left Meneghini for an even richer man, the Greek shipping magnate Aristotle Onassis.

Longtime Callas admirers say her voice was at its peak when she was singing with the ill-fated Italian opera company, organized by New York lawyer-impresario Edward Bagarozy, which ran aground in Chicago in 1947–1948. At that time she weighed 190 pounds. When she reached the Metropolitan ten years later, the change in her appearance was so dramatic that rumors were soon circulating that she was suffering from a tapeworm. Callas brushed aside inquiries about her figure by saying that if she had a secret reducing formula, she would be as rich as Helena Rubinstein. Many admirers felt Callas had taken off too much too quickly. Generally speaking, and all else being equal, it is safer vocally for a singer to err on the stout rather than the slender side.

When Callas arrived at the Metropolitan, her voice was already beginning to show the strain of her early singing days. As Maria Callogeropoulos, born and brought up in the Fort Washington section of Manhattan, she had been an unhappy, overweight schoolgirl with a promising voice. At thirteen she had gone with her mother to Athens, to study with the great Elvira de Hidalgo. Trapped by the war, they spent five years in Athens.

The Athens Opera continued functioning, for an audience composed mainly of the opera-loving Italian army of occupation. At seventeen, Callas made her debut with the company, singing Tosca on twenty-four hours' notice. It was typical of the engagements with which she made her earliest successes. At La Fenice in Venice, she learned, rehearsed and sang Isolde in one month. When she was preparing another Wagnerian role, Brünnhilde in *Die Walküre*, the soprano scheduled for the staggeringly difficult coloratura role of Elvira in *I Puritani* became ill a few days before the performance. Since it was impossible to get a replacement on such short notice, Callas took over Elvira as well as Brünnhilde.

When Callas auditioned for de Hidalgo, she had sung "Ocean, Thou Mighty Monster" from *Oberon*. "Now that you have sung 'Ocean' so well," de Hidalgo told her, "you must put this music away. In ten years' time you can look at it again. This is no music for a young voice."

But Callas in her teens and early twenties was singing some of the most taxing roles of the dramatic soprano repertoire — Santuzza in *Cavalleria rusticana*, the title roles in *Turandot, La Gioconda* and *Aida*, Brünnhilde in *Die Walküre*, and Isolde in *Tristan und Isolde*. She was also singing lyric and coloratura roles. She would sing anything to get a performance. If someone needed a dramatic soprano, she was a dramatic soprano; if they needed a coloratura, she was a coloratura.

It is all very well if one has that kind of voice; but it can be a spend-thrift use of vocal resources for which one must pay later on.

Callas was driven by the attribute which every prima donna needs and of which she possessed enough for several: an obsessive desire to succeed, at whatever cost. It was the propulsive power that would send her through her first *Gioconda* in spite of a sprained ankle — a mishap that is painful out of all proportion to its seriousness as an injury — and that in later seasons would cause her to rehearse thirteen hours at a stretch if there was no other way to get the effect she wanted.

It would also send her into a screaming tantrum when a maitre d'hotel, quite courteously and respectfully, informed her that the New York Board of Health regulations would not permit her to bring her miniature poodle to dinner at his restaurant. And, in Chicago, it produced what was perhaps the most unflattering photograph of a prima donna ever made — Callas's strident denunciation of a process server who had just handed her a summons.

When reporters were around, Meneghini wore a somewhat apprehensive look, as if uneasy about what Callas would do or say next. Callas was "good copy" because she answered questions off the top of her head, without stopping to think how the answers would look in cold print next day. Consequently she was always stumbling into the traps laid for her by crafty newsmen. Once, being questioned about Renata Tebaldi, Callas said she admired Tebaldi's fine musicianship and did not regard her as a rival. That was a gracious thing to say and Callas could well have stopped there. But she went on to add: "It's like comparing champagne and Coca-Cola."

The life of a prima donna's husband is not all beer and skittles. For Meneghini it meant giving up time from his construction-materials business to accompany Callas about Europe, South America, Mexico and the United States, sitting through endless rehearsals and coping with the crises that were precipitated around her with clocklike regularity.

A bystander recalled seeing Meneghini at a Metropolitan rehearsal that had been going on for hours. Meneghini was asleep in a folding chair backstage. Presently he awoke with a start. He looked around, realized where he was and sighed. He took a large roll of bills from his pocket and began to count the money. He counted again to be sure he had the amount correctly. Then he sighed again, happily, and went back to sleep.

For Callas's first season at the Metropolitan, Bing had craftily scheduled her performances so as not to coincide too closely with those of Tebaldi and Milanov. The previous season, Carol Fox in Chicago had presented Callas in *I Puritani* one evening, Tebaldi in *Aida* the next. Callas, magnificently gowned, attended her rival's performance. In the Nile Scene, as Tebaldi approached the dreaded high C, listeners were distracted by a flurry in the Callas box. Callas had dropped a diamond bracelet and was looking for it with a flashlight.

After two seasons at the Metropolitan, Callas demanded a new production staged especially for herself. To keep Tebaldi happy, the Metropolitan had presented her in a handsome new *Traviata*, and Milanov had starred in a revival of *Ernani*. By contrast, *Norma* was no longer new, the *Tosca* sets were shabby and those for *Lucia* were almost in tatters. Bing proposed *Macbeth*, which he planned to revive in 1958–1959, followed by *La Traviata*. Callas demurred; Bing's proposed schedule would require alternating the dark, dramatic role of Lady Macbeth too closely with the florid, almost coloratura music of Violetta. As a compromise, Bing proposed Lucia instead of Violetta.

While the negotiations were still going on, Callas had gone to Texas (CALLAS IN DALLAS, the *Times* couldn't help headlining) to appear in Cherubini's *Medea*. Time was growing short. Bing sent Callas a peremptory telegram asking to know her plans and demanding an answer by ten o'clock next morning. Immersed in *Medea*, Callas didn't reply. In midafternoon Bing fired off a telegram of dismissal and released a statement to the press. The Metropolitan, while "grateful for her artistry for two seasons . . . is nevertheless also grateful that the association is ended."

Callas had left the Athens Opera after a tiff with the management. She had held the Chicago Opera Company personally responsible for her encounter with the process server and had vowed never to sing there again. She had abruptly canceled in Vienna and Edinburgh. She had canceled a San Francisco performance on the ground of being indisposed and had then gone to Venice to attend a party Elsa Maxwell was giving in her honor.

Maxwell, whose syndicated column appeared in San Francisco, was indiscreet enough to write that it was the first time a star had ever canceled a performance to attend one of her parties. At the San Francisco Opera, Callas's stock tumbled to zero. Callas, Bing ironically observed, was "burning her opera houses behind her."

Callas was frequently singing badly. Two days after Christmas, 1957, she sang a Norma at the Rome Opera before a gala audience that included President Gronchi and other Italian government officials. Her high notes were tired and unsteady, and soon her low notes gave out as well. She was barely able to finish the first act. The performance ended there; the management had not provided an understudy. Neither the management nor anyone representing Callas appeared to explain to the audience what had happened. Callas escaped through an underground passage to the Hotel Quirinale and took refuge in her suite. Operagoers gathered outside the hotel, denouncing Callas and demonstrating wildly. Despite Callas's apology to President Gronchi, newspapers protested the "affront" to the head of the Italian Republic. Rome, too, was now off limits.

Callas left La Scala after bickering with superintendent Antonio Ghiringhelli. Her last appearance was in Bellini's *Il Pirata*. At the opera's end, the heroine bemoans the fate of her lover, now captured, with the words "*Vedete il palco funesto*" ("Behold the fatal scaffold."). *Palco* in Italian also means "seats for spectators," and the "palco" to which Callas pointed with a bitter smile, to underscore her reason for leaving La Scala, was the proscenium box occupied by superintendent Ghiringhelli.

Ghiringhelli got even. While Callas was still taking curtain calls, he had the asbestos fire curtain lowered.

One place in which Callas could still sing was Paris. At four o'clock on the afternoon of a *Norma* performance there, Callas had a sudden, alarming drop in blood pressure. But after an injection of nikethamide, she insisted on singing. She wanted no repetition of the Roman disaster. She went on stage even though she could hardly walk straight; one of the drug's side effects is that it sometimes upsets the sense of balance. "I'll never forget that performance," said a singer who was there. "I don't like

Callas, but I have to hand it to her. The first two acts were awful. Then she picked herself up off the floor, by sheer nerve and will power, and carried the audience with her. At the end, she had them eating out of her hand."

During one of Callas's infrequent trips to New York, Bing heard a familiar voice on the telephone: "Hello, Rudy" — Bing detests being called Rudy — "this is Maria."

The phone call paved the way for a reconciliation. Exasperating as Bing might find Callas to deal with, he was too astute to ignore her demonstrated pulling power at the box office.

After negotiations between New York and the home in Paris to which Callas had moved since divorcing Meneghini, the date of Callas's return to the Metropolitan was fixed. She would sing two performances of *Tosca* in March, 1965. Bing saw to it that they would be special gala performances at special gala prices.

Callas's return on March 19 was one of the big events of the 1964–1965 season. The ticket scalpers, those infallible box-office indicators, had been busy. Standees had begun lining up outside the building days before the tickets went on sale. They hung out a large banner reading: "Welcome home, Callas." When Callas made her first appearance in Act I, the normal spatter of applause became a demonstration that lasted four minutes. The performance itself was page-one news in both the *Times* and the *Herald Tribune*, something that normally happened only after opening night.

The voice was smaller than listeners remembered it as being and it had lost some of its freshness. In good voice or bad, however, it was clear that the public still wanted Callas.

When Callas's long and well-publicized association with Aristotle Onassis came to an end, she was said to have summed up her career with the rueful observation: "First I lost weight, then I lost my voice, then I lost Onassis."

As for Onassis, a story that made the rounds paid tribute to the *savoir faire* of that astute financier:

"How did Onassis get rid of Callas, when he wanted to marry Jackie Kennedy?"

"Easily. He took Callas to the airport and put her on a plane."

Maria Callas

36

Nilsson

ONE OF THE GREAT OCCASIONS in Metropolitan history was the December night in 1959 on which subscribers first heard the voice of Birgit Nilsson.

For listeners backstage, the event was given added impressiveness by the realization that the Swedish soprano's voice was sending its vibrations through the Metropolitan's four-foot brick walls.

What makes a well-produced big voice like Nilsson's exciting is not loudness per se. Old-fashioned steam calliopes were loud — it was said the organists who played them were eventually deafened by the tremendous racket — but that did not make them enjoyable listening. Nilsson's voice exhibited the quality that Italians call *raccolta* — the quality of being compact or focused like a beam of light. The thrill of hearing a big voice properly zeroed in is comparable to a backswing in which every ounce of energy goes into a cleanly hit shot that sends the ball 250 yards down the fairway. And the singer's focus, or "placement," must be as microscopically accurate as the golfer's backswing, or he will find himself hitting vocal hooks and slices, and landing knee-deep in the rough.

Nilsson's superb singing technique was not natural and instinctive, like Ponselle's; she had to work hard to acquire it. The first obstacle was her father, a prosperous farmer of Västra Karup in southern Sweden. Disappointed at not having a son to take over the family farm, he sent his daughter to agricultural school, reasoning that she could at least become a farmer's wife. Nilsson's mother, however, a fine soprano who could still sing high C's at sixty, wanted her daughter to have the career she had wished for herself.

Nilsson's first and, as it turned out, only teacher was a local organist and choirmaster named Ragnar Blennow. He was obviously a capable and conscientious voice teacher, but the crucial factor in Nilsson's development was Nilsson herself. One night she was experimenting to find a way of singing above a heavy cold. She found it, and made the discovery of proper breath support. Blennow, like any teacher worth his salt, must have stressed breath support from the opening lesson; but it was Nilsson's own investigations that enabled her to put theory into practice.

With proper support, Nilsson found her range, which had been limited, going up and up. High notes no longer held any terrors. One of her earliest successes at the Royal Opera in Stockholm was as Lady Macbeth, a role dreaded by many sopranos because of the D flat above high C at the end of the Sleep-walking Scene. Not only is the note attacked, but also it is sustained as the soprano walks offstage.

As a safety measure, conductor Fritz Busch had assigned the high note to another soprano, standing in the wings. At rehearsals, the offstage soprano cracked repeatedly. Nilsson thought the arrangement ridiculous; nobody should be expected to start from scratch with a high D flat. It would be easier to work up to it by singing the aria. She would be blamed anyway if the note was cracked, said Nilsson; why not let her crack her own D flat? She sang a number of performances and never cracked once.

Nilsson was engaged by the San Francisco Opera in 1956 for her American debut. She had auditioned for Bing in Berlin without success. Later, after hearing her as Salome in Munich, he had again decided against engaging her. Not until he heard her Isolde in Vienna did the Metropolitan general manager offer her a contract.

Nilsson was philosophical about the delay but could not resist pointing out that if Bing had engaged her earlier, she might have been a good deal less expensive.

In her first month with the Metropolitan, Nilsson's ruggedness was underscored by a *Tristan* which she sang with three ailing tenors, each of whom believed his strength would hold out for one act. Explaining the arrangement to the audience in a brief curtain speech, Bing added matter-of-factly: "Fortunately, the opera has only three acts."

The indisposed *Heldentenoristen* were Karl Liebl, Ramon Vinay and Albert da Costa, all six-footers and, in costume backstage, looking rather like the center of the Green Bay Packers' line. Nevertheless, at the end of the performance, all three went back to bed. Nilsson, however, was still going strong. "Now," she said, "I feel as if I could sing Turandot!"

But pride goes before a fall. That was before Nilsson found out what it was like to rehearse for and perform on the Ed Sullivan show. She was so knocked out by the telecast that she had to cancel her next two Metropolitan performances.

Bing was incensed, not only by the loss of his star soprano but also by her public juxtaposition with vaudeville and an animal that proved imperfectly housebroken. "A Metropolitan artist," said the general manager bitterly, "between a ventriloquist and a peeing dog."*

Once at the Metropolitan, Nilsson rapidly became indispensable to the German wing. A first-rate *Ring* cycle depended on the availability of Nilsson; there was no one else in her class. She sang Elsa, Isolde, and once accomplished the *tour de force*, never before attempted at the Metropolitan, of singing Venus in the first act of *Tannhäuser* and Elisabeth in the other two. She performed the strenuous title roles in Strauss' *Salome* and *Elektra*, and turned to Italian repertoire to sing Aida, Tosca, Turandot, and Amelia in *Un Ballo in maschera*. Possibly not since the days of Lilli Lehmann had so large and varied a share of the season's burden been carried by a single artist.

A story relished at the Metropolitan concerned the accountant, helping Nilsson with her income tax, who asked whether she had any dependents. "Yes," she replied, "Mr. Bing."

Nilsson disclosed an extraordinary ability to vary the texture of her voice to suit a particular role or occasion. In her *Tannhäuser* dual performance, she differentiated sharply between the sultry, sensuous music of Venus and the fresh, girlish singing of Elisabeth; it was almost as if two different voices were performing the roles. In *Turandot*, she used a cold, almost metallic vocal quality to portray the frigid Princess.

One of Nilsson's most remarkable vocal feats took place after she had finished singing Brünnhilde in *Die Götterdämmerung*. In her dressing room, to amuse a group of friends, she sang the Queen of the Night aria from

---

* Sullivan defended his mishmash variety programming as a matter of sheer survival. Once, he said, when he presented a scene from opera that lasted eighteen minutes, his rating dropped six points.

The Magic Flute, complete with runs, staccato leaps and repeated F's above high C. When conductor Karl Böhm heard the story, he refused to believe it. After the next *Götterdämmerung*, Nilsson repeated the feat, with the incredulous Böhm at the piano.

Nilsson's powerful top tones proved able to hold their own with the heaviest Wagnerian orchestration, but she could scale down her voice to more modest dimensions if the occasion called for it. Once she was announced for a *Tosca* in Philadelphia, with Ferruccio Tagliavini. Operagoers expected Tagliavini to be annihilated; his voice, although suave and well produced, was the lightest of lyric tenors. But Nilsson matched her volume to Tagliavini's to create a remarkably well-balanced performance.

But when anyone attempted to outdo Nilsson, it was another story. Her powers in that respect earned her in Italy the nickname of *"La voce di vendetta"* ("The voice of revenge").

In the second-act duet *In questa reggia*, from *Turandot*, there is a high C for tenor and soprano which, since it occurs at the end of a phrase, can be held for bravura effect. At one performance, Franco Corelli made the tactical mistake of holding the C after Nilsson had let go.

Later, according to a story that became part of Metropolitan lore, the two were singing *Turandot* in Boston during the Metropolitan's spring tour. Long after Corelli had given out, Nilsson was still holding the high C of *In questa reggia*.

Corelli, the story goes, left the stage, sulked in his dressing room and declared that he would not come out again. At that point, Bing was said to have offered a suggestion.

"In America, a man cannot retreat before a woman," Bing reportedly said. "Continue! And in the next act, when the time comes to kiss her, *bite* her instead."

Corelli, according to the story, followed instructions and Bing fled to New York, where he received a phone call from Nilsson, saying that she could not complete the tour.

"I cannot go on to Cleveland," said Nilsson. "I have rabies."

Birgit Nilsson, wearing the 1883 golden wreath, singing Brünnhilde's Immolation from GÖTTERDÄMMERUNG *at the Gala Farewell*

37

The New House

"At first sight of the Metropolitan Opera House," said Frances Alda, "I gasped. Then I laughed.

"*That* an opera house?

"It looked more like a storage warehouse. Dirty brown brick. Shabby. Old, weather-stained posters hanging in tatters in the sleety winter wind. The sordid everyday business of Broadway — the hawkers, the actors and actresses out of jobs, the hotel touts, out-of-town sightseers, sandwich men, dope peddlers, gangsters, the thousands who make a living off the ignorance and weakness of other human beings — swirling in a greasy tide about its doors.

"I remembered the stately Opéra in Paris; the dignity of La Scala — a palace dedicated to music and as noble as the *palazzo* of any Visconti in Milan. I thought of the magnificent opera house in Buenos Aires where I had sung that summer. . . .

"And this was New York. The richest, most modern, most progressive city in the world."

Most newcomers had a similar reaction on seeing the Metropolitan for the first time, particularly as its once-yellow brick grew more and more dingy with the years. The shortcomings of the house had been evident ever since the opening-night *Faust* of 1883. At frequent intervals, voices were raised to demand that the house be replaced by a new and better-equipped building. One of the most insistent voices was that of Otto Kahn. Kahn launched his twenty-year campaign for a new Metropolitan Opera House in 1908. His conviction that a new house was needed, however, was not shared by the Metropolitan Opera and Real Estate Company. Boxholders were happy with the status quo.

By 1924, with operating profits over $50,000 a year and still rising, Kahn felt it was time for an all-out drive on behalf of the new house. He prepared a pamphlet, distributed to subscribers at the end of the season, in which he set forth the reasons why a new house was necessary. All through 1925, rumors circulated about the site of the new opera house. It was to be on Seventy-second Street and Fifth Avenue, facing Central Park, or Seventy-second Street and Central Park West, or on West Fifty-seventh Street. The last rumor proved to be the correct one. In January, 1926, came the formal announcement that Otto Kahn had assembled a plot on West Fifty-seventh Street as the location for the new Metropolitan Opera House.

The announcement brought a statement from Fulton Cutting, chairman of the board of directors of the Metropolitan Opera and Real Estate Company, that would have daunted a less hardy soul than Kahn. If New York music-lovers wished to build a new opera house, said Cutting, the members of the Opera and Real Estate Company would put no obstacle in their way. "They are not, however, of the opinion that the present house is antiquated or that its site is undesirable. It is producing opera more superbly than anywhere else in the world. The acoustic properties of its auditorium are unsurpassed. . . ."

In other words, if Kahn and other opera-lovers wanted to build a new house, they were free to do so; but they could count on no help from the Opera and Real Estate Company. That was not quite what Kahn had in mind. His idea was to finance the building of a new Metropolitan Opera House by selling the old one. It was a tribute to Kahn's persuasive powers that by early 1926 he had convinced Vincent Astor, Edward S. Harkness, E. Roland Harriman and other boxholders of the soundness of his plan.

Kahn's idea was to abolish the outright ownership of boxes. Instead, boxes would be leased to a list of "eligibles" to be compiled by the Kahn and Cutting groups. The Opera and Real Estate Company made a counter-proposal: Boxholders would still own the boxes, and would have un-limited use of them on Monday nights and either Thursdays or Saturday afternoons. For other performances, the boxes would be leased to a group chosen by a "box committee." To finance the project, the existing house would be sold and each of the thirty-five boxholders would reinvest $145,-000, making a total of $4,640,000 with which to build the new house.

The negotiations consumed more than a year, but by April, 1927, it was possible to announce that a majority of the boxholders had agreed to surrender their stock and permit the Opera House Committee to proceed. Benjamin Wister Morris, designer of the Morgan Library on Madison Avenue, was named as architect, with the Metropolitan's Joseph Urban as assistant.

So far, so good. No one can guess what might have happened had not Deems Taylor, then editor of *Musical America*, happened to visit Urban's studio one day in the summer of 1927. He found Urban hard at work on plans for the new opera house. Urban's design called for a wide stage with an extended stage apron, a curved proscenium and sight-lines radiating out into a wide fan-shaped auditorium. It was in fact remarkably like what later took shape as Radio City Music Hall. Urban's theatre, of course, might have turned out to have acoustical properties like the Music Hall's, requiring microphones and amplification.

Taylor asked for permission to publish Urban's designs, and they appeared in *Musical America* for October 8, 1927. The publication created a furor. Urban apparently had drawn up his plans without consulting Morris, and the senior architect was offended. No site had yet been chosen for the new opera house, said Morris, and until the site was chosen there could be no plans. If Morris was correct, Kahn had not made the use of his West Fifty-seventh Street property a condition of the agreement.

Two days after the designs were published, it was announced that a committee consisting of J. P. Morgan, Fulton Cutting, Cornelius N. Bliss, Jr., Robert S. Brewster and De Lancey Kountze had been named to choose a suitable site. Between October and January, the group considered Central Park South, the Century Theatre location on Central Park West, and half a dozen other sites, including one on West 110th Street, facing the park and accordingly backing on Harlem.

In November, Kahn offered to keep his Fifty-seventh Street property available if desired. He also made a statement that contradicted Morris. The plan for the distribution of boxes at the new house, the financing details and the Fifty-seventh Street site, he said, had all been approved the previous February by the unanimous vote of both his own group and the Opera and Real Estate Company board. Kahn was borne out by a 1927

Metropolitan ledger entry that listed $40,000 under "Architect's fees for 57th street site." The unanimous vote had been overturned by Mrs. Cornelius Vanderbilt III and others in favor of maintaining the status quo.

Kahn, seeing that the game was up, on January 19, 1928, instructed his brokers to put the Fifty-seventh Street property up for sale. The prospect of a new opera house gradually evaporated. Kahn did not mention the matter again and three years later he left the Metropolitan altogether. It was an unhappy ending for his twenty-year-old dream of a new opera house. On the other hand, as some dissidents pointed out at the time, the proposed Fifty-seventh Street location *was* a grubby neighborhood, made even more objectionable in those days by the Ninth Avenue "El."

In any case, those who believed Kahn had used his position as a Metropolitan director to take a trading turn in real estate at the company's expense (garbled versions of the story kept cropping up for years) were completely mistaken. First and last, the Fifty-seventh Street property netted Kahn a loss of $1,600,000.

Almost immediately — in mid-May — reports began circulating of another plan to build a new Metropolitan Opera House. This plan, it was soon learned, had the very solid backing of John D. Rockefeller, Jr. His interest in the Metropolitan's housing problem had been aroused, it is said, by a vice-president of William A. White & Sons, the real estate brokers. As the site for a new Metropolitan Opera House, Rockefeller had leased from Columbia University the block bounded by Fifth and Sixth Avenues, West Forty-ninth and West Fiftieth streets. It was an area of brownstone houses, some of which, on the Fifth Avenue side, were still imposing and some of which, in the shadow of the Sixth Avenue "El," had seen better days. Envious nonparticipating brokers said that "Rockefeller has bought a thousand speakeasies."

Architects' drawings published in the newspapers showed how the proposed new opera house would look. It would dominate the square, facing across an open space to Saks Fifth Avenue and Saint Patrick's Cathedral. Space for other buildings would be leased in the square, but their designs would have to conform to that of the opera house. A company known as the Metropolitan Square Corporation had been formed to manage the property.

Rockefeller's proposal was cordially received at the Metropolitan. "Everything looks very promising," Cutting said. There were still problems to be solved, however. Rockefeller expected the Metropolitan to pay for the construction of the new opera house, and to pay him an annual ground rent thereafter. The Metropolitan Opera and Real Estate Company would raise the money for the new building by selling the old one. Anything realized in this way over and above the building costs would be a profit for the Opera and Real Estate Company stockholders. On the other hand, if the sale price didn't cover the cost of building, the stockholders would have to make up the difference out of their own pockets.

It was announced that the Opera and Real Estate Company would consider an offer of $13,000,000 for the Metropolitan Opera House. The figure was high, even by the optimistic standards of January, 1929. What the boxholders were selling was, in effect, their land. The opera house was merely a liability which any conceivable purchaser, barring the appearance of another Oscar Hammerstein, would be certain to tear down and replace with a commercial structure. And, twenty-five years later, the value of the Metropolitan's irregular plot was estimated at around $4,000,000. Not surprisingly, at $13,000,000 there were no buyers.

When the stock-market bubble burst in October, it ended Metropolitan Square as far as the opera company was concerned. It was a bad time to sell; the real estate market was dropping as sharply as everything else. Moreover, the Metropolitan Square Corporation would need two years to clear out the bootleggers and start building. Early in December, it was announced that the move to Metropolitan Square had been abandoned.

Rockefeller evidently hoped the company would change its mind. Space for an opera house was retained in the plans as Metropolitan Square became Rockefeller Center, and finally, with the advent of RCA and NBC as major tenants, Radio City.

The development as completed included Radio City Music Hall, planned from the start as a movie and variety theatre, and the Center Theatre, with a seating capacity about the same as the Metropolitan's. There were periodic rumors that the Metropolitan was on the point of moving to the Center Theatre. The Center, however, was a white elephant from the start. Its seats were comfortable, and each had an unobstructed view of the stage. But its acoustics were so poor that microphones and amplifiers were required. Backstage facilities were as cramped as the Metropolitan's and had as little room for expansion. For several years,

Fortune Gallo and his San Carlo Opera presented a spring season at the Center Theatre after the Metropolitan had left town; but it was at best a makeshift arrangement.

The Center Theatre was no better suited to the spoken drama. In fact, trial-and-error experimentation showed that virtually the only spectacle to which it was well adapted was an ice show. Eventually the theatre was dismantled and replaced by a bank.

On the whole, the Metropolitan could congratulate itself on not having made the move to Radio City. The Center Theatre showed how imperfectly the science of theatre acoustics was understood, and an obsolete theatre with good acoustics was better than an up-to-date one without.

The Rockefellers had money and patience. In the summer of 1955, John D. Rockefeller III showed that his family had not given up on a new home for the Metropolitan Opera. He announced plans to transform a rundown section of upper Broadway into a civic asset — a performing-arts center with quarters for the Metropolitan, the Philharmonic and other groups.

Bing was strenuously opposed to the idea of moving to Lincoln Center, even though he had complained of the shortcomings of the old house as vehemently as everyone else. But at Broadway and Thirty-ninth Street he was master of all he surveyed, whereas at Lincoln Center he would be merely one of several equals — the vice-president, in effect, in charge of Metropolitan Opera performances.

Bing was also uneasy about the proximity of the New York City Opera, whose performances would be taking place only a few yards from the Metropolitan's. "Suppose somebody says, 'I heard a lousy opera at Lincon Center last night,'" Bing suggested. "Maybe it was the other house's opera, or maybe it was ours. Under the umbrella of Lincoln Center, each of the two houses is bound to be deprived of its individual image, and that is the most important asset an opera house can have."

But Bing was realistic enough to recognize an irresistible force when he saw one and he yielded to Rockefeller pressure with good grace. "You can't fight the Royal Family," Bing said philosophically.

Rockefeller engaged Wallace K. Harrison, the architect of Radio City, to design the new Metropolitan Opera House. The two of them, with stage director Herbert Graf, who was also an expert on opera-house design, and

Herman Krawitz of the Metropolitan's technical staff set off on a tour of European opera houses.

Whatever Harrison's fee, the architect doubtless felt he earned it. Design after design was submitted, modified or scrapped. One beautifully wrought scale model after another was constructed for the directors and the Opera Guild. Time after time, the date of opening night was pushed back another season; it had been agreed from the start that Philharmonic Hall was to have priority. And with each postponement, the cost of the building mounted higher. The original budget had been set at $40,000,000. Unforeseen contingencies, however, such as striking water in the building site, raised the final cost to $45,700,000.

Harrison must have been thinking long, long thoughts as the costly acoustical gamble neared completion. The poor acoustics of newly completed Philharmonic Hall in particular had caused a scandal. Its acoustical "clouds" had not worked as they were supposed to. After performing there, one major orchestra had announced its intention to return to Carnegie Hall for part of its New York season.

On Monday, April 11, 1966, a student matinee performance of *La Fanciulla del West* was presented at Lincoln Center. It was the first actual performance in the new house. The regular Metropolitan season was to end on Saturday, and before bidding a permanent farewell to the old Metropolitan, the directors thought it prudent to try out the new. Reporters were barred; only a few observers sworn to secrecy were allowed inside.

Before the performance, technicians startled the student audience by firing blank cartridges to test the hall's reverberation time. Then the music began.

Newspapers reported next day that Metropolitan officials had entered the new opera house looking grim. They came out beaming.

38

"L'Ultima Canzone"

THE METROPOLITAN'S LAST DAY as an opera house began on April 16, 1966, with business as usual — a broadcast matinee of *La Bohème*, with Gabriella Tucci as Mimi, Heidi Krall as Musetta, Richard Tucker as Rodolfo, and Mario Sereni, Clifford Harvuot and Jerome Hines as the other Bohemians.

La Bohème had been performed 444 times at the Metropolitan, and this performance was fully up to Metropolitan standards. In the last act, however, there was one difference. Hines's *Vecchia zimarra* farewell was addressed not to an old coat but to an old theatre: *"Vecchio teatro, addio."*

Then it was time to hurry home and change. All the principals were performing again in the evening.

Around six P.M., the Rolls Royces and Cadillacs began arriving with people who, for twelve dollars each and with reservations made a year in advance, were having dinner at Sherry's for the last time. Mrs. Belmont. Gene Tunney, a member of the Metropolitan Opera Club since 1927, the year he beat Jack Dempsey in Chicago. Mrs. John Barry Ryan, Otto Kahn's daughter. Cornelius Vanderbilt Whitney, whose grandfathers Cornelius Vanderbilt II and William C. Whitney had been among the Metropolitan's original founders. Mrs. Whitney, wearing a diamond and ruby tiara that had belonged to the Empress Elisabeth of Austria. General David Sarnoff, recalling the 1908 opening-night *Aida* he had heard from the topmost balcony.

Princess Marina of Greece. Mrs. C. Ruxton Love, Jr., with her arm in a sling but wearing the largest diamonds to be seen at the dinner. Roger M.

Waiting to buy standing-room tickets for the Gala Farewell

Blough, board chairman of United States Steel. Mrs. Albert D. Lasker, with Mrs. Joseph P. Kennedy, mother of the late President, as one of her guests.

A boxful of Mellons, in from Pittsburgh for the occasion. A Murchison from Texas, a Cooledge from Atlanta and a Weyerhaeuser from St. Paul.

Lewis W. Douglas, former Ambassador to the Court of St. James. Walter J. Kohler, Jr., former governor of Wisconsin. James Cash Penney, founder of the department-store chain that bears his name. Alfred A. Knopf, Mrs. Nelson Doubleday and George T. Delacorte, Jr., from the world of publishing.

Katharine Cornell, Ethel Merman, who sat in the front row, and Ed Sullivan, who called the evening "a very good show."

In Sherry's kitchen, Louis Sismondo, the seventy-year-old manager of the restaurant, was busy supervising last-minute preparations. "This is the grandest, biggest, maddest night we've ever had," said Sismondo. "But we'll make it."

In anticipation of the evening's festivity, Sismondo had iced five hundred bottles of champagne instead of the usual twenty-four to thirty-six. He refused to feel sentimental about leaving the old house. In fact, he said, he could hardly wait to get to Lincoln Center.

"The kitchen here, she is lousy," Sismondo said. "Very, very lousy. Most of the time, to get the dinners out, we had to do some miracles."

Outside, pickets were demonstrating, carrying their "Save-the-Met" placards. A stubbornly hopeful faction still hoped for a repetition of the near-miracle that had saved Carnegie Hall.

The house had been sold out, at prices ranging from twelve to two hundred dollars. Scalpers were doing a brisk business. Since the artists were contributing their services, the evening would net the opera company $292,000.

More limousines were arriving. Top-hatted and evening-gowned patrons emerged, while a crowd gawked on the sidewalk. Reporters, behind the rope barrier, were busy taking notes, and photographers' flashbulbs popped. It was much like any opening night, except that tonight everything was for the last time.

The performance began almost on time, although seating was slow;

souvenir hunters had stolen most of the metal number plates from the seats.

Bing welcomed the audience with a gracious curtain speech. "This is a farewell," he said, "and every farewell hurts, however long one may have been looking forward to it. Fortunately it is a goodbye to brick and mortar only, and not to friends. A building is replaceable. Friends are not. . . .

"Thank you for decades of loyal help and support. I would like to feel that it was meant for the company rather than for a building. The company goes on, and will do all we can to deserve your continued support. The Queen is dead. Long live the Queen."

The curtain rose on a stage filled with vacant chairs. It had been Bing's happy thought to invite former members of the company as special guests. One by one, in alphabetical order, they came onstage — Marian Anderson, "First of her race" at the Metropolitan. Conductor Giuseppe Bamboschek. Rose Bampton, the unforgettable Donna Anna who made the transition successfully from mezzo- to dramatic soprano. Baritones Richard Bonelli and John Brownlee. Anna Case, who left the Metropolitan in 1920 to marry Clarence H. Mackay, head of the Postal Telegraph Company, and whose daughter married Irving Berlin.

Tenors Mario Chamlee, Eugene Conley* and Richard Crooks. Mezzo-sopranos Vilma Georgiou and Herta Glaz. Nanette Guilford, onetime "Baby of the Met" and still charming. Indestructible Frederick Jagel. Blonde, appealing Helen Jepson. Raoul Jobin, who liked Paris better. Alexander Kipnis, fine operatic basso and even finer recitalist (some enthusiasts maintain his recording of Brahms's "Von ewiger Liebe" is the finest performance of that difficult song ever heard). Charles Kullman, onetime pride of the Yale Glee Club.

Marjorie Lawrence, unforgettable Salome, superb horsewoman who actually rode her mount, as Wagner's score directs, into the flames in the Immolation Scene of *Götterdämmerung*; stricken with polio at the height

---

* Some listeners recalled with amusement Conley's New York debut, at a Salmaggi production of *Rigoletto* years earlier. At the conclusion of *La donna e mobile*, the tenor tosses a pack of cards into the air, the traditional signal to the conductor that he is about to release the high note. Conley ended the aria with a high B that was like a shower of stars. The house went wild. Under easygoing Salmaggi rules, an encore was not only permissible but almost inevitable. Nodding to the conductor, Conley reached into his doublet and produced a second deck of cards.

Picketers protesting the planned demolition of the opera house

of her career, but smiling gallantly from a wheelchair. Lotte Lehmann, beloved Marschallin in *Der Rosenkavalier,* silver-haired, silver-gowned and wearing a row of medals. Mezzo-soprano Martha Lipton. White-haired Giovanni Martinelli, who had sung leading tenor roles on this stage for thirty-two years. Sopranos Edith Mason and Ruth Miller. Nina Morgana, who toured with Caruso and married Caruso's secretary, Bruno Zirato.

Nicola Moscona, basso and incorrigible backstage humorist. Patrice Munsel, no longer at the Metropolitan but in great demand for summer musicals. Irra Petina, who also made it in musicals after leaving the Metropolitan. Lily Pons, as stunning as ever (gossip said she would have liked to perform). Elisabeth Rethberg, looking frail and tired, but blooming at the tremendous roar that went up from the audience.

Sopranos Stella Roman and Bidu Sayao. Risë Stevens, no longer singing but still active as manager of the Metropolitan's National Company.

A few couldn't make it. Farrar and Ponselle almost never left their homes. Farrar sent Mrs. Belmont a telegram of good wishes. Jeritza, in mourning for her husband, sent Bing a handsome floral tribute. Melchior and Traubel sent regrets.

The musical program began on a somewhat jarring note. After a rousing performance of the National Anthem, Leopold Stokowski conducted the opening chorus from the Wartburg Scene in *Tannhäuser,* "Happily We Salute the Noble Hall." At its conclusion, he turned to the audience. Stokowski had always been a great maker of impromptu speeches and he made one now.

"What a beautiful house!" A ripple of surprise, and a patter of applause, went through the audience. "What splendid acoustics!" More applause and a few chuckles. "Help us to save this magnificent building!" There was great applause in some quarters and stunned quiet in others. From the balcony, a raucous voice shouted: "Save the Met!"

Had Stokowski removed his pants, he could hardly have created greater consternation. If there was one thing the Metropolitan wanted no part of, it was the "Save-the-Met" campaign. If any lingering doubt remained on that score, Bing's curtain speech had dispelled it. Bing had bitterly opposed the move to Lincoln Center, but the issue had been fought to a finish, the death sentence had been pronounced and now nothing remained but to get the execution over with in as decent a manner as possible.

Bing was furious with the octogenarian maestro. "It was rude," he snapped. "He was invited here to conduct, not to make a speech."

But Francesco Molinari-Pradelli entered the pit and the show went on, with the Sextet from *Lucia* with Anna Moffo, Carlotta Ordassy, Arturo Sergi, Charles Anthony, Justino Diaz, William Walker; *Eri tu*, from *Un Ballo in maschera*, sung by Robert Merrill, and the *Otello* duet, sung by James McCracken and Anselmo Colzani.

Backstage, looking sadly at the grimy brick walls, McCracken said: "La Scala and Covent Garden are old, too, but they wouldn't tear *them* down."

Cesare Siepi, in *Ella giammai m'amo*, from *Don Carlo* (in which he had made his Metropolitan debut), was followed by Dorothy Kirsten's *Depuis le jour* and the *Carmen* Quintet, with Regina Resnik, Thelma Votipka, Marcia Baldwin, Paul Franke and George Cehanovsky. It was Cehanovsky's fortieth season with the company, and he had undoubtedly appeared there oftener, in more different roles, then anyone else on the stage. He had made his debut in 1926 and had sung de Brètigny with three generations of Manons.

An odd fact was that if one entered the house in the midst of an ensemble, it was always possible to tell when one of the voices was Cehanovsky's. Odd, because it was not an especially big voice nor was it piercing or strident. Cehanovsky never forced; that was one reason why he lasted so long. It was just a voice that would go through anything.

Un bel di was sung by Licia Albanese. As she bowed to the applause, she bade the house a sentimental farewell by kissing her fingertips and touching them to the stage.

Fernando Corena, not usually heard in German, sang *Heil diesem Hause*, from Cornelius's *Barber of Bagdad*. Roberta Peters's *Una voca poco fa* was followed by the final trio from *La Forza del destino*, with Delia Rigal, Jan Peerce and Giorgio Tozzi; *L'amo come il folgor*, from *La Gioconda*, with Regina Crespin and Biserka Cvejik, and *D'amor sull' ali rosee*, from *Il Trovatore*, sung by Leontyne Price.

Price beamed to acknowledge the applause but, backstage, burst into tears.

"The new house is wonderful," she told Bing, "but it will never be the same."

Renata Tebaldi and Franco Corelli offered *Vieni! Colle tue braccia*, from

Leopold Stokowski about to begin conducting the Gala Farewell

Manon Lescaut. Sandor Konya sang the Prize Song for *Die Meister-singer,* Birgit Nilsson the Immolation Scene from *Götterdämmerung.*

When Nilsson appeared, a gasp of surprise and pleasure went through the house. She was wearing the massive golden girdle-wreath, with its twin masks representing Tragedy and Comedy, that had been presented to her namesake (but no relation) Christine Nilsson on opening night eighty-three years before. After the earlier Nilsson's death, the wreath had gone to the Museum of Musical History in Stockholm. The museum had loaned it for the evening, and it had been flown to New York in time for the performance.

The Triumphal Scene from *Aida,* without which a Metropolitan season would have been unthinkable, offered Mary Curtis-Verna, Jean Madeira, Kurt Baum, Mario Sereni, John Macurdy and Norman Scott. The Farewell Trio from *Così fan tutte* had Teresa Stratas, Mildred Miller and Frank Guarrera. The *Magic Flute* quintet was sung by Mary Ellen Pracht, Joann Grillo, Gladys Kriese, George Shirley, and Theodore Uppman. Another quintet, from *Vanessa,* presented Eleanor Steber, Mignon Dunn, Blanche Thebom, John Alexander and Clifford Harvuot. The final trio from *Der Rosenkavalier* was performed by Montserrat Caballé, Judith Raskin and Rosalind Elias.

An especially enthusiastic welcome went to Zinka Milanov, who had sung her official farewell performance earlier in the week. She was heard with Richard Tucker in the final duet from *Andrea Chénier.*

Now the end of the program had come. The Metropolitan was ending its life cycle, as it had begun it, with the concluding trio of the Prison Scene in *Faust.* Nicolai Gedda was the tenor, Jerome Hines the bass, Gabriella Tucci's the soprano voice soaring upward in the radiant phrases sung by the demented, dying Marguerite as she sees the heavens opening:

> *Anges purs, anges radieux,*
> *Portez mon âme au sein des cieux . . .*

The curtains came down. When they opened again, the stage was packed. Singers, ballet dancers, choristers, prompters, *corrépétiteurs,* carpenters, stagehands, front-office staff and backstage crew — everybody who could find a place to stand was there.

Performers onstage, patrons in the audience, linked hands to form a great human chain for the singing of "Auld Lang Syne."

Birgit Nilsson had a moment of panic. "But I don't know the words," she gasped.

It didn't matter. Everyone else did.

Then, very slowly, the gold curtains came down for good.

As if reluctant to leave, the audience began filing out. Nearly everyone paused in the doorway for a final backward glance. There were many who wept openly as they looked for the last time at the red-and-gold house, rich with memories of the great voices and great performances of eighty-three years.

The souvenir hunters were already busy. In a balcony, a student was surreptitiously unscrewing a light bulb from one of the carved rosettes.

It was nearly one-thirty in the morning. As the performers filed out, Bing greeted each one with the famous last word from *Pagliacci*: *"Finita."*

There were still to come three weeks of the Bolshoi Ballet. Then the "Save-the-Met" campaign would begin to gather momentum. Huntington Hartford contributed $100,000 to the cause; another $100,000 was raised by lovers of the old house. Joseph Gimma, husband of Licia Albanese and a partner in the Stock Exchange firm of Hornblower & Weeks, directed the drive from an office at 87 Beaver Street. Wreckers' deadlines were pushed back again and again by the sympathetic new owners as it appeared that the campaign to save the Metropolitan had a fair chance of succeeding. What with one thing and another, the death throes of the Metropolitan were to last until after Christmas.

But when the gold curtains came down on April 16, the party was over. Then the iron ball started swinging, and the Metropolitan was gone. In the world's long history, it had been only a moment. But it had been a moment not without grandeur.

*Metropolitan performers, other personnel and friends join the audience in
singing "Auld Lang Syne" at the end of the Gala Farewell.*

Picture Credits

Culver Pictures, Inc.: pages 13, 73, 83, 95 (bottom), 113, 129, 143, 149, 173, 181 (top), 189 (bottom), 209 (top), 239, 267 (both), 271, 275, and 289

The Bettmann Archive: pages 18-19, 47, 65, 95 (top), 103, 155, 167, 189 (top), 193, 201, 209 (bottom), 247, 251, and 263

Metropolitan Opera Archives: pages 25 and 121

From the collection of Steven B. Facett: pages 55, 69 (both), and 181 (bottom)

Courtesy of Eugene Cook: page 139

Wide World Photos: pages 293 and 313

Photo by E. Fred Sher: pages 319, 333, and 341

The New York Times: frontispiece and pages 329 and 337

Index

343

January 31, 1920 — World premiere of Henry Hadley's *Cleopatra's Night* (Alda, Orville Harold, Jeanne Gordon).

December 24, 1920 — *La Juive* (Easton, Caruso, Leon Rothier, Harrold). Caruso's 607th and last appearance at the Metropolitan.

March 24, 1922 — First American performance of *Così fan tutte* (Easton, Lucrezia Bori, de Luca, Didur).

March 21, 1925 — First Metropolitan performance of *Pelléas et Mélisande* (Bori, Edward Johnson, Whitehill, Rothier).

November 16, 1926 — First American performance of *Turandot* (Maria Jeritza, Giacomo Lauri-Volpi, de Luca).

February 17, 1927 — World premiere of Deems Taylor's *The King's Henchman* (Easton, Johnson, Lawrence Tibbett).

January 25, 1930 — First American performance of Rimsky-Korsakoff's *Sadko* (Ina Bourskaya, Gladys Swarthout, Johnson).

February 7, 1931 — World premiere of Taylor's *Peter Ibbetson* (Bori, Johnson, Tibbett).

December 25, 1931 — *Hänsel und Gretel* (Editha Fleischer, Queena Mario, Dorothee Manski) is first opera to be broadcast complete from the Metropolitan. Its coast-to-coast and international shortwave network is largest ever assembled up to that time.

December 3, 1932 — First Metropolitan performance of *Elektra* (Karin Branzell, Gertrud Kappel, Rudolf Laubenthal, Friedrich Schorr).

January 7, 1933 — World premiere of Gruenberg's *The Emperor Jones* (Tibbett, Marek Windheim).

February 25, 1933 — Public fund-raising campaign begins during matinee broadcast of *Manon* (Bori, de Luca, Richard Crooks). Deficit from previous season is $497,213, the largest in many decades.

February 10, 1934 — World premiere of Howard Hanson's *Merry Mount* (Göta Ljungberg, Swarthout, Arnold Gabor, Tibbett).

March 19, 1935 — Farewell gala for retiring Gatti-Casazza. Acts and scenes from six operas performed by twenty-seven artists.

May 10, 1935 — Herbert Witherspoon, named as Gatti's successor, dies of a heart attack. Edward Johnson takes over as general manager.

July–August, 1935 — Metropolitan Opera Guild founded under leadership of Mrs. August Belmont.

December 16, 1935 — First Johnson season opens with *La Traviata* (Bori, Crooks, Tibbett).

May 12, 1937 — World premiere of Walter Damrosch's *The Man Without a Country* (debut Helen Traubel; Arthur Carron, George Rasely).

February 26, 1938 — Giovanni Martinelli collapses during matinee broadcast of *Aida* (Zinka Milanov, Bruna Castagna, Carlo Tagliabue). Performance resumes in less than half an hour. Frederick Jagel hurries to the Metropolitan to fill in.

1939–1940 season — Million-dollar fund campaign raises $1,042,000. Largest sum from a single source — $327,000 — comes from radio audience.

June 28, 1940 — Metropolitan Opera Association takes title to Metropolitan Opera House from Metropolitan Opera and Real Estate Company.